THE COURSE OF HUMAN EVENTS

THE REVOLUTIONARY AGE
Francis D. Cogliano, Christa Breault Dierksheide,
Eliga H. Gould, and Patrick Griffin, Editors

*Winner of the Walker Cowen Memorial Prize
for an outstanding work of scholarship
in eighteenth-century studies*

The Course of Human Events

*The Declaration of Independence and the
Historical Origins of the United States*

STEVEN SARSON

UNIVERSITY OF VIRGINIA PRESS
Charlottesville and London

The University of Virginia Press is situated on the traditional lands of the Monacan Nation, and the Commonwealth of Virginia was and is home to many other Indigenous people. We pay our respect to all of them, past and present. We also honor the enslaved African and African American people who built the University of Virginia, and we recognize their descendants. We commit to fostering voices from these communities through our publications and to deepening our collective understanding of their histories and contributions.

This book is published with the support of the Institut d'études transtextuelles et transculturelles of Jean Moulin University-Lyon 3 / Ouvrage publié avec le soutien de l'Institut d'études transtextuelles et transculturelles (UR 4186 IETT) de l'université Jean Moulin Lyon 3.

University of Virginia Press
© 2025 by the Rector and Visitors of the University of Virginia
All rights reserved
Printed in the United States of America on acid-free paper

First published 2025

9 8 7 6 5 4 3 2 1

Library of Congress Cataloging-in-Publication data is available for this title.

ISBN 978-0-8139-5396-0 (hardback)
ISBN 978-0-8139-5397-7 (paperback)
ISBN 978-0-8139-5398-4 (ebook)

Cover art: Declaration of Independence (1819) by John Trumbull. (Courtesy of Architect of the Capitol)
Cover design: Cecilia Sorochin

For Nathalie Morello

CONTENTS

Acknowledgments   ix

Introduction: The Facts and Principles Advanced in That Declaration   1

Part I. The Past: To Secure These Rights

1. The Laws of Nature and of Nature's God   15
2. Our Emigration and Settlement Here   42

Part II. The Past and the Present: The History of the Present King of Great Britain

3. Unfit to Be the Ruler of a Free People   77
4. A History of Repeated Injuries and Usurpations   107

Part III. The Past, the Present, and the Future: To Institute New Government

5. The Right of the People   143
6. The Rest of Mankind   175

Postscript: We Hold These Truths to Be Self-Evident   207

Notes   213
Works Cited   241
Index   261

ACKNOWLEDGMENTS

Ten years ago, I started teaching a second-year master's degree course on the Declaration of Independence, and somewhere along the way I stopped being surprised that every year I learn new things about this endlessly rich and fascinating document. That is in large part thanks to the countless conversations I have had in classes with students who have taken the course and without whom this book could not have been written—most from my home institution, Jean Moulin University in Lyon, but many too from neighboring Lumière University and the Ecole Normale Supérieure de Lyon. I wish I could name them all, but special thanks for particularly inspiring contributions are owed the following (in year order): Julien Agostini, Claire-Anne Ferriere, Adrien Halliez, Elizabeth Ramey (formerly Hargrett), Loic Henry, Narimene Ibrahim, Guillaume Braquet, Caroline Laplace, Marwa Maghrabi, Léa Berne, Diego Dos Santos Alves, Domitille Dubois-Athenor, Etienne Gimenez, Clara Griffiths, Stella Rofi, Baptiste Arnoux, Luye Zhang, Ilona Albertino, Anissa Bounouara, Ender Calman, Natacha Bardy, Clément Courberand, Pierre Court, Agathe Enezian, Théo Knopfer, Mouna Mulder, Eloise Noblet, Lena Osty, Marie Philippe, Thomas van Woerden, Clementine Bourgue, Sarah Hellali, Juliette Héritier-Pingeon, Marylou Parabis, Mendy Ali Aichouba, Tieno Barbance, Maxence Brin, Noé Delnord, Néhémie Landes, Amandine Tête, Léo Depierre-Arzimanoglou, Sebastian Benone, Valentin Carme, Clara Davi, Inès Kadem, Louise Noilhac, Juliette Pregnard, Noé Ringeard, Lessa Bonnet, Nina Broyer, Blandine Colas, Solen Ducheman, Pauline Genest, Laura Kenny, Radhuiya Maoulida, Perrine Paccard, Al Santos-Filipe, Gabrielle Tarrit, Pauline Tauzin, and Liam Thiercelin. A special mention is in order for other students or former students who did not take the course but who otherwise inspired me: Leslie Tassery (ENS and Jean Moulin) and Amy Weitzman (College of William and Mary).

I am also immensely grateful to numerous colleagues and friends who have made enormously useful comments either privately or at conferences and seminars. Many thanks to Jim Ambuske, Megan Bee, Anna Berkes, Trevor Burnard, Jane Calvert, Lindsay Chervinsky, Frank Cogliano, Nicholas Cole, Jean-Daniel Collomb, Jon Delogu, Christa Dierksheide, Max Edelson, Hans Eicholz, Julie Flavell, Julia Gaffield, Anne Giribone-Mackay, Sara Georgini, John Stuart Gordon, Lige Gould, Philip Gould, Annette Gordon-Reed, Jack Greene, Patrick Griffin, Steven Grow, Sandra Gustafson, Kevin Gutzman, Augustin Habran, John Harpham, Emma Hart, Michael Hattem, Lauric Henneton, Philip Herrington, Rachel Herrmann, Gérard Hugues, Tom Humphrey, Holly Hurd, Catherine Kelly, Ed Larson, Benoit Leridon, Jeff Looney, Nell MacCarty, Brendan McConville, Stephen McLeod, Ben Marsh, Philip Mead, Simon Middleton, Emilie Mitran, Estelle Morali-Silver, Hiram Morgan, Nathalie Morello, John Patrick Mullins, Angel Luke O'Donnell, Peter Onuf, Andrew O'Shaughnessy, Hélène Parent, Robert Parkinson, Jessica Parr, Chris Pearl, Pierre-François Peirano, John Ragosta, Liam Riordan, Jessica Roney, Barry Shain, Adam Smith, Emily Sneff, Samantha Snyder, Hannah Spahn, Endrina Tay, Fredrika Teute, Peter Thompson, Lenora Warren, Andrew Wegmann, Esther Wright, Craig Yirush, Serena Zabin, Natalie Zacek, and Rosemarie Zaggari. I am especially thankful for readings by and long conversations with Max Edelson, Hans Eicholz, Jack Greene, Lige Gould, John Harpham, Michael Hattem, Peter Onuf, John Ragosta, Rob Parkinson, Hannah Spahn, Andrew Wegmann, Craig Yirush, and Serena Zabin.

I have given numerous papers at various conferences and seminars on the Declaration and related subjects that are relevant to this book. I thank all the organizers and audiences at University College Cork, the British Group in Early American Studies at Cardiff University, the Wilberforce Centre for the Study of Slavery and Emancipation and the Cultures of Incarceration at the University of Hull, the Rothermere American Institute at the University of Oxford, the European Early American Studies Association at Paris Cité University and the University of Poitiers, the French Association for American Studies at the University of Strasbourg, the Société d'études anglo-américaines des XVIIe et XVIIIe siècles at Paris Nouvelle Sorbonne University, the University of Aix-Marseille, Paris Sorbonne University, the

University of Rouen, the University of Toulouse, the University of Tours, Ecole Normale Supérieure de Lyon, Institut Stanislas de Cannes, the James Madison Center at Delta State University, Cleveland, Mississippi (where I was honored to give the Howorth Constitution Day Lecture—yet more thanks to Andrew Wegmann), the Massachusetts Historical Society, the McNeil Center for Early American Studies and Museum of the American Revolution, the Omohundro Institute for Early American History and Culture, Williamsburg, the Robert H. Smith International Center for Jefferson Studies (twice), the George Washington Presidential Library (twice, once sponsored by the David Center for the American Revolution and American Philosophical Society), the William L. and Ruth Dunfey Endowment for the Study of History at the University of New Hampshire, Portsmouth, the American Historical Association, and the Society of Early Americanists at the University of Notre Dame. I have also benefited immeasurably from participating in three Liberty Fund conferences (and from organizing one of them with Hannah Spahn), and have been privileged to spend time at Monticello thanks to two Peter Nicolaisen International Fellowships and at Mount Vernon thanks to a George Washington Presidential Library Fellowship. Many thanks too for financial support from my home research center, the Institute d'Etudes Transtextuelles et Transculturelles at Jean Moulin University. Also, huge thanks to everyone at the University of Virginia Press involved with this book. I wanted to publish the book with UVA Press from the moment I conceived of it, mostly for reasons of the head—the well-earned professional reputation of the press—but also for reasons of the heart—to publish the book with the academic press of the university founded by the principal author of the Declaration of Independence. I am immensely happy as well as honored that UVA Press agreed and indulged me. Special thanks to Frank Cogliano, Christa Dierksheide, Lige Gould, and Patrick Griffin, editors of The Revolutionary Age series published by the Press; to Ellen Sartrom, for her superb management of the publishing process; to Marjorie Pannell, for thoughtful copyediting; and in particular to the amazing Nadine Zimmerli, a brilliant historian and editor, who helped me see this project through from beginning to end—a million thanks!

Last but not least, infinite thanks go to my wife, Nathalie Morello, for her patient sufferance while this book extended an unwarrantable jurisdiction over us, and for three decades and counting of companionship and love. This book is dedicated to her.

THE COURSE OF HUMAN EVENTS

INTRODUCTION

The Facts and Principles Advanced in That Declaration

The Declaration of Independence is best known today for the following inspiring words:

> We hold these truths to be self-evident, that all men are created equal, that they are endowed by their Creator with certain unalienable Rights, that among these are Life, Liberty and the pursuit of Happiness.[1]

These apparent promises were far from fulfilled in 1776, or for many years after. Some therefore see the Declaration's authors as hypocrites for failing to abide by their self-evident truths, though others see them as visionaries for establishing ideals to be realized in the future. Whatever the case, later generations of reformers used the Declaration as a charter for universal equality and liberty. As a consequence, the Declaration has become sacralized, described by activists, politicians, and historians alike as a "creed," an "American Scripture," a "revolutionary prophecy," and "even a kind of prayer."[2]

Historians disagree on the ideological origins of the Declaration and of the American Revolution more generally—on whether they were founded on this philosophy or that, or on constitutional imperatives, or on religious convictions. Some see American independence as inspired less by ideas than by political imperatives such as easing socioeconomic conflict in the colonies or securing foreign aid and recognition of the United States among the powers of the earth. Yet there is broad agreement that the Declaration's proclamations on equality and liberty promised a break with the past and a new kind of future. The founder of modern Declaration studies, Carl Becker, wrote over a century ago that its authors "were not writing history, but making it." The founder of modern nation studies, Benedict Anderson, notes that the document makes "no reference to Christopher Columbus, Roanoke, or the Pilgrim Fathers, nor are the grounds put forward to justify independence in any way 'historical,' in the sense of highlighting the antiquity of the American people" but convey instead a "profound feeling that a radical break with the past was occurring." Some have acknowledged that the document included some historical content, if only to dismiss it as often vague or erroneous, even disingenuous, and only there anyway to serve the grander purposes of the present and future—of independence and of founding a nation dedicated to equality and liberty for all.[3]

Yet the Declaration does not begin with its self-evident truths. It begins, in fact, as follows:

> When in the Course of human events, it becomes necessary for one people to dissolve the political bands which have connected them with another, and to assume among the powers of the earth, the separate and equal station to which the Laws of Nature and of Nature's God entitle them, a decent respect to the opinions of mankind requires that they should declare the causes which impel them to the separation.

Rather than breaking with the past, then, the Declaration's opening sentence references the British empire's past political bands, arrives at the present necessity of separation, and forecasts a future American place among the powers of the earth. The document's introduction thus conveys an interconnected past, present, and future—a history. It also conveys a historical consciousness by advancing a theory that "the Course of human events" should be analyzed according to entitlements derived from "the Laws of Nature and of Nature's God." And this history and historical consciousness become even more apparent on rereading the rest of the Declaration with this opening framing in mind.[4]

First, in light of this introduction, the preamble looks less like abstract theory and more like a general depiction of the ages and stages of human history. The idea that "all men are *created* equal"—my emphasis—and "endowed by their Creator with certain unalienable Rights" takes the reader back to the beginning of time and the state of nature. For John Locke and the later authors of the Declaration, the state of nature was not theoretical but invoked a real time and place where all were equal and free in the sense of possessing self-sovereignty and a right to the earth and its sustaining resources—a historical argument Locke made to counter Robert Filmer's claim that God granted absolute power over people and proprietorship over the earth to Adam and all succeeding kings. But, with only the unwritten laws of nature and God to guide them, and with no earthly authority to enforce those laws except one or a few individuals alone, people left the state of nature and formed governments to secure their lives, liberties, and estates, thus inaugurating the next stage of human history, the origins of government, which Locke and the Declaration's authors also believed to be a real historical phenomenon. The equality and liberty of the state of nature meant that government could only be created by consent, and the "unalienability" of certain rights meant that people retained a collective if not individual sovereignty and, if necessary, could replace any government that was destructive of its ends. "All experience hath shewn," the Declaration says, that people will "suffer, while evils are sufferable," but "when a long train of abuses and usurpations, pursuing invariably the same Object evinces a design to reduce them under absolute Despotism, it is their right" and "duty, to throw off such Government, and to provide new Guards for their future security."[5]

This general history of humankind then segues into a particular history of the American colonies: "Such has been the patient sufferance of these Colonies; and such is now the necessity which constrains them to alter their former Systems of Government." The preamble then describes the "history of the present King of Great Britain" as "a history of repeated injuries and usurpations, all having in direct object the establishment of an absolute Tyranny over these States," and concludes by promising to prove this by submitting facts to a "candid world." The purpose of the first part of the preamble was not therefore to invent ideals for an imagined future but to present a general history of humankind as a context and model for a particular history of colonial and revolutionary America that, seen in the light of the laws of nature and God, would explain and justify independence.[6]

The right to revolution inhered in those laws of nature and God, but natural and sacred law was believed to be eternal and unchanging, ahistorical, and as such could never be the cause of revolution. The reasons for revolution could therefore lie only in a disjuncture between the laws of nature and the course of human events—in history. Hence the Declaration's grievances—proofs that the "history of the present King of Great Britain" was indeed "a history of repeated injuries and usurpations"—were as essential in explaining "the causes of the separation" as natural law was in explaining the right to revolution. The grievances are mostly presented thematically rather than chronologically, although the final five mark a revolutionary turning point foreshadowed in the preamble. The first seven address the king's injuries and usurpations of the colonists' legislative rights, the next five his abuses of the judicial system, customs services, and military forces, and the thirteenth his unlawful collaboration with the British parliament, listing nine separate complaints arising from that collaboration. These assaults on "Liberty and the pursuit of Happiness" justified colonial protest and armed resistance before independence. The final five grievances, however—describing the king declaring the colonies out of his protection and waging war against them—represented direct threats to "Life" and thus invoked the first law of nature and God: the natural right and sacred duty of self-defense that almost, but not quite, justified revolution.

Almost, but not quite: the question remained of whether there was "a design" or "direct object" of establishing tyranny. The Declaration's conclusions thus begin by noting that colonists had petitioned the king against his oppressions and that he had responded only with repeated injury, proving he had acted knowingly and therefore intentionally and was thus "unfit to be the ruler of a free people." The Declaration also observed that the colonists had warned the British people of attempts by their legislature to extend a jurisdiction over the colonies that was unwarrantable owing to "the circumstances of our emigration and settlement here." That referred to a then well-known and much-recounted history according to which the first settlers had earned inviolable rights to property and self-government under their own representative assemblies by undertaking colonization themselves, without British help, and that these rights had been written into colonial charters and thus into the imperial constitution from the beginning. The British people, too, however, were deaf to the "voice of justice and of consanguinity." With war raging across the colonies, with all attempts at resolution made, and with the king's tyrannical intentions proven, revolution became "necessary" as the only way to preserve a people's lives, liberty, property, safety, and happiness. It was at this moment, then, that a long train of abuses and usurpations finally *evinced a design* to reduce the colonists under absolute despotism. The time for patient sufferance was therefore over, and it was now the colonists' right and indeed "duty" to overthrow their government and establish a new one. This was thus the "when" it was "in the Course of human events" that it became "necessary for one people to dissolve the political bands which have connected them with another."

The final paragraph of the conclusions brought the Declaration back to its first one, the introduction, with Americans acquiescing in the necessity of separation and declaring the colonies to be free and independent states. The authors finished by pledging their lives, fortunes, and sacred honor to each other and to the cause of independence, doing so with an appeal to "the Supreme Judge of the world" and the "protection of divine Providence" that reaffirmed their commitment to the laws of nature and of God.

The above description of the Declaration sketches out the history embedded in each of the document's sections in turn—the introduction, preamble, grievances, and conclusions. The rest of this book, however, rearranges the Declaration's "Course of human events" chronologically—past, present, and future. Part I begins by exploring natural law historiography and its application to the Declaration's general history of humankind from Creation and the state of nature through the origins of government and historical revolutions. A second chapter examines the Declaration's particular history of "emigration and settlement" and thus the origins of American colonial and British imperial government—how inherent natural rights and inherited English rights evolved into acquired American rights that centered on legislative autonomy and property rights under the protection of the crown. Part II shows the influences of the Declaration's past on the revolutionaries' present. Chapter 3 explores colonists' perceptions that property rights and self-government under the crown persisted, despite occasional disruption, and how the Declaration's blaming of the king for the colonists' grievances therefore made historical sense. Chapter 4 shows how the grievances represented recognizable violations of natural rights and of English and American civil rights in a highly sophisticated argument for independence that culminated in proof of the king's intent to impose absolute tyranny. Part III explores the influences of the Declaration's past and present on the future, as far as that could be foreseen in 1776. Chapter 5 examines the form of government and society the Declaration forecasted—potentially but not necessarily federal, republican (representative) but not necessarily Republican (nonmonarchical), and based on popular sovereignty but not necessarily democratically inclusive. Chapter 6 explores how the Declaration's logic excluded certain people from America's "one people" altogether, most notably enslaved people and Native Americans, and how its ideas about history and natural law rationalized the violations of other people's natural rights in the cause of self-defense. A brief postscript reflects on how the original history and natural law historiography of the Declaration was gradually forgotten and replaced by the natural rights and creedal interpretation of the document that prevails today.

This book thus reveals the original Declaration of Independence before later generations' interpretations transformed it into the one we are now familiar with. The principal author of the Declaration told us how to read the Declaration in its original form. In 1825, Thomas Jefferson wrote a letter to the Virginia historian Henry Lee that has since been frequently cited and yet much ignored in some of its meaning. Jefferson confirmed that certain "historical documents" in Lee's possession—the 1776 Virginia Constitution and Bill of Rights—were "corroborative of the facts and principles advanced in that Declaration." And he explained how purposely unoriginal the document was in advancing them. The "object of the Declaration of Independence" was, he wrote,

> not to find out new principles, or new arguments, never before thought of, not merely to say things which had never been said before; but to place before mankind the common sense of the subject; [in] terms so plain and firm, as to command their assent, [. . .] it was intended to be an expression of the american mind, and to give to that expression the proper tone and spirit called for by the occasion. all it's authority rests then on the harmonising sentiments of the day, whether expressed, in conversns in letters, printed essays or in the elementary books of public right, as Aristotle, Cicero, Locke, Sidney Etc.[7]

Many historians have paid heed to Jefferson's words and explored the influence of various "books of public right" on the Declaration. This book does so too, and agrees with the orthodox view that John Locke was the Declaration's most significant philosophical forebear, or at least that the document's authors relied on a Lockean synthesis of older ideas about natural law and history. That said, this book differs from most previous studies in emphasizing Lockean history and historiography rather than Locke's supposedly abstract theory, Lockean natural law rather than natural rights, and Lockean concepts of the rights of a people collectively rather than as individuals.

Historians have also extensively explored the influence of "conversations... letters, printed essays" on the American Revolution generally but have paid little heed to Jefferson's words about their influence on the Declaration of Independence specifically. Indeed, today's prevailing historiography supposes that earlier colonial and revolutionary political writing and oratory emphasized the colonists' inheritance of historical English civil rights, and it was only as abandonment of that inheritance began that colonists started defining American rights as natural rights. The Declaration is thus seen as emerging from late revolutionary writing produced from 1774 onward but largely detached from the longer traditions of colonial and revolutionary protest. This book proposes, in contrast, that the Declaration emphasized historical civil law and rights, and that earlier colonial and revolutionary writings and oratory emphasized natural law and rights, more than historians have generally appreciated. There was certainly a change in emphasis from "the rights of freeborn Englishmen" to American and natural rights from 1774, but there was an essential continuity in the belief, expressed in colonial political literature from the seventeenth century and reiterated in the Declaration of Independence, that natural and sacred law should be the basis of civil law and that natural rights accruing to people as "men" were the basis of colonists' civil rights as Britons and Americans. Indeed, recognizing the older colonial and revolutionary literature as based on natural law and on natural, English, and American rights allows us to read between the Declaration's lines and recover its historical content and consciousness. This new reading of the Declaration thus returns the document to its original place in the traditions of American thought and restores it to its place in a continuing rather than abruptly changing narrative of the American Revolution.[8]

Jefferson's recounting of documents, conversations, letters, essays, and books makes clear that the Declaration was not advancing "new principles, or new arguments." But the letter to Lee also tells us why that was so. The Declaration, Jefferson wrote, "was intended to be an expression of the american mind" and "to place before mankind the common sense of the subject." And the authors therefore had to rest "it's authority . . . on the harmonising sentiments of the day." Jefferson certainly exaggerated the extent of consensus. As this book shows, there was broad agreement on the Declaration's "principles," and neither the "committee of five" charged with drafting a declaration—Jefferson, John Adams, Benjamin Franklin, Robert Livingston, and Roger Sherman—nor the Continental Congress altered the substance of Jefferson's draft statements on natural law or the nature of his theory or methods of historical analysis. Indeed, the changes they did make reinforced rather than revised Jefferson's original statements on these matters.

The "facts," however, were another matter. The committee and Congress together, but mostly Congress, deleted about a third of Jefferson's first draft, some of it to eliminate wordiness, but much of it to edit out controversial or disputed facts or else to render them ambiguous enough for others to interpret them as they wished. The committee and Congress especially edited many of Jefferson's grievances, not least his attack on the slave trade. Congress also reduced his explanation of the origins of the colonies as "states" and the empire as a "league & amity" to an unexplained reference to "the circumstances of our emigration and settlement here," into which people could read a less radical version of early American history. On these and other issues, then, the final Declaration was less an expression of the American mind, as Jefferson conceived it, than an expression of Americans' many minds. The Declaration's authority therefore rested less on "the harmonising sentiments of the day" than on an artful harmonizing of the often discordant sentiments of the day.[9]

The need for the Declaration to appeal to as many people as possible made writing it an inclusive process, though far from an all-inclusive one. In addition to Thomas Jefferson, the committee of five (or at least Adams and Franklin), plus the fifty other delegates to the Continental Congress, there was also a fourth kind of author, and another one with varying opinions: the intended audience on whom the winning of independence ultimately depended and whose views therefore had to be accommodated. That is not quite to say that the Declaration was the product of "democratic writing," as one scholar has argued; the process of authorship and the resulting content excluded too many people at the time to warrant that description. But the document was certainly polyphonic, including many but not all voices in its production, and polysemic, including many but not all meanings in its expression. And, through its elisions and ambiguities, it often expressed two or more different and even contradictory meanings at once. Yet that variety of meanings did not lead to meaningless variety, for the Declaration contained its meanings in both senses of the term—by including as many of them as possible within the text, but also by trying to limit them within certain interpretative boundaries. It was, in short, a carefully crafted compromise, broadly appealing enough for a wide range of people to agree to, yet also meaningful and coherent enough to make a powerful case for independence.[10]

This book argues, then, that the Declaration based its case for independence on a known if contested past rather than on an imagined future. The document's original meanings therefore lie in its first sentence rather than its second one, in "the Course of human events" and "the Laws of Nature and of Nature's God" of the introduction rather than in the "self-evident" truths of the preamble. The authors thus presented the ideas "that all men are created equal, that they are endowed by their Creator with certain unalienable Rights, that among these are Life, Liberty and the pursuit of Happiness," and "That to secure these rights, Governments are instituted among Men, deriving their just powers from the consent of the governed" as historical facts dating from Creation and the origins of government, not as new ideas for an unprecedented future. And when they stated that "all experience hath shewn, that mankind are more disposed to suffer, while evils are sufferable," but "when a long train of abuses and usurpations, pursuing invariably the same Object evinces a design to reduce them under absolute Despotism, it is their right, it is their duty, to throw off such Government," they were not writing a new theory of revolution but drawing parallels between past "experience" and current events.

Reading the Declaration as grounded in contemporary understandings of the past also helps us understand its relationship to the present as it appeared in 1776. Its "circumstances of our emigration and settlement here," for example, explains how colonial charters established inviolable rights to property and legislative autonomy under the crown and therefore why it presented the "history of repeated injuries and usurpations" as "a history of the present King of Great Britain," and why the "Facts . . . submitted to a candid world" blamed George III rather than Parliament for "having in direct object the establishment of an absolute Tyranny over these States." Historicizing the Declaration also helps us resolve another of the Declaration's supposed mysteries, the contents of the grievances. The Declaration's presentation of those grievances in general terms rather than as specific actions by the king prompted anti-independence partisans then and some historians since to say that they were opaque and even deliberately misleading. As some of those historians admit, however, listing every offense would have made a cumbersome document indeed. Moreover, while the grievances' claims may seem obscure to us two and a half centuries later, they were easily recognizable to those who had lived through the Declaration's events or read about them in the copious pamphlets, newspapers, declarations, and petitions and discussed them in speeches, sermons, and conversations in the streets, coffee houses, and taverns that hosted the vibrant public political culture of the time. Furthermore, generalization allowed the king's actions to be placed in historical contexts, as violations of the colonists' inherent rights as men, inherited rights as Englishmen, and acquired rights as American colonists. Last, appreciating contemporary understandings of the laws of nature and God, in particular the natural right and sacred duty of self-preservation, helps explain how the final five grievances and the beginning of the conclusions—depicting the war that began at Lexington Green and the king's refusal to heed colonial petitions—mark a turning point from resistance and rebellion to revolution and independence.[11]

Seeing the Declaration as grounded in contemporary understandings of the past and present also helps us understand its relationship to the future the revolutionaries envisioned. Indeed, it helps us understand the apparent contradiction between the principles of equality and liberty on which the United States was supposedly founded and the vast inequalities and illiberalities that nevertheless survived independence. If the Declaration's strictures about universal equality and liberty applied only in a state of nature and only to individual sovereignty and rights to subsistence and therefore the earth and its produce, they were not intended to apply in full in civil society. Certainly, natural equality and liberty meant that the origins of government must be by consent and for the securing of certain unalienable rights. But the social contract also required that people subject themselves to the authority of civil government and law. And it also required that some people surrender more of their alienable rights than others, in accord with their supposedly unequal natural and circumstantial capacities and competences. The notion that all were *created* equal applied to self-sovereignty and property rights in a state of nature but did not mean that all were or would be equal in any other sense. Women, for example, were deemed to be naturally dependent and therefore incapable of exercising such public responsibilities as voting. Men with little or no property were deemed circumstantially dependent and therefore similarly unsuited to enfranchisement. And the government was authorized and indeed required to provide for its people's safety and happiness by depriving criminals of life, liberty, or property by execution, imprisonment, or fines, according to the severity of their offenses. None of the historical societies included in the Declaration's general history of humankind or in its particular history of the British colonies and empire had ever provided indiscriminate equality or unconditional unalienable rights for their subjects or citizens. Nor did the Declaration's authors envision such things for the future United States.

And inequality and the alienability of certain rights applied all the more to those outside the social contract. The origins of government took those who consented to it out of the state of nature, the realm of "all men," and reconstituted them as a particular people whose government was entrusted with protecting them against all external enemies. The Declaration's "circumstances of our emigration and settlement here" originally created thirteen peoples, but their common experience forged them into the "one people" referenced in the document's introduction. Yet emigration and settlement also separated European Americans from those they enslaved and from Native Americans, with enmities against "domestic" insurrectionaries and "the inhabitants of our frontiers" exacerbated in the War of Independence. Yet slavery was also a state of war in any case, according to the laws of nations, and as such it could legally continue after the Revolution, in line with the first law of nature and God—self-defense. Furthermore, as the Declaration's authors' use of the term "Savages" connotes, Native Americans supposedly lived in a state of nature and therefore did not own the lands within or beyond the thirteen colonies' frontiers, supposedly leaving the continent open to settlement from the Appalachian Mountains to the Mississippi River and possibly beyond, in line with the natural right to subsistence and in line with God's injunction to "mankind" in Genesis 1:28: "Be fruitful and multiply, and fill the earth, and subdue it; and have dominion over the fish of the sea and over the birds of the sky and over every living thing that creeps on the earth."

Far from breaking with history, then, the original Declaration of Independence portrayed a past and present that would continue into the future.

Indeed, the inequalities and iniquities that persisted after the American Revolution were not contradictions *of* the Declaration but reflections of the complexities of the laws of nature and God and the contingencies of the course of human events *within* the Declaration, as originally written and read. The document's authors were therefore neither hypocrites nor visionaries. They simply never intended to institute the civil equality and liberty for all or the "natural rights republic" that we imagine they promised. They aimed instead to create a *natural law republic* in which the inherent inequalities of its citizens would be codified for the better ordering of things and which would secure the lives, liberty, property, and happiness of its "one people," even at the expense of the natural rights of others, for as long as the future course of human events continued to require it.[12]

This book thus offers a new interpretation of the Declaration of Independence (or at least a renewed original interpretation) that has important implications for our understanding of the American Revolution and the founding of the nation. Parts of the book may seem bleak, in particular its argument that the Declaration's "Course of human events" and "Laws of Nature and of Nature's God" rationalized past, present, and future inequalities and iniquities. I stress here, then, that I celebrate the rereading of the Declaration as a charter for universal equality and liberty. Let me likewise stress that while this book does not call for a return to an original understanding of the Declaration, it does call for an understanding of the original Declaration. And it does so because, for all the good that a creedal reading of the document has done, its self-evident truths have also been used as excuses for inaction, as if they depicted existing realities rather than aspirations, and even as reasons for reaction, as if questioning their reality were seditious or sacrilegious. The creedal reading has thus been both a means of perpetuating historical iniquities and an argument for abolishing them. If new interpretations of the "self-evident" truths of universal equality and liberty help explain certain changes in the United States in the two and a half centuries since independence, old interpretations of "the Course of human events" and the "Laws of Nature and of Nature's God" help explain certain continuities. To prove this, let the Declaration's original facts and principles be submitted once again to a candid world.

PART I

The Past
To Secure These Rights

1

The Laws of Nature and of Nature's God

When in the Course of human events, it becomes necessary for one people to dissolve the political bands which have connected them with another, and to assume among the powers of the earth, the separate and equal station to which the Laws of Nature and of Nature's God entitle them, a decent respect to the opinions of mankind requires that they should declare the causes which impel them to the separation.

The Declaration of Independence begins by framing the separation of the American colonies from Great Britain as both historic and historical, an epic moment in the grandest possible narrative—a veritable "when" in nothing less than "the Course of human events." That course of events begins with the founding of the laws of nature and of God at Creation, addresses the colonial American past by referencing the political bands of empire, and includes the more recent revolutionary era with its promise to declare the causes of the separation of the colonies from Britain. And this first paragraph not only takes the reader from the beginning of time to the present but also looks to the future, forecasting a separate and equal American station among the powers of the earth.[1]

As well as framing independence as historic and historical, the Declaration's introduction signals its authors' historical consciousness. One form of historical consciousness is evident in the epical time frame itself; another lies in the idea that the event is significant enough to be declared to "mankind." More than that, though, the introduction reveals the document's theory of history and method of historical analysis. The key statement in this regard is that the laws of nature and of nature's God entitle Americans to independence. As that statement indicates, the founders believed that natural law was not an abstract concept but a set of legal entitlements under the laws of nations. As such, natural law was both a set of rules for how human beings should behave and a measure for judging whether they had done so correctly—a theory for how the world should work and a method for analyzing how the world works or has worked in practice. The laws of nature and God were thus the basis for analyzing the course of human events.

The history and historical consciousness evident in the Declaration's introduction provide a context and a framework, as introductions usually do, for understanding everything that follows, including the more famous second paragraph, the preamble, which comes next. In light of the introduction, the beginning of the preamble looks less like a set of abstract philosophical principles and more like a general history of humankind. Its "self-evident" truths describe the conditions of a state of nature in which all were "created equal" in the sense of each being a sovereign individual and having liberty to gain sustenance from the earth. Without a superintending magistrate, however, lives, liberty, property, and happiness were in perpetual danger, and so people formed governments in order "to secure these rights." It is worth noting here that the Declaration states that it was to secure these rights that "Governments are instituted among Men, deriving their just powers from the consent of the governed." Not should be instituted or will be instituted but "are" instituted—a simple present tense, but one that indicates the continuation of norms derived from the past. If a government was later "destructive of these ends," then natural and sacred law allowed it to be replaced. The Declaration signaled such revolutions as historical phenomena by noting that "all experience hath shewn" that people had suffered while evils were sufferable. "But," the Declaration states next, in line again with natural law, "when a long train of abuses and usurpations, pursuing invariably the same Object evinces a design to reduce them under absolute Despotism, it is their right, it is their duty, to throw off such Government, and to provide new Guards for their future security." And at that point the preamble's general history of humankind segues into its particular history of British America, using an em-dash followed by similar wording to highlight the parallels: "—Such has been the patient sufferance of these Colonies; and such is now the necessity which constrains them to alter their former Systems of Government. The history of the present King of Great Britain is a history of repeated injuries and usurpations, all having in direct object the establishment of an absolute Tyranny over these States." "To prove this, let Facts be submitted to a candid world," the preamble concludes, leading its readers into the grievances. And each of those grievances, for the founders, represented a violation of English and American civil laws that were grounded on the laws of nature and of God, as explored in chapter 4.

Thomas Jefferson later claimed that "all American whigs" agreed on "the facts and principles advanced" in the Declaration of Independence. That was certainly untrue regarding the Declaration's facts, and later chapters in this book detail significant disagreements among the authors and intended readers over the document's historical content. But Jefferson's claim was substantially true regarding the Declaration's principles, reflecting a broad consensus that the laws of nature and God should be the rules of human behavior and thus the basis for analyzing the course of human events. The committee of five and the Continental Congress made some changes to the statements of principle Jefferson enunciated in his first draft, but all of them reinforced rather than revised his original assertions. In the introduction, for example, the committee substituted "a people" for "one people," and Congress agreed, confirming that the Declaration was not philosophizing about theoretical peoples but depicting a real American people. Similarly, the committee substituted the general term "change" for the more specific "separation" to describe the independence they were declaring. It also altered Jefferson's "equal & independant station" to "separate and equal station," perhaps to distinguish the complete independence from Britain they were now claiming from the independence from the British Parliament that they had previously claimed. Otherwise, except for adding some commas and capital letters, Congress accepted the statements of principle submitted by the committee on June 28.[2]

The committee and Congress also altered Jefferson's preamble, but again, to enhance rather than detract from Jefferson's original statements of principle. The committee clarified Jefferson's phrasing by changing "We hold these truths to be sacred & undeniable; that all men are created equal & independant, that from that equal creation they derive rights inherent

& inalienable, among which are the preservation of life, & liberty, & the pursuit of happiness" to "We hold these truths to be self-evident that all men are created equal; that they are endowed by their creator with inherent & inalienable rights, that among these are life, liberty, and the pursuit of happiness." Congress in turn dropped "inherent," perhaps because natural rights were inherent by definition, and it added "certain" to indicate that its list of unalienable rights was not exhaustive. It also changed "inalienable" to "unalienable." It may be that one or more grammarians argued that inalienable was too absolute a term, signifying that certain rights could never be alienated in any circumstances. Unalienable, on the other hand, suggests that it was in the act of entering into society that certain rights could not be alienated, rather than through other acts—by committing crimes, for example, or by making war against a people. This was not a matter of mere pedantry as it clarified, first, that criminals might be punished by loss of their life, liberty, or property by execution, imprisonment, or fines—all considered essential to a system of law enforcement that was one of the principal reasons for consenting to government. Also, outsiders, such as Britons, Loyalists, Native Americans, and enslaved people, could and supposedly did alienate their natural rights as they had not entered into the American social contract but instead threatened the safety of those who had.

Congress also made some notable orthographical alterations for the engrossed, parchment copy of August 2. Or rather its printer, Timothy Matlack, did, as early modern printers were also interpreters, entrusted with making visual changes to texts to emphasize their meanings and enhance their impact. Matlack added capital letters to the "Course" of human events and to "Laws of Nature and of Nature's God," for example, apparently signaling these as especially important words and concepts. He also added to the number of hyphens included in previous versions of the document, and converted some into em-dashes. Matlack's first em-dash falls between the self-evident truths of the state of nature and the section on the origins and purposes of government, the second between those origins and purposes of government and the section on the right to revolution, and the third in the transition between that generalized history of revolutions and the particulars of the American Revolution. These additions emphasized the logical progression of the argument, reinforcing the idea that natural law was the basis of historical analysis and highlighting the connections between its general history of humankind and its particular history of the American colonies and revolution.³

The rest of this book explores how the Declaration's authors' history and natural-law historical consciousness manifested in the document's interpretation of the American past and the implications of that for the future United States. The rest of this first chapter, however, explores the origins of that historical consciousness and the general history of humanity it depicted. That exploration begins with Thomas Jefferson's ideas on natural law and history, and then examines those who influenced him, especially John Locke. It then shows how ideas about natural law and history informed English jurisprudence and also American colonial and revolutionary political literature before 1776. The history and natural law historiography of the Declaration of Independence had long histories of their own.

Thomas Jefferson thought deeply throughout his life about how subjects such as natural and sacred law, civil law, history, politics, and moral philosophy were constituted and how they related to each other. Though his ideas on these subjects developed over time, there were essential continuities in them, not least because he synthesized them from previous thinkers, most notably Francis Bacon, Isaac Newton, and John Locke, whom Jefferson esteemed as "the three greatest men that ever lived." It is from all three, but mainly from Locke, that the principal author of the Declaration of Independence got the ideas about natural law and history that he wrote into the American nation's founding document.⁴

When Jefferson organized his personal library after the War of Independence, he arranged large parts of it under the categories of "History," "Philosophy," and "Fine Arts," which roughly aligned with Bacon's description of the different "faculties of the mind" as "Memory, Reason, and Imagination." He also subdivided "History" into "Human history" and "Natural history" and "Philosophy" into "Human philosophy" and "Natural philosophy." When he sold his by then 6,487 books to the Library of Congress in 1815, to replace those burned by the British during the War of 1812, he refined the subcategories. This time, "History" included "Civil History (ancient; foreign; British; American; ecclesiastical)" and "Philosophy" included "Moral Philosophy (law of nature and nations; religion; law; politics; economics)." These categories remained in place for Jefferson's recommendations for the library of the new University of Virginia in the 1820s, and his suggestion of ten professorships also reveals much about his intellectual taxonomies. The eighth professor, for example, would cover the following subjects: "Government[,] Political Economy[,] Law of Nature and Nations[,] History, being interwoven with Politics and Law."[5]

What is significant here is not only the categories themselves but the relationships among them. Most striking, perhaps, are the subcategorizing of "Human history" and "Natural history" under the single heading "History" and the subcategorizing of "Human philosophy" and "Natural Philosophy" under the single heading "Philosophy," linking natural science to human action and thought. And while Jefferson separated "Civil History" and "Moral Philosophy," the two came together again under the "law of nature and nations." In turn, the putative professor was expected to teach "Law of Nature and Nations" alongside "Political Economy," "Government," and indeed "History," the last of which Jefferson saw as "interwoven with Politics and Law."

Jefferson's sense of what we now call intellectual disciplines illustrates that he did not see the laws of nature and God as abstract concepts but rather as related to all aspects of human thought and endeavor. The "law of nature and nations; religion; law; politics; economics" related to "Moral Philosophy." These in turn related to the subcategories of "Civil History": "ancient; foreign; British; American; ecclesiastical." It should not surprise us, perhaps, that the empirically minded materialist Jefferson should stress the utility of philosophy not as an isolated and abstruse subject but as a foundation for understanding such tangible matters as political economy, government, law, and history. Or that someone who took a razor to a Bible to cut out the miracles and leave only what he called "The Life and Morals of Jesus of Nazareth" should see religion not as mysterious ethereality but as teachings to be put to practical uses. Nor should it surprise us, therefore, that he saw the laws of nature and God that he wrote into the Declaration of Independence as material phenomena to be drawn on for understanding the course of human events.[6]

As Danielle Allen and Hannah Spahn have shown, the connection between Jefferson's ideas about natural law and history are written into the Declaration's opening phrase. The word "Course" evoked such natural phenomena as rivers and, combined with "human events," implied the ebbs, flows, and occasional torrents of human history. And, as that implies,

Jefferson's historical thought was shaped by two concepts of time deriving from Isaac Newton, once again linking nature to human behavior. Newton's "absolute, true and mathematical time" corresponded to Jefferson's eternal natural law, while his "relative, apparent and common time" corresponded to the temporalities of human events. Eighteenth-century "philosophical history," furthermore, posited an idealized convergence of absolute time and relative time, with Enlightenment knowledge of natural law advancing to where its principles could be better integrated into civil law and governance. History itself could reveal "the constant and universal principles of human nature," according to David Hume, and was therefore a form of "philosophy teaching by examples," according to Henry Bolingbroke. Jefferson's early faith in this optimistic philosophical history was challenged by the disruptions of the revolutionary era, however, and a more pessimistic viewpoint entered his historical thinking, one placing greater weight on divergences between absolute and relative time. Those divergences, between natural law and human actions, were indeed fundamental to the Declaration's reasons for independence.[7]

If Jefferson derived his ideas about the faculties of the mind from Bacon and about the dualism of time from Newton, he derived his application of them to the course of human events primarily from Locke. It is true that disputes over Locke's influence on Jefferson date back to the latter's own lifetime. Jefferson himself complained to James Madison, for example, that "Richard Henry Lee has charged" that he had copied the Declaration of Independence "from Locke's treatise on Government," stating "that I turned to neither book nor pamphlet while writing it." Jefferson thus denied copying, but he did not deny deriving; an equivocation that acknowledges that authors frequently inserted memorized ideas and phrases into their own writings when they wished to condense arguments into commonplaces that readers could recognize.[8]

It is also true that ideas about natural law as a foundation for civil law long predated Locke. Cicero (106–43 BCE) pronounced "that right is founded not in opinion but in nature. There is," he said, "a true law, right reason, agreeing with nature and diffused among all, unchanging, everlasting, which calls to duty by commanding, deters from wrong by forbidding. . . . It is not allowable to alter this law nor to deviate from it. Nor can it be abrogated." Natural law must therefore "bind all nations and all times" and must be the "one common lord and ruler of all, even God, the framer and proposer of this law." Theologians, jurists, and philosophers such as Richard Hooker, Edward Coke, Hugo Grotius, Algernon Sidney, and Samuel von Pufendorf expressed similar ideas before Locke, and Jean-Jacques Burlamaqui, Emer de Vattel, and William Blackstone did so after him. It is therefore true that the Declaration's ideas were a synthesis of many writings over many centuries. Yet it was very much a Lockean synthesis, one mirroring Locke's particular accounts of equality in a state of nature, consent of the governed, the purposes of government, and the right to revolution, as well as his and older views on the relations between natural law, the laws of nations, civil law, government, and history.[9]

John Locke's first major publication was *Questions Concerning the Law of Nature* (1664), but he developed his ideas on the relationship between natural law and civil law and governance most thoroughly in his more famous later works. In his *Second Treatise of Government*, he argued that "The *State of Nature* has a Law of Nature to govern it, which obliges everyone: And Reason, which is that Law, teaches all Mankind . . . that being all equal and independent, no one ought to harm another in his Life, Health, Liberty, or Possessions." Furthermore, "The Obligations of the Law of Nature, cease not in Society, but only in many Cases are drawn closer, and have by Humane [i.e. civil] Laws known Penalties annexed to them, to inforce their observation." Thus "the Law of Nature stands as an Eternal Rule to all Men, *Legislators* as well as others." Indeed, "The *Rules* that" legislators "make for other Mens Actions, must, as well as their own and other Mens Actions, be conformable to the Law of Nature, *i.e.* to the Will of God, of which that is a Declaration." And "Princes" too "owe subjection to the Laws of God and Nature. No Body, no Power can exempt them from the Obligations of that Eternal Law."[10]

As the laws of nature and God were standards for human conduct, they were also standards for judging that conduct. Locke made that point best in his *Essay Concerning Human Understanding* when addressing the "*laws* that men generally refer their actions to, to judge of their rectitude, or obliquity." These comprised "*First*, The *divine* law, whereby I mean, that law which God has set to the actions of men, whether promulgated to them by the light of nature, or the voice of revelation." And "*Secondly*, the *civil* law, the rule set by the commonwealth to the actions of those who belong to it. . . . engaged to protect the lives, liberties, and possessions of those who live according to its laws." And "*Thirdly*, the *law of opinion or reputation*.

Virtue and vice are names pretended, and supposed everywhere to stand for actions in their own nature right and wrong," Locke concluded, "and as far as they really are so applied, they so far are coincident with the *divine law*."[11]

As that indicates, Locke considered the laws of nature and God not as abstract concepts but as actual laws. Indeed, as for the later American founders, it would have been out of intellectual character for an empiricist like Locke to view them as merely theoretical, and it was the same with the state of nature and the social contract, which he regarded as real phenomena and not just theoretical or heuristic devices. Locke indeed subscribed to the contemporary orthodoxy that a state of nature existed between nations and that relations between them were governed by natural law. Answering the "mighty Objection, *Where are*, or ever were, there any *Men in such a State of Nature*," Locke asserted that "all *Princes* and Rulers of *Independent* Governments all through the World, are in a State of Nature" in relation to each other. Even "in a Commonwealth" and under "the Laws of the Society," individuals remain "in the State of Nature with the rest of Mankind," so any "Community is one body in the State of Nature, in respect of all other States or persons out of its Community." Natural law "therefore, contains the Power of War and Peace, Leagues and Alliances, and all the Transactions, with all Persons and Communities without the Commonwealth." Even "Promises and Bargains for Truck, *&c.* between the two Men in the Desert Island, mentioned by *Garcilasso De la vega*, in his History of *Peru*, or between a *Swiss* and an *Indian*, in the Woods of *America*, are binding to them, though they are perfectly in a State of Nature, in reference to one another." Locke also argued that "*Absolute Monarchy* . . . is *inconsistent with Civil Society*, and so can be no Form of Civil Government at all." As the "*end of Civil Society*" was to eliminate "those inconveniences of the State of Nature, which necessarily follow from every Man's being Judge in his own Case, by setting up a known Authority to which every one of that Society may Appeal upon any Injury received, or Controversy that may arise," it followed that those "who have not such an Authority to Appeal to . . . are still *in the state of Nature*. And so is every *Absolute Prince* in respect of those who are under his *Dominion*."[12]

Locke also called on the sixteenth-century theologian Richard Hooker as a witness against "those that say, There were never any Men in the State of Nature," citing "the Judicious *Hooker, Eccl. Pol. Lib.* I. *Sect.* 10. where he says . . . the Laws of Nature, *do bind Men . . . although they have never any settled fellowship, never any Solemn Agreement amongst themselves what to do or not to do.*" Locke then affirmed in his own words "That all Men are naturally in that State, and remain so, till by their own Consents they make themselves Members of some Politick Society." Hooker was also one of Locke's sources for the self-evident character of equality in the state of nature. The "*equality of Men by Nature,*" Locke wrote, in words that would echo in the Declaration of Independence, "the Judicious *Hooker* looks upon as so evident in it self, and beyond all question, that he makes it the Foundation of that Obligation to mutual Love amongst Men, on which he Builds the Duties they owe one another, and from whence he derives the great Maxims *of Justice* and *Charity.*" Locke otherwise said little about what later came to be called "moral sense," and Thomas Jefferson and others may have been influenced by later Scottish philosophers on this matter. That said, if the Declaration's self-evident truth of equality had any personally affective quality to it, any sense of a "moral sense," it most likely derived from Locke and Hooker.[13]

Above all, though, Locke made the case for the reality that all were created equal and endowed with liberty in a state of nature, with all the implications of that for the origins and purposes of government, in historiographic opposition to Robert Filmer's divine-right argument for the absolute power and proprietorship of Adam and all kings who succeeded him. The *Two Treatises* together read indeed like a modern historical essay in which the author begins by debunking an earlier thesis before revealing their own. In the lesser-read *First Treatise*, the title tells us, "The False Principles and Foundation OF Sir *Robert Filmer*, And His FOLLOWERS, ARE Detected and Overthrown," while the *Second Treatise* is described as "an ESSAY CONCERNING The True Original, Extent, and End OF Civil-Government." Early in the *First Treatise*, Locke positioned himself "In opposition" to Filmer's "Doctrine" that "*Adam was Monarch of the whole World*" and promised to show "1. That by this grant, I Gen. 28 God gave no immediate power to *Adam* over Men, over his Children, over those of his own Species; and so he was not made Ruler, or *Monarch*, by this Charter," and "2. That by this Grant God gave him not *Private Dominion* over the Inferior Creatures, but right in common with all Mankind; so neither was he *Monarch* upon the account of the Property here given him." The *First Treatise* is thus largely a biblical exegesis countering Filmer's divine right argument for the absolute power and proprietorship of kings in favor of an original, natural, and God-given equality and liberty of all.[14]

Locke thus began his argument for natural liberty and equality with the beginning of time, opposing Robert Filmer's claim for a "*Fatherly Authority* . . . first vested in *Adam*." And toward the end of his lengthy "Scripture History," Locke once again dismissed Filmer's claim that through "*Abraham, Isaac, and* Jacob, *until the* Egyptian Bondage . . . *we may trace this Paternal Government unto the* Israelites *coming into* Egypt . . . of Absolute Monarchical Power descending from *Adam*," arguing that "for 2290 Years . . . he cannot produce any one Example of any Person who claim'd or Exercised Regal Authority by right of *Fatherhood;* or shew any one who being a King was *Adams* heir."[15]

Locke's argument for an original equality of all and against the divine-right absolute power of kings included a case for common and individual rights to property (whether in common or in private ownership) for their subsistence, and thus the natural and God-given right to life. This form of Lockean equality was also anti-Filmerian. Locke quoted Filmer's claim, as per Genesis 1:28, that "Adam" was "*commanded to Multiply and People the Earth, and to subdue it, and having Dominion given him over all Creatures, was thereby the Monarch of the whole World*" and that "*none of his Posterity had any Right to possess any thing, but by his Grant or Permission, or by Succession from him.*" Locke claimed instead that "*God said, Let us make Man in our Image, after our likeness, and let them have Dominion over the Fish,* &c."—meaning that all "were to have Dominion" and to "signify *Adam* singly" as proprietor of everything "is against both Scripture and Reason." Hence, "Whether we consider natural *Reason,* which tells us, that Men, being once born, have a right to their Preservation, and consequently to Meat and Drink, and such other things, as Nature affords for their Subsistence: Or *Revelation,* which gives us an account of those Grants God made of the World to *Adam,* and to *Noah,* and his sons, tis very clear, that God, as king *David* says, *Psal.* CXV. xvi. *has given the Earth to the Children of Men,* given it to Mankind in common."[16]

Locke's argument for equal access to the earth and its resources thus relates to the first law of nature and God—the unalienable right to life. "God having made Man," Locke wrote, "and planted in him . . . a strong desire of Self-preservation, and furnished the World with things fit for Food and Rayment and other Necessaries of Life," it would be a "curious . . . piece of Workmanship" if "by its own Negligence, or want of Necessaries" people "should perish." Locke believed it must therefore be that "I *Gen.* 28, 29" meant that "Man's *Property* in the Creatures, was founded upon the right he had, to make use of those things, that were necessary or useful to his Being." Therein also lay the historical origins of private property. "God, who hath given the World to Men in common," Locke wrote, "hath also given them reason to make use of it to the best advantage of Life, and convenience." There must therefore "of necessity be a means *to appropriate*" it for better use by "any particular Man." Hence anything "he removes out of the State that Nature hath provided, and left it in, he hath mixed his *Labour* with it, and joyned to it something that is his own, and thereby makes it his *Property*. It being by him removed from the common state Nature placed it in, it hath by this *labour* something annexed to it, that excludes the common right of other Men . . . at least where there is enough, and as good left in common for others" (a caveat that defies characterizations of Locke as an advocate of selfish individualism).[17]

The idea that people are "born equal" followed from the same natural law principles that determined that they were originally created equal. "Men are not," Locke explained, "Proprietors of what they have, merely for themselves," as "their Children have a Title to part of it, and have their Kind of Right joyn'd with their Parents, in the Possession which comes to be wholly theirs, when death having put an end to their Parents use of it." Hence no one could legitimately alienate their children's liberty or property, and nor could any conqueror legitimately claim it, a point to be explored further in chapter 2.[18]

The absolute equality and liberty of Creation and the state of nature would determine the proper origins of civil government and law but would also be circumscribed by that civil government and law. First, the inherent dangers of absolute equality and liberty were what motivated people to form civil government and law. But the fact that all were created equal by nature and God meant that people could only create civil government and laws that would limit their equality and liberty by their own consent and for their greater security and happiness. "IF Man in the State of Nature be so free," and "absolute Lord of his own Person and Possessions, equal to the greatest, and subject to no Body, why," Locke asked, "will he part with his Freedom? Why will he give up this Empire, and subject himself to the Dominion and Controul of any other Power?" He answered "that though in the state of Nature he hath such a right, yet the Enjoyment of it is very uncertain, and constantly exposed to the Invasion of others." For "all being Kings as much as he, every Man his Equal . . . the enjoyment of the property he has in this state is very unsafe, very unsecure." And so "'tis not without reason," Locke continued, "that he seeks out, and is willing to joyn in Society with others . . . for the mutual *Preservation* of their Lives, Liberties and Estates, which I call by the general Name, *Property*." Hence Locke explained the difference between the two states in the following terms: "THE *Natural Liberty* of Man is to be free from any Superior Power on Earth, and not to be under the Will or Legislative Authority of Man, but to have only the Law of Nature for his Rule." Whereas "The *Liberty of Man, in Society*, is to be under no other Legislative Power, but that established, by consent, in the Common-wealth, nor under the Dominion of any Will, or Restraint of any Law, but what that Legislative shall enact, according to the Trust put in it." The first lines of the preamble of the Declaration of Independence do not therefore predict the future adoption of equality and liberty for all under a new American government but instead depict a general history of humankind in which the absolute equality and liberty of the state of nature were abandoned, by consent, for greater security of life, liberty, property, and happiness.[19]

Once again, for Locke, the origins of government by consent and for the purposes of securing life, liberty, property, and happiness were not theoretical propositions but historical facts. As an empiricist, Locke admitted but attempted to reckon with problems of evidence to support his claim that the origins of government by consent had "been the practice of the World from its first beginning to this day." To the idea that "the consent of any number of Freemen capable of a majority to unite and incorporate" was the "*beginning* to any *lawful Government* in the World," Locke heuristically proposed "two Objections." First, "*That there are no Instances to be found in Story* [history], *of a Company of Men independent and equal one amongst another, that met together, and in this way began and set up a Government*." Locke answered this objection by stating that "it is not at all to be wonder'd, that *History* gives us but a very little account of Men, *that lived together in the State of Nature*" as the "inconveniences of that condition, and the love, and want of Society, no sooner brought any number of them together, but they presently united and incorporated." Hence "Government is every where antecedent to Records, and Letters seldome come in amongst a People, till a long continuation of Civil Society has . . . provided for their Safety, Ease, and Plenty." Hence "both *Common-wealths*" and "*Persons* . . . are commonly *ignorant of their own Births* and *Infancies*." Locke thus sometimes relied on retrospective conjecture to demonstrate the historical realities of the state of nature and the social contract. He wrote, for example, that "if we may not suppose *Men* ever to have been *in the State of Nature,* because we hear not much of them in such a State, we may as well suppose the Armies of *Salmanasser,* or *Xerxes* were never Children, because we hear little of them, till they were Men, and imbodied in Armies." Locke added that "He must shew a strange inclination to deny evident matter of fact . . . who will not allow that the *beginning* of *Rome* and *Venice* were by the uniting together of several Men free and independent one of another, amongst whom there was no natural Superiority or Subjection."[20]

Locke's second hypothetical objection was, "*'Tis impossible of right that Men should*" consent to be governed because "*being born under Government, they are to submit to that, and are not at liberty to begin a new one.*" His response was once again conjectural and rhetorical. but also historically irrefutable: "how came so many lawful Monarchies into the World?" he asked. He added too that "there are no Examples so frequent in History, both Sacred and Prophane, as those of Men withdrawing themselves, and their Obedience, from the Jurisdiction they were born under, and the Family or Community they were bred up in, and *setting up new Governments* in other places; from whence sprang all that number of petty Commonwealths in the beginning of Ages, and which always multiplyed." One specific example he cited was the founding of Tarentum in eighth-century Italy, and he added his hope that "those who went away from *Sparta* with *Palentus,* mentioned by *Justin* . . . , will be allowed to have been *Freemen* independent one of another, and to have set up a Government over themselves, by their own consent."[21]

With secular evidence in short supply, however, Locke deployed scriptural sources. He noted, for example, that the "*Gileadites*" called on "*Jephtha* to assist them against the *Ammonites,* to make him their Ruler." And he cited chapter and verse for empirical validation: "*And the people made him head and captain over them,* Judg. 11. 11 . . . *And he judged Israel,* Judg. 12. 7. that is, was their *Captain-General, six Years.*" Locke gave several other examples from "Scripture History," including cases of people rejecting rulers. When "the Children of *Israel* desired a King . . . *to fight their battels* I Sam. 8. 20," for instance, "God granting their Desire, says to *Samuel, I will send thee a Man* . . . *to be Captain over my People Israel, that he may save my People out of the hands of the Philistines,* c. 9. v. 16." However, "those, who after *Saul's* being solemnly chosen and saluted *King* by the *Tribes* at *Mispah*, were unwilling to have him as their King," claiming that "This Man is unfit to be our *King*, not having Skill and Conduct enough in War, to be able to defend us," and God then "resolved to transfer the Government to *David*." Even God, it seems, obeyed the laws of nature and Himself.[22]

Locke thus claimed that "I have given several Examples out of History, of *People free and in the State of Nature*, that being met together incorporated and *began a Common-wealth*." And he concluded: "Reason being plain on our side, that Men are naturally free, and the Examples of History shewing, that the *Governments* of the World . . . had their beginning laid on that foundation, and were *made by the Consent of the People*." Hence "There can be little room for doubt, either where the Right is, or what has been the Opinion, or Practice of Mankind, about the *first erecting of Governments*."[23]

Locke supplemented his historical evidence with what he saw as contemporary repetitions of the origins of government, describing "the *Kings* of the *Indians* in *America*" as "a Pattern of the first Ages in *Asia* and *Europe*." Citing Josephus Acosta's *The naturell and morall historie of the Indies* (1604), Locke wrote "that in many parts of *America* there was no Government at all. *There are great and apparent Conjectures*, says he, *that these Men*, speaking of those of *Peru*, *for a long time had neither Kings nor Common-wealths, but lived in Troops, as they do this day in* Florida, *the* Cheriquanas, *those of* Bresil, *and many other Nations, which have no certain Kings, but as occasion is offered in Peace or War, they choose their Captains as they please*." He also argued that Native Americans practiced consent, as when an "Heir for want of Age, Wisdom, Courage, or any other Qualities" was "less fit for Rule," people "used their natural freedom, to set up him, whom they judged the ablest, and most likely, to Rule well over them." And, "Conformable hereunto we find the People of *America*, who . . . enjoy'd their own natural freedom, though . . . they commonly prefer the Heir of their deceased King; yet if they find him any way weak, or uncapable, they pass him by and set up the stoutest and bravest Man for their Ruler." Locke's famous assertion that "in the beginning all the World was *America*" was therefore not a metaphorical but a historical claim.[24]

The equality and liberty of the state of nature also premised the right to revolution, although that right could only be acted on if necessitated by the course of human events. "The Reason why Men enter into Society, is the preservation of their Property" (in the wider sense of lives, liberties, and estates), Locke explained. And since people would not give government "a Power to destroy that, which every one designs to secure, by entering into Society, and for which the People submitted themselves to the Legislators of their own making," it followed that *"whenever the Legislators endeavour to take away, and destroy the Property of the People,* or to reduce them to Slavery under Arbitrary Power, they put themselves into a state of War with the People, who are thereupon absolved from any farther Obedience, and are left to the common Refuge, which God hath provided for all Men against Force and Violence." If indeed "the *Legislative* shall transgress this fundamental Rule of Society; and . . . *endeavour to grasp* themselves, *or put into the hands of any other an Absolute Power* over the Lives, Liberties, and Estates of the People," they "*forfeit the Power* the People had put into their hands for quite contrary ends, and it devolves to the People, who have a Right to resume their original Liberty, and," in words echoed in the Declaration of Independence, "by the Establishment of a new Legislative (such as they shall think fit) provide for their own Safety and Security, which is the end for which they are in Society." And this applied too, Locke noted, "concerning the *supreame Executor,* who having a double trust put in him, both to have a part in the Legislative, and the supreme Execution of the Law, Acts against both, when he goes about to set up his own Arbitrary Will as the law of the Society."[25]

Locke added caveats to the right to revolution, however, as the Declaration of Independence later would. He acknowledged first that "it will be said, that the People being ignorant, and always discontented, to lay the Foundation of Government in the unsteady Opinion, and uncertain Humour of the People, is to expose it to certain ruine; And *no Government* will be *able long to subsist,* if the People may set up a new Legislative, whenever they take offence at the old one. To this, I Answer," Locke continued, "Quite the contrary. People are not so easily got out of their old Forms" as some suggest. "They are hardly to be prevailed with to amend the acknowledg'd Faults, in the Frame they have been accustom'd to," he noted, adding that "This slowness and aversion in the People to quit their old Constitutions, has, in the many Revolutions which have been seen in this Kingdom, in this and former ages, still kept us to, or, after some interval of fruitless attempts, still brought us back again to, our old Legislative of King, Lords and Commons." These examples may account for the Declaration's claim that "all experience hath shewn" that people will suffer much before resorting to revolution. Locke thus stated, in accord with the later Declaration's dictums, that until "mischief be grown general, and the ill designs of the Rulers become visible, or their attempts sensible to the greater part, the People, who are more disposed to suffer, than to right themselves by Resistance, are not apt to stir." But, he added, "if a long train of Abuses, Prevarications, and Artifices, all tending in the same way, make the design visible," then people "have a Right to resume their original Liberty, and, by the Establishment of a new Legislative . . . provide for their own Safety and Security." Thomas Jefferson may not have turned to any book or pamphlet when writing his draft declaration, but he remembered John Locke's words well enough.[26]

The Declaration of Independence had to get its message across as concisely as possible. There was therefore no room to detail the historical examples Locke provided of the natural equality of all men, unalienable rights, the social contract, consent of the governed, purposes of government, and the right to revolution, or to explain the historical theory and methods in which natural law was the basis of analysis of human history. The authors therefore relied on readers' prior knowledge and capacities for inference to make those connections themselves. And they had good reason to believe that their intended audience would do so, as many of the Declaration's readers were familiar with Lockean natural law historiography, if not directly from Locke then from one or more of the many exegeses or other similar writings that appeared in colonial and revolutionary America before 1776.[27]

As Craig Yirush has shown, early advocates of colonists' rights to property and political autonomy invoked Edward Coke's ruling in *Calvin's Case* in 1608 that the Scottish Robert Colville, born after the 1603 Union of the Crown, had the right to inherit English land as a subject of King James VI of Scotland (who became James I of England on the death of Elizabeth I), a judgment that rested on the laws of nature and nations rather than on common law. And many American colonists evidently agreed with Coke's statements that "the law of nature is immutable," that it came "before any judicial or municipal law in the world," and was "part of the laws of England." Daniel Dulany the Elder, perhaps the most widely read of colonial political writers before the revolutionary era, cited Coke, Hugo Grotius's *On the Law of War and Peace* (1625), Samuel Pufendorf's *On The Law of Nature and of Nations* (1672), Henry Care's *English Liberties* (1682), and other works predating Locke in his 1728 reflections on the rights of American colonists to English laws as laws of nature. He thus applied the idea that "Common Law, takes in the Law of Nature, the Law of Reason, and the revealed Law of God; which are equally binding, at All times, in All Places, and to all Persons" as premises for his opposition to prerogative powers deployed by the Lords Baltimore following the restoration of the Maryland proprietorship in 1715. And he cited "that great Man . . . the Learned Mr. Locke" when detailing the evolution of natural law into civil law, writing that "Men, from a state of Nature and Equality, formed themselves into Society, for mutual Defence, and Preservation, and agreed to submit to Laws that should be the rule of their Conduct," before applying these principles to his history of the settlement of Maryland, as explored further in chapter 2.[28]

Many of the revolution's most famous writers made the same connections between natural law and human institutions and events. As early as 1762, James Otis laid out ten principles and facts of government in opposition to Governor Francis Bernard extending prerogative powers by appropriating public funds to fit out a vessel to defend Cape Breton fishermen from privateers. The last five were components of the British constitution, but the first five were principles upon which that constitution supposedly rested:

> 1. God made all men naturally equal. 2. The ideas of earthly superiority, preheminence and grandeur are educational . . . not innate. 3. Kings were (and plantation Governor's should be) made for the good of the people, and not the people for them. 4. No government has a right to make hobby horses, asses and slaves of the subject. . . . 5. Tho' most governments are *de facto* arbitrary, and consequently the curse and scandal of human nature; yet none are *de jure* arbitrary.

The above extended over four pages as it was accompanied by footnotes comprising several long extracts from "Locke's DISCOURSE on GOVERN'T," an indulgence Otis justified by reckoning Locke as "not only one of the most wise, as well as most honest, but the most impartial man that ever lived." And on that basis he argued that colonists' claim "to all the privileges of the people of Great Britain" were "a declaration of what they are intitled to by the common law, by their several charters, by the law of nature and nations, and by the law of God."[29]

Two years later, with the Sugar Act enacted and the Stamp Act impending, Otis began his *Rights of the British Colonies* with a twenty-page

"Introduction" on "the Origin of Government" that extensively quoted Grotius, Pufendorf, Vattel, and most of all Locke, before applying their ideas to the origins "Of Colonies in General," then "the natural Rights of Colonists" and "the Political and Civil Rights of the British Colonists," as he subtitled each section. Otis did not believe that a state of nature had existed as people were born dependent. But for him that only confirmed that government was "founded *on the necessities of our nature*," that "an original supreme Sovereign, absolute, and uncontroulable, *earthly* power *must* exist in and preside over every society," but also that it "is *originally* and *ultimately* in the people." As "the people" cannot "*rightfully* make an absolute, unlimited renunciation of this divine right," government "is ever in the nature of the thing given in *trust*, and on a condition . . . that the person or persons on whom the sovereignty is confer'd by the people, shall *incessantly* consult *their* good." So, he argued, "The *end* of government being the *good* of mankind, points out its great duties . . . to provide for the security, the quiet, and happy enjoyment of life, liberty, and property." It followed for Otis that "Every British subject born on the Continent of America, or in any other British dominions, is by the law of God, and nature, by the common law, and by act of parliament . . . entitled to all the natural, essential, inherent, and inseparable rights of our fellow subjects in Great-Britain." The "imposition of taxes" was thus "irreconcileable with the rights of Colonists, as British subjects, and as men."[30]

Otis also argued that "the *community* perpetually retains a supreme power of saving themselves from the attempts and designs of any body, even of their legislators whenever they shall be so foolish, or so wicked, as to lay and carry on designs, against the liberties and properties of the subject." And he extensively quoted "Mr. Locke" to argue that "there remains still, '*in the people, a supreme power to remove, or alter, the legislative when they find the legislative act contrary to the trust reposed in them,*'" explaining that "a dissolution of government, Locke says, may be done, '. . . 1st. When the legislative is altered. Which is often by the prince, but sometimes by the whole legislative." That, as Otis added, continuing to quote Locke, might be "by invading the *property* of the subject, and making themselves arbitrary disposers of the lives, liberties and fortunes of the people; reducing them to slavery under arbitrary power" whereby "they put themselves into a state of war with the people, who are thereupon absolved from any further obedience, and are left to the common refuge which GOD hath provided for all men, against force and violence." Government then "devolves to the *people*, who have a right to *resume* their original liberty, and by the establishment of a *new* legislative (such as they shall think fit) provide for their own safety and security, which is the end for which they are in society."³¹

Others were less loquacious, perhaps because Otis had done so much work for them. Even so, Daniel Dulany the Younger noted in his 1765 considerations on taxes that "In the Opinion of a great Lawyer, 'an act of parliament may be void,' and of a great Divine, 'all Men have natural, and Freemen legal Rights, which they may justly maintain, and no legislative Authority can deprive them of.'" And, he said, colonial charters were "founded upon the unalienable Rights of the Subject, and upon the most sacred Compact" that ensured "Exemption from Taxes *not imposed with their Consent.*" William Hicks, also writing during the Stamp Act crisis, although he published his pamphlet on the nature and extent of parliamentary power during the Townshend Acts crisis, drew his arguments against British parliamentary taxation "from general principles," stating that "the distinguishing characteristic of the *English* constitution" is "that no free man shall be restrained in the exercise of his natural liberty, or, in the use of his acquired property but by those regulations to which he has *really* or *virtually* subscribed." It followed therefore that "The natural right which every man possesses, to restrain, by every possible method, the progress of arbitrary, lawless government, is not at this day to be controverted."³²

James Wilson also began his considerations on parliamentary authority, written during the Townshend Acts crisis but published after passage of the Coercive Acts, with first principles: that "ALL men are, by nature, equal and free: No one has a right to any authority over another without his consent: All lawful government is founded on the consent of those, who are subject to it: Such consent was given with a view to ensure and to encrease the happiness of the governed above what they could enjoy in an independant and unconnected state of nature." Therefore, "the happiness of the society is the FIRST law of every government." And, he added, "THIS rule is founded on the law of nature: It must control every political maxim: it must regulate the Legislature itself." Wilson cited Burlamaqui's statement that "'civil liberty is nothing else but natural liberty, divested of that part which constituted the independance of individuals by the authority which it confers on sovereigns, attended with a right of insisting upon their making a good use of their authority.'" Popular sovereignty is therefore "founded on the law of nature ... must control every political maxim" and "regulate the legislature itself," and he cited "BLACKSTONE 41" to the effect that "The law of nature is superiour in obligation to any other." He further argued that "The people have a right to insist that this rule be served; and are entitled to demand a moral security that the Legislature will observe it. If they have not the first, they are slaves; if they have not the second, they are, every moment, exposed to slavery." He therefore hoped that the colonists would "be re-instated in the enjoyment of those rights, to which we are entitled by the supreme and uncontroulable laws of nature, and the fundamental principles of the British constitution."[33]

Some advocates of colonists' rights circulated these ideas to wider audiences that were not directly reachable through learned pamphlets. Boston Massacre Orations, also published as pamphlets, were particularly apt for such popularization. Joseph Warren's 1772 Oration observed that "man is formed for *social life* . . . an observation which, upon our first inquiry, presents itself immediately to our view, and our reason approves that wise and generous principle which actuated the first founders of civil government; an institution which hath its origin in the weakness of individuals, and hath for its end, the *strength and security* of all." Warren reached into the ancient past to argue that "It was *this* noble attachment to a free constitution, which raised ancient Rome from the smallest beginnings, to *that* bright summit of happiness and glory to which she arrived; and it was the loss of *this* which plunged her from *that* summit, into the black gulf of infamy and slavery." And he added that it "was *this* attachment to a constitution, founded on free and benevolent principles, which inspired the first settlers of this country," a theme he then explored at some length in this oration and at even greater length in another Boston Massacre Oration three years later, as explored in chapter 2.[34]

But no one did more to popularize these ideas and to portray them as historical realities than Thomas Paine, whose *Common Sense*, published in early January 1776 and soon the most widely circulated pamphlet of the era, presented the natural law origins of society in almost pictorial terms: "let us suppose," he wrote:

> a small number of persons settled in some sequestered part of the earth, unconnected with the rest; they will then represent the first peopling of any country, or of the world. In this state of natural liberty, society will be their first thought. A thousand motives will excite

them thereto; the strength of one man is so unequal to his wants, and his mind so unfitted for perpetual solitude, that he is soon obliged to seek assistance and relief of another, who in his turn requires the same. Four or five united would be able to raise a tolerable dwelling in the midst of a wilderness, but *one* man might labor out the common period of life without accomplishing anything.[35]

Paine's portrait of the origins of government was equally visualizable, and he added arboreal imagery that evoked a continuity between natural phenomena and the constitution of government, as the Declaration would use riverine imagery in its depiction of history as a "Course" of human events. "Some convenient tree will afford them a statehouse," Paine wrote, "under the branches of which the whole colony may assemble to deliberate on public matters." And "in this first parliament every man, by natural right will have a seat" until the colony's growth would require a system of representation by "a select number chosen from the whole body" but "who will act in the same manner as the whole body would act were they present." Eventually "it will be found best to divide the whole into convenient parts," although "prudence will point out the propriety of having elections often," and "this frequent interchange will establish a common interest with every part of the community . . . and on this . . . depends the *strength of government and the happiness of the governed.*" For all that Paine was a radical republican, then, and thus distinct from previous revolutionary writers, he subscribed as others did to the notion that civil law and institutions should accord with the fundamental laws of nature and of God.[36]

The natural law foundation of civil government and law was also the official doctrine of colonial assemblies, congresses, and conventions long before the Declaration of Independence. In 1762, the returning Massachusetts agent in London, William Bollon, informed the colony's General Court that the crown intended to require their laws to include a suspending clause pending approval by the Privy Council. It was therefore time, Bollon wrote, "for a thorough examination . . . of the Original, inherent and just Title of the Colonies in America to the Rights, Liberties and Benefits of the State, whereof they were Members." The General Court duly sent "instructions" to its new agent in London, Jasper Manduit, stating that "The natural Rights of the Colonists" are "the same with those of all other British subjects, and indeed of all Mankind." They then quoted Locke on the state of nature to the effect that "The Principal of these Rights is to be 'free from any superior power on Earth, and not to be under the Will or Legislative Authority of Man, but to have only the Law of Nature for his Rule.'" They also distinguished natural from civil rights, but linked the two. Quoting Locke again, they wrote, "Our political or Civil Rights will be best understood by beginning at the Foundation":

> The Liberty of all Men in society is to be under no other legislative power but that established by Consent in the Commonwealth, nor under the Dominion of any Will or Restraint of any Law, but what such legislative shall enact, according to the trust put in it. In General freedom of Men under Government, is to have standing fundamental Rules to live by, common to everyone of that Society, and made by the legislative power erected in it; a Liberty to follow my own will in all things where that Rule prescribes not, and not to be subject to the inconstant, uncertain, unknown arbitrary will of another Man; as freedom of Nature is to be under no Restraint but the law of Nature.

"This Liberty," furthermore, "is not only the right of Britons, and British Subjects, but the Right of all Men in Society, and is so inherent, that they Can't give it up without becoming Slaves, by which they forfeit even life itself." The instructions further argued that "the Charter of King William and Queen Mary" guaranteed "all the Liberties and Immunities, of free and natural Subjects, within any of the Dominions" and was thus "declaratory of the Common Law" and "the Law of nature and nations."[37]

The idea that natural law should translate into civil government and law, including in the constitutions of the colonies and empire, was also the doctrine of the 1765 Declaration of Rights and Grievances of the Stamp Act Congress, which stated, first, "That his Majesty's Liege Subjects in these Colonies, are entitled to all the inherent Rights and Liberties of his Natural born Subjects, within the kingdom of *Great-Britain*." Historians have traditionally supposed that the "inherent Rights" and "Liberties" mentioned here were one and the same and derived from English civil law only, yet the use of the words "inherent" and "Natural born" imply derivation from natural law. Indeed, in Calvin's Case of 1608, Edward Coke observed that "Whosoever are born under one natural ligeance and obedience, due by the Law of Nature to one Sovereign are natural-born Subjects." Moreover, the document stated next, "That it is inseparably essential to the

Freedom of a People, and the undoubted rights of *Englishmen*, that no Taxes be imposed on them, but with their own Consent." The "Freedom of a People" thus appears as distinct from and yet related to the "undoubted rights of *Englishmen*"—a distinction emphasized by the comma and a relationship emphasized by the "and"—indicating a distinction between natural and civil rights while confirming the former as the basis of the latter.[38]

The South Carolina and New Jersey Resolves of November 1765 repeated those words, and other colonial assemblies also indicated both a distinction and a relation between natural and civil laws and rights. The Pennsylvania Provincial Assembly asserted "that the Constitution of Government in this Province is founded on the natural Rights of Mankind, and the noble Principles of *English* Liberty," and it is "the inherent Birth-right, and indubitable Privilege, of every *British* Subject, to be taxed only by his own Consent, or that of his legal Representatives." Massachusetts stated "That there are certain essential Rights of the *British* Constitution of Government, which are founded in the Law of God and Nature, and are the Common Rights of Mankind—Therefore . . . the Inhabitants of this province are *unalienably* entitled to those essential Rights in common with all Men: And that no Law of Society can consistent with the Law of God and Nature divest them of those Rights." The Virginia Resolves did not state explicitly that colonists' "Liberties, Privileges, Franchises, and Immunities" were based on natural law, but the Virginia General Assembly had previously described the "Right of being governed by such Laws respecting their internal Polity and Taxation as are derived from their own Consent" as "A Right which as" both "Men, and Descendants of *Britons*, they have . . . possessed" since "they left the Mother Kingdom." The Sugar Act and then impending Stamp Act were therefore "subversive . . . of that Freedom which all Men, especially those who derive their Constitution from *Britain*, have a right to enjoy."[39]

Colonists also argued that natural law and rights were the bases of English and American civil rights during the Townshend Acts crisis. The 1768 Massachusetts Circular Letter stated that "it is an essential, unalterable Right in nature, grafted into the British Constitution, as a fundamental Law, and ever held sacred & irrevocable by the Subjects within the Realm, that what a man has honestly acquired is absolutely his own" and "cannot be taken from him without his consent: That the American Subjects may, therefore . . . assert this natural and constitutional right." And the House thus complained to the King that the British Parliament could not violate "the fundamental Rights of Nature & the Constitution to which your majesty[']s happy Subjects in all parts of your Empire conceive they have a just & equitable Claim."[40]

Following the outbreak of war in April 1775, many colonies cited natural right as well as historical reasons for abandoning their old constitutions and adopting new ones. The Constitution of New Hampshire of January 5, 1776, complained of "the British Parliament, depriving us of our natural and constitutional rights and privileges" and of an abdication of government "whereby the lives and properties of" the people were at risk. Hence, "for the security of the lives and properties of the inhabitants of this colony, we conceive ourselves reduced to the necessity of establishing A FORM OF GOVERNMENT." That of South Carolina, of March 26, complained that Governor William Campbell, "having used his utmost efforts to destroy the lives, liberties, and properties of the good people here, whom by the duty of his station he was bound to protect, withdrew himself from the colony and carried off the great seal and the royal instructions to governors," rendering it "indispensably necessary that . . . some mode should be established by common consent, and for the good of the people, the origin and end of all governments, for regulating the internal polity of this colony." The New Jersey Constitution of July 2 declared that "all civil authority under" George III "is necessarily at an end, and a dissolution of government in each colony has consequently taken place." And because "some form of government is absolutely necessary, not only for the preservation of good order, but also . . . in their own necessary defence," the constitution created "such government as shall best conduce to" the people's "happiness and safety."[41]

Most famously, Virginians incorporated their Declaration of Rights of June 12, which Jefferson had to hand as he wrote his draft Declaration of Independence, into a constitution of June 29, which was published in Philadelphia a few days later. It stated, "That all men are by nature equally free and independent, and have certain inherent rights, of which, when they enter into a state of society, they cannot, by any compact, deprive or divest their posterity, namely, the enjoyment of life and liberty, with the means of acquiring and possessing property, and pursuing and obtaining happiness and safety." Hence "all power is vested in, and consequently derived from, the people," "government is, or ought to be, instituted for the common benefit, protection, and security," and "when any government shall be found inadequate or contrary to these purposes, a majority of the community hath an indubitable, inalienable, and indefeasible right to reform, alter, or abolish it, in such manner as shall be judged most conducive to the public weal." It then listed its grievances and proclaimed that by these "several acts of misrule, the government of this country, as formerly exercised under the crown of Great Britain, is TOTALLY DISSOLVED."[42]

The First Continental Congress's Declaration and Resolves of October 14, 1774, had similarly stated "That the inhabitants of the English colonies in North-America, by the immutable laws of nature" and "the principles of the English constitution, and the several charters or compacts, have the following RIGHTS." The first was "That they are entitled to life, liberty and property," which "cannot be legally taken from them, altered or abridged by any power whatever, without their own consent." The Congress's October 20 Articles of Association instituted its "Non-Importation, Non-Consumption, and Non-Exportation" agreement in order "To obtain redress of these Grievances, which threaten destruction to the Lives, Liberty, and Property of his Majesty's subjects in *North America.*"[43]

The Second Continental Congress's Declaration of the Causes and Necessity of Taking Up Arms, of July 6, 1775, similarly invoked natural law as superseding civil institutions when necessary. The titular "Necessity" signaled the first law of nature—self-preservation. The first paragraph denied absolute *dominium* and *imperium* on the part of any ruler, echoing Locke's arguments against Filmer: "IF IT was possible for Men who exercise their Reason to believe that the Divine Author of our Existence intended a Part of the human Race to hold an absolute Property in, and an unbounded Power over others, marked out by his infinite Goodness and Wisdom, as the Objects of a legal Domination never rightfully resistible, however severe and oppressive, the Inhabitants of these Colonies might at least require from the Parliament of Great-Britain some Evidence, that this dreadful Authority over them has been granted to that Body." It then invoked natural and sacred law to describe the true nature and purpose of government: "a Reverence for our great Creator, Principles of Humanity, and the Dictates of Common Sense, must convince all those who reflect upon the Subject, that Government was instituted to promote the Welfare of Mankind, and ought to be administered for the Attainment of that End." It was the moderate John Dickinson, rather than his more radical fellow drafter of the 1775 Declaration, Thomas Jefferson, who first suggested these opening lines. As much as they disagreed about important aspects of British imperial and colonial American history, as shown in subsequent chapters, they agreed that natural law accounted for the origins and purposes of government and remained the measure for analyzing the course of human events.[44]

The authors of the Declaration of Independence broadly agreed on certain principles—notably the role of natural and sacred law as the basis of and standard for civil government and law. That idea was old—dating back to Cicero and incorporated into early modern English jurisprudence, theology, and philosophy, and then into American political writings, long before the revolutionary era. The Declaration's introduction thus presented its "Laws of Nature and of Nature's God" as a long-established doctrine. And the preamble presented them as self-evident truths that underwrote a general history of humankind that was similarly familiar—from Creation and the state of nature to the origins of government, and through occasional revolutions.

That general history of humankind was also a model for the Declaration's particular history of British America. The preamble thus followed its general statement that "all experience hath shewn, that mankind are more disposed to suffer, while evils are sufferable, than to right themselves by abolishing the forms to which they are accustomed" by noting particularly "Such has been the patient sufferance of these Colonies." The preamble also stated in general terms that "when a long train of abuses and usurpations, pursuing invariably the same Object evinces a design to reduce" a people "under absolute Despotism, it is their right, it is their duty, to throw off such Government, and to provide new Guards for their future security." It followed that with the particular point that "such is now the necessity which constrains" the American people "to alter their former Systems of Government" because "The history of the present King of Great Britain is a history of repeated injuries and usurpations, all having in direct object the establishment of an absolute Tyranny."

The "history of the present King of Great Britain," foreshadowed in the preamble and detailed in the grievances' facts "submitted to a candid world," are the subjects of this book's chapters 3 and 4. But the next chapter shows that the Declaration's American history went further back than that, to the origins of colonies and empire—to "our emigration and settlement here"—when the inherent, inherited, and acquired rights of the colonists that King George would injure and usurp were supposedly initially established.

2

Our Emigration and Settlement Here

Nor have We been wanting in attentions to our Brittish brethren. We have warned them from time to time of attempts by their legislature to extend an unwarrantable jurisdiction over us. We have reminded them of the circumstances of our emigration and settlement here.

Buried in the conclusion of the Declaration of Independence is a brief reference to "the circumstances of our emigration and settlement here." Its placement in the document, following the long list of complaints against the king, was determined by the need to show that the colonists had explained their rights and grievances before resorting to revolution. The document's conclusion thus began by noting that colonists' petitions to the king had "been answered only by repeated injury," which proved he had acted knowingly and therefore intentionally, proving him "unfit to be the ruler of a free people" (a matter explored further in chapter 3). The Declaration's authors then turned to the British people, who had repeatedly voted for members of Parliament who had attempted to extend that unwarrantable jurisdiction over the colonies, ignoring colonists' reminders of "the circumstances of our emigration and settlement here."[1]

But the placement, context, and brevity of the reference to emigration and settlement belie its importance in the colonists' arguments for independence. That importance is clearer in Thomas Jefferson's draft Declaration, where he wrote that we have warned them from time to time of attempts by their legislature to extend a jurisdiction over these our states. we have reminded them of the circumstances of our emigration & settlement here, no one of which could warrant so strange a pretension: that these were effected at the expence of our own blood & treasure, unassisted by the wealth or the strength of Great Britain: that in constituting indeed our several forms of government, we had adopted one common king, thereby laying a foundation for perpetual league & amity with them: but that submission to their parliament was no part of our constitution, nor ever in idea, if history may be credited.

The Declaration's history of emigration and settlement was thus key to understanding two fundamental and related issues of the American Revolution: the historical origins of the colonists' rights and the nature of the imperial constitution. They supposedly showed, first, that the earliest emigrants and settlers had founded the colonies through their own effort and expense and had thereby, by natural law and right, earned exclusive entitlements to property and self-government, which their descendants duly inherited, again by natural right—a set of ideas that I am calling settler imperialism. Second, the colonists therefore governed themselves under the legislative authority of their own elected assemblies in conjunction with governors acting under the authority of the crown (but not of the British Parliament), a set of ideas that Jack P. Greene has styled "settler constitutionalism."[2]

But Jefferson had attempted to draft into the Declaration a radical theory of settler imperialism and settler constitutionalism. He ascribed to what I call a "free state theory" of the origins of colonies and empire according to which emigrants had abandoned English or British jurisdiction and thus their subjection to the crown, and had thereby become free and stateless individuals, as per the natural right of expatriation. They then settled supposedly new lands and mixed their labor with it, making it their own property and theirs alone, again by natural right. As these lands were also supposedly unclaimed or at least unconquered by the crown or any other British authority, and supposedly unsettled or unused by Indigenous peoples, they constituted a state of nature wherein settlers formed new societies and governments of their own—effectively independent "states," as Jefferson consistently called the colonies. Jefferson's "circumstances of our emigration and settlement" were thus an American enactment of John Locke's history of the origins of property, society, and government. Crucially, the English or British crown played no part in Jefferson's portrait of the origins of the colonies but did have a role in the imperial constitution. After forming their own governments, he argued, the colonists adopted secondary compacts with the crown, consenting to a new layer of authority that would better secure their independent states, although the British Parliament remained "no part of our constitution." Jefferson's settler-imperial history thus claimed that free emigrants had formed independent states and had founded the empire from the outside in, arguing that these new peoples created a "league & amity" or confederation of sovereign states coequal with each other and with the state of Great Britain, all independent of each other except for sharing a monarchy.

Jefferson added the phrase "if history may be credited" to his description of emigration and settlement, a phrase that at first sight may suggest confidence in his ideas but was in fact a rhetorical assertion against a historiographic and political opposition that he undoubtedly anticipated. Others, most notably John Dickinson, agreed that the efforts and expenses of colonization gave the first settlers extensive and inviolable rights to property and self-government that their descendants inherited by right. But they subscribed to a more traditional charter theory of the origins of colonies and empire wherein emigrants (actually migrants, in these terms) had settled lands already claimed by the crown under royal charters, and had therefore never left crown jurisdiction or abandoned their subjecthood. Because the crown thus had an original jurisdiction over the colonists and their territories, it followed that the British Parliament, through its constitutional relationship to the crown, had the right to regulate trade in the empire (though the charters forbade raising revenues in the colonies) and held an ultimate (if never clearly defined) sovereignty throughout British dominions. Dickinson's settler-imperial history thus argued that migrants had founded the colonies not as free or independent states but as part of a preexisting empire. Accordingly, the colonists were members of an empire that was a federation of more or less self-governing polities, each with its own legislature, sharing authority under the sovereignty of the British crown and, to a more limited extent, Parliament.

These internal disagreements over the facts of emigration to and settlement of the colonies, and therefore over the constitution of the empire, had been aired before, both in the Continental Congress and in often angry exchanges in revolutionary pamphlet literature and oratory from the mid-1760s. The most pressing question in the middle of 1776, however, was how to reference the important but contested matter of the origins of colonies and empire as an argument for independence in a Declaration that needed to express "the harmonising sentiments of the day" and a "common sense of the subject." Jefferson's initial answer to that question was that his version of "history" should be "credited." However, knowing that some delegates in Congress and others outside might object to the apparently total negation of British parliamentary jurisdiction that the original passage asserted, either Jefferson added, or Benjamin Franklin or John Adams suggested adding, a qualifying "unwarrantable" to the reference to Parliament's jurisdiction over these states, implying that *some* such jurisdiction might in fact be legitimate. The committee submitted the passage to Congress otherwise unaltered, except for adding capital letters.[3]

That concession, however, was not enough to get the committee's history fully credited by Congress. First, delegates replaced the words "over these our states" with "over us," divesting the sentence of its implication that the empire was a mere league and amity or confederation of sovereign states. Congress also eliminated Jefferson's description of emigration and settlement, leaving the term unexplained. The radical nature of these revisions did not mean, though, that the final Declaration failed to include a history of the colonies and empire. It meant, in fact, that it included two, for the elision created a strategic ambiguity that allowed readers to interpret the circumstances of emigration and settlement as a reference either to Jefferson's version of settler imperialism and constitutionalism or to Dickinson's, as they preferred. Hence Congress, if not Jefferson in this instance, helped to harmonize the discordant "sentiments of the day."[4]

Furthermore, if that strategic ambiguity elided what colonists disagreed on, it still pointed to what they agreed on: that the colonies had been created by settlers who, through their own efforts and expenses, unassisted by Britain, had earned inviolable rights to property and at least some degree of self-government that their descendants inherited by natural right. Agreement on those points and their inclusion in the Declaration was crucial to the colonists' arguments against certain ideas about British imperial authority. British jurists from Edward Coke to William Blackstone had debated the meanings of conquest and settlement for the legal and constitutional status of Wales, Scotland, Ireland, and the American colonies based on historical circumstances, including who had conquered whom and how. These legal-historical debates and rulings culminated in Lord Chief Justice Mansfield declaring in 1774, in relation to Grenada but with implications for other colonies: "A Country, conquered by the British Arms, becomes a Dominion of the King in Right of his Crown, and therefore, necessarily subject to the Legislature, the Parliament of Great Britain." Grenada was deemed to have been conquered by British arms; hence both versions of settler imperialism embedded in the Declaration implied that the colonies were not conquered by "British Arms" but by the settlers, by the circumstances of "our" emigration and settlement here.[5]

The circumstances of "our" emigration and settlement were important for other reasons, too. First, combined with shared tribulations under George III, the common history of emigration and settlement helped Americans become the "one people" referenced in the Declaration's introduction. Second, emigration and settlement marked that "one people" out as originally European. Native Americans were clearly not part of the same historical process, though they too had shared the expenses of blood and treasure that Jefferson's draft mentioned. Nor were Africans a part of the one people so created, having arrived in America as victims of the slave trade. These issues are explored in greater detail in chapters 5 and 6. The rest of this chapter focuses on how Jefferson and others arrived at their different ideas on the origins of colonies and empire and how the Declaration of Independence mediated those disagreements. It argues that the final Declaration espoused Jefferson's views, though not so explicitly as to alienate Dickinson and his allies. Ultimately, the Declaration's circumstances of emigration and settlement bridged the preamble's general history of humankind and its particular history of the American Revolution. It signified, drawing on a long tradition in colonial and revolutionary protest literature, a process in which the colonists' inherent rights as "men," inherited rights as Englishmen, and acquired rights as American colonists were established at the founding of the colonies—rights that would later be injured and usurped by George III and Parliament.

In the summer of 1774, Thomas Jefferson authored a set of "Instructions" for the Virginia delegates to the First Continental Congress, which convened in Philadelphia that September. His fellow members of the Virginia

Assembly declined to give his ideas official approval, but his friends had them printed as a pamphlet titled *A Summary View of the Rights of British America*. Published in Williamsburg and Philadelphia, in the latter city by John Dunlap, who would later produce the July 4 broadside of the Declaration of Independence, the pamphlet was distributed across the colonies and established Jefferson's reputation as a "masterly Pen" with "a peculiar felicity of expression," in the words of John Adams. Those words appear to stress qualities of form rather than content, although in the eighteenth century such language implied substance as much as style, including an ability to express agreeable opinions as well as to express them agreeably. Jefferson's opinions were agreeable enough that the Virginia House of Burgesses, despite withholding official approval of his instructions, appointed him a delegate to the Second Continental Congress. That Congress subsequently appointed him to committees to draft documents of enormous importance, including the Declaration of the Causes and Necessity of Taking Up Arms of 1775 and the Declaration of Independence. Congress rejected and revised many of Jefferson's suggestions, but his was nonetheless an opinion that other delegates valued, and they often found his expressions of them felicitous in every sense of the term.[6]

Jefferson's *Summary View*, in many ways a reader's guide to the Declaration of Independence, concerned itself with the "unwarrantable encroachments and usurpations, attempted to be made by the Legislature of one part of the empire, upon those rights which God and the laws have given equally and independently to all." It is not clear whether Jefferson's "laws" were natural or civil laws, but, as the rest of the pamphlet made clear, he deployed "God and the laws" in the same way that his draft and the final Declaration of Independence would deploy "the Laws of Nature and of Nature's God": as the basis of people's rights and of governmental obligations that should be incorporated in civil society. And on those grounds, he proposed that "in order that these our rights, as well as the invasions of them, may be laid more fully before his Majesty," he would "take a view of them from the origin and first settlement of these countries." Also, the pamphlet's argument accorded with the free state settler imperialism that Jefferson would attempt to insert into the Declaration of Independence: that original rights to American property and territory—dominium and imperium—originally belonged entirely to settlers, according to both natural law and the course of human events.[7]

The pamphlet dealt first with emigration, aiming to "remind" the king that "our ancestors, before their emigration to America, were the free inhabitants of the British dominions in Europe, and possessed a right which nature has given to all men, of departing from the country in which chance, not choice, has placed them, of going in quest of new habitations, and of there establishing new societies, under such laws and regulations as to them shall seem most likely to promote public happiness." Jefferson thus rejected the doctrine of *nemo potest exuere patriam*—"No one can cast off their country"—in favor of a natural right of expatriation—emigration from a native land and abandonment of former subjecthood. This right and historical practice had been asserted by John Locke, but Jefferson also built it into a history of America that linked back to German migration to ancient Britain. Americans' "Saxon ancestors," Jefferson argued, "had under this universal law . . . left their native wilds and woods in the north of Europe" and "possessed themselves of the island of Britain, then less charged with inhabitants, and . . . established there that system of laws which has so long been the glory and protection of that country." Jefferson added that no "claim of superiority or dependence" was made "over them by that mother country from which they had migrated."[8]

Jefferson supported his account of free emigration with claims that settlers had colonized America without assistance from the British crown or people. "Not a shilling was ever issued from the public treasures of his Majesty, or his ancestors, for their assistance," he wrote, until the Seven Years' War, "after the colonies had become established on a firm and permanent footing . . . valuable to Great Britain for her commercial purposes" and "to the great aggrandizment of herself, and danger of Great-Britain." While "those aids . . . were doubtless valuable," Jefferson argued that, coming long after settlement, they "cannot give a title to that authority which the British Parliament would arrogate over us" and had in any case been "amply repaid" via the "exclusive privileges in trade" that Britain had enjoyed with the colonies.[9]

"America was conquered," then, "and her settlements made, and firmly established, at the expence of individuals, and not of the British public," Jefferson asserted. And the colonists' "own blood was spilt in acquiring lands for their settlement, their own fortunes expended in making that settlement effectual; for themselves they fought, for themselves they conquered, and for themselves alone they have right to hold." Settlers thus possessed exclusive rights to dominium and imperium in the lands they conquered. Regarding property rights, Jefferson wrote, "From the nature and purpose of civil institutions, all the lands within the limits which any particular society has circumscribed around itself are assumed by that society, and subject to their allotment only." On self-government, he added, "That settlements having been thus effected in the wilds of America, the emigrants thought proper to adopt that system of laws under which they had hitherto lived in the mother country, and to continue their union with her by submitting themselves to the same common Sovereign, who was thereby made the central link connecting the several parts of the empire thus newly multiplied."[10]

Jefferson knew that his free state history of emigration and settlement was controversial, defying the orthodoxy that emigrants had settled lands that were already claimed by the crown and under the authority of royal charters. He therefore attempted to buttress his case with some rather heavy-handed historical revisionism. Toward the end of his *Summary View*, he urged readers to "take notice of an error in the nature of our land holdings, which crept in at a very early period of our settlement," referring to the ideas that the crown had prior ownership of American territories and lands and could therefore impose charters and quitrents. These, Jefferson charged, were vestiges of feudalism, which he argued had been introduced in post-Conquest England and then in America only partially and largely illegally. "In the earlier ages of the Saxon settlement," Jefferson claimed, "feudal holdings were certainly altogether unknown; and very few, if any, had been introduced at the time of the Norman conquest." Jefferson thus associated feudalism with foreign conquest and in turn freehold land tenure with freedom itself. "Our Saxon ancestors held their lands," he continued, "as they did their personal property, in absolute dominion, disencumbered with any superior, answering nearly to the nature of those possessions which the Feudalists term Allodial. William, the Norman, first introduced that system generally."[11]

Jefferson insisted, though, that William's English feudalism was violently oppressive and illegally imposed, thus discrediting its implied extension to America. "The lands which had belonged to those who fell in the battle of Hastings, and in the subsequent insurrections of his reign, formed a considerable proportion of the lands of the whole kingdom," he wrote. "These" William "granted out, subject to feudal duties, as did he also those of a great number of his new subjects, who, by persuasions of threats, were induced to surrender them for that purpose." Even then, "much was left in the hand of his Saxon subjects; held of no superior, and not subject to feudal conditions," although these freeholds "were made liable to the same military duties as if they had been feuds" and "Norman lawyers soon found means to saddle them also with all the other feudal burthens." But, Jefferson asserted, "still they had not been surrendered to the king, they were not derived from his grant, and therefore they were not holden of him. A general principle . . . was introduced, that 'all lands in England were held either mediately or immediately of the crown,' but this was borrowed from those holdings, which were truly feudal, and only applied to others for the purposes of illustration." For Jefferson, then, "Feudal holdings were . . . exceptions out of the Saxon laws of possession, under which all lands were held in absolute right." Freehold tenure thus remained the true inheritance of Englishmen and thus Americans, and of the latter not only as the descendants of Englishmen but as emigrants to and settlers of new lands. As he added, "America was not conquered by William the Norman, nor its lands surrendered to him, or any of his successors. Possessions there are undoubtedly of the allodial nature."[12]

At that point, Jefferson returned to the "error" he aimed to correct. "Our ancestors," he said, "who migrated hither, were farmers, not lawyers. The fictitious principle that all lands belong originally to the king, they were early persuaded to believe real; and accordingly took grants of their own lands from the crown." The misunderstanding had remained tolerable as long as "the crown continued to grant [lands] for small sums, and on reasonable rents." But, as "his majesty has lately taken on him to advance the terms of purchase, and of holding to the double of what they were, by which means the acquisition of land being rendered difficult, the population of our country is likely to be checked. It is time, therefore," he concluded, "for us to lay this matter before his majesty, and to declare that he has no right to grant lands of himself." He was also laying the matter before his fellow countrymen, some of whom continued to believe in an original crown title to American lands and territories that made quitrents and restrictions of settlement legal.[13]

In early 1776, furthermore, Jefferson wrote in his notebook a long précis of Humphrey Gilbert's attempts to settle Norumbega and of Walter Raleigh's missions to Roanoke, largely derived from Richard Hakluyt's writings. Jefferson's "Refutation of the Argument that the Colonies were Established at the Expense of the British Nation" was inspired by George III's speech to Parliament of October 1775, in which the king claimed that the stakes in the current conflict were too high "to give up so many colonies which she [Britain] has planted with great industry, nursed with great tenderness, encouraged with many commercial advantages, and protected and defended at much expence and treasure." Jefferson wrote at the end that "this short narration of facts, extracted principally from Hakluyt's voiages, may enable us to judge of the effect which the charter to Sr. Walter Ralegh may have on our own constitution and also on those of the other colonies within it's limits, to which it is of equal concernment. It serves also," he continued, "to expose the distress of those ministerial writers, who, in order to prove that the British parliament may of right legislate for the colonies, are driven to the necessity of advancing this palpable untruth that 'the colonies were planted and nursed at the expence of the British nation': an untruth which even majesty itself, descending from it's dignity, has lately been induced to utter from the throne."[14]

Jefferson's views on land tenure, conquest, and emigration also echoed those of John Locke. Locke had shown how rights to the self, self-government, free emigration, and property related to each other, principally through the idea that all are born equal and free and thus a parent cannot alienate an offspring's inheritance. "Every Man is born with a double Right," Locke wrote, "*First, A Right of Freedom to his Person*, which no other Man has a Power over. . . . *Secondly* . . . to *inherit* . . . his Fathers Goods." Both rights meant that whatever "Engagements or Promises any one has made for himself, he . . . *cannot*, by any *Compact* whatsoever, bind *his Children* or Posterity. For this Son, when a Man, being altogether as free as the Father, any *act of the Father can no more give away the liberty of the Son*, than it can of any body else." Someone might therefore "forfeit but his own Life, but involves not his Children in his guilt or destruction" because "his goods, which Nature, that willeth the preservation of all Mankind as much as is possible, hath made to belong to the Children to keep them from perishing, do still . . . belong to his Children" who "have done nothing to forfeit them." And neither therefore "*has the Conqueror any right* to take them away." A conqueror might have "*a right over a Man's Person* to destroy him if he pleases," but he "has *not* thereby a right *over his Estate* to possess and enjoy it. For it is the brutal force the Aggressor has used, that gives his Adversary a right to take away his Life, and destroy him if he pleases, as a noxious Creature; but 'tis damage sustain'd that alone gives him Title to another Mans Goods." Hence, "even in a just War," the conqueror "hath, *by his Conquest, no right of Dominion*."[15]

Locke applied these rules specifically to the Norman Conquest, making the same historiographic corrections that Jefferson would make. "We are told by some, that the *English* Monarchy is founded in the *Norman*

Conquest," Locke wrote, "and that our Princes have thereby a Title to absolute Dominion: Which if it were true, (as by the History it appears otherwise) and that *William* had a right to make War on this Island; yet his Dominion by Conquest could reach no farther, than to the *Saxons* and *Britains* that were then Inhabitants of this Country." In other words, the conquest would affect those who surrendered in 1066, but not their descendants, and not "The *Normans* that came with him, and helped to Conquer, and all descended from them." Indeed, as shown below, colonists argued that they themselves were the conquerors of American lands and thus inviolably entitled to their property and self-governance.[16]

That double natural right to person and property also meant that the idea "that *by being born under any Government, we are naturally Subjects to it*" was wrong and that expatriation was therefore a natural right. Locke pointed to examples "frequent in History ... of Men withdrawing themselves, and their Obedience, from the Jurisdiction they were born under, and the Family or Community they were bred up in, and *setting up new Governments* in other places; from whence sprang all that number of petty Common-wealths in the beginning of Ages." Indeed, this was historically self-evident, as "it was impossible ... there should have been so many little Kingdoms ... if Men had not been at *liberty to separate* themselves from their Families, and the Government ... and go and make distinct Commonwealths and other Governments, as they thought fit." The rights of conquest to property could only therefore apply to a single generation, and any subsequent feudal tenure thus defied the laws of nature and God.[17]

Settler-imperial history first appeared in colonial political writing a century before American independence. In 1675, the Virginia General Assembly sent agents to London to oppose the royal granting of the colony's Northern Neck to Lords Culpeper and Arlington. The assemblymen requested that all land in the colony be "assured to the present possessors and owners of it," who had relied on a royal grant "to lay out their estates, and employ their industry ... for the improvement and advancement" of the "country." And "both the acquisition and defense of this country hath been, for the most part, at the country's charge" in "an uncultivated part of the world." Nine years later, the same assembly petitioned Charles II against Governor Lord Howard of Effingham's insistence that colony laws be reviewed by the Lords of Trade and Privy Council. The burgesses argued that the colony's first settlers had earned self-governing rights as they had left their "Natiue Soyle" and "Aduentured" their "Liues, fortunes and all that are deare to us" in "Inhabiting a Barbarous and Malanchoply part of the world" where they had been "subject to the Incursions . . . and depredations of a Skulking, Cruell, inhumane . . . Enemie."[18]

The Dominion of New England of 1685–1689 inspired longer and more detailed histories of settlers' rights to property and self-government that were well recollected in the revolutionary era. Edward Rawson's 1691 *The Revolution in New-England Justified*, reprinted in Boston in 1773, asserted that by "*an original contract* between the king and the first planters in *New-England* . . . at their own cost and charge would subdue a wilderness, and enlarge his dominions" and so "they and their posterity . . . should enjoy such privileges as are in their charters expressed," including "not having taxes imposed on them without their consent." Governor Edmund Andros had asserted, however, that "*where-ever an Englishman sets his foot, all that he hath is the king's*" and that "either you are subjects or you are rebels." He thus "gave out, that *now their charter was gone, all their lands were the king's* . . . and that therefore men that would have any legal title to their lands must take *patents* of them." Andros and his counselors then "made what laws they pleased *without any consent of the people, either by themselves or representatives*," including "the *levying* [of] *monies without the consent of the people either by themselves or by an assembly*" and thereby "did invade the property as well as liberty of the subject." And, Rawson asked, "What people that had the spirits of Englishmen could endure this? That when they had at *vast charges of their own conquered a wilderness* . . . that now a parcel of strangers . . . must come and inherit all that the people now in *New-England* and their fathers before them, had laboured for!" Rawson thus concluded that "Had not an happy *revolution* happened in *England*, and so in *New-England*, in all probability those few ill men would have squeezed more out of the poorer sort of people there, than half their estates are worth, by *forcing them to take patents.*"[19]

Jeremiah Dummer's 1721 *A Defence of the New-England Charters*, reprinted in Boston in 1765, contained detailed accounts of the "blood and treasure" expended by migrants and settlers. The charters, he argued first, guaranteed "Patentees their Title to the Soil" and the rights "to call General Assemblies" and "make Laws" because Settlers had suffered "Dangers in their Voyages over the *Atlantick*" and "arriv'd at an Inhospitable Shore and a waste Wilderness" where they "found themselves inevitably engag'd in a War with the Natives. So that by Fatigue and Famine, by the Extremity of the Seasons, and by a War with the Savages, the first Planters soon found their Graves, leaving the young Settlements to be perfected by their Survivors." They did all this also at their own expense, "which was above 200,000 *l*. in setling the single Province of the *Massachusets Bay*." Dummer even itemized those expenses. "The Freight of the Passengers cost 95000 *l*.," then "The Transportation of their first Stock of Cattle came to 12000 *l*. The Provisions laid in for Subsistance, till by Tillage more could be rais'd, cost 45000 *l*. The Materials for Building their first little Cottages came to 18000 *l*. Their Arms and Ammunition cost 22000*l*. . . . These several Articles amount to 192000 *l*. . . . not taking into the Account the very great Sums which were expended in Things of private Use, that People could not be without, who were going to possess an uninhabited Land." Charters were thus "Praemiums for Services to be perform'd" and so "to strip the Country of their Charters after the Service . . . is abhorrent from all Reason, Equity and Justice." Dummer even leaned precociously toward a free state version of settler imperialism by arguing that the crown "neither did nor could grant the Soil, having no right in it self." While "Queen *Elisabeth* gave out the first patent to Sir *Walter Rawleigh* in 1584," she had no "*Right of Inheritance*, because those Countries did not descend to her from her Ancestors," or of "*Conquest*, because she neither conquer'd, nor attempted to conquer" the Indigenous peoples, and nor was there any "preceding Injury or Provocation" that might have given a right of conquest. Nor did right "arise by *Purchase*, there being no Money or other valuable Consideration paid. Nor could she claim by the *prior Discovery or Pre-occupancy* . . . because that gives a Right only to *derelict Lands*, which these were not, being full of Inhabitants, who undoubtedly had as good a Title to their own Country." Colonial property rights had only thereby been acquired by settlers' conquering it or purchasing it from its "Inhabitants"—an issue explored further in chapter 6.[20]

Daniel Dulany the Elder similarly wrote in 1728 that "The First Settlers of Maryland, left their Native Country, with the Assent and Approbation of their Prince; to enlarge his Empire in a remote Part of the World, destitute of almost all the Necessaries of Life, and inhabited by a People, savage, cruel, and inhospitable," and "at great expence; ran all the Hazards, and underwent all the Fatigues incident to so dangerous and daring an Undertaking;

in which Many perished, and Those that survived, suffered All the Extremities of Hunger, Cold, and Diseases." Dulany the Younger similarly wrote in 1765 that "The *English* subjects, who left their *native* country to settle in the wilderness of *America,* had the privileges of *other Englishmen*" and "knew their value, and were desirous of having them perpetuated to their posterity." In order to protect "the property they should earn by the utmost hazard and fatigue," they "entered into a compact with the crown" so that "*their privileges as English subjects, should be effectually secured to themselves, and transmitted to their posterity.* . . . CHARTERS were accordingly framed and conferred by the crown, and accepted by the settlers," which were "founded upon the unalienable rights of the subject, and upon the most sacred compact." Thus "the colonies," he concluded, "claim a right of exemption from taxes *not imposed with their Consent.*—They claim it upon the principles of the constitution . . . upon principles on which their compact with the crown was originally founded."[21]

James Otis went further than the Dulanys, endorsing expatriation and thus signaling a free state theory of the founding of the colonies. He argued that "it is left to every man as he comes of age to chuse *what society* he will continue to belong to," and also argued that the American colonies were new societies. "A plantation or colony," he wrote, "is a settlement of subjects in a territory *disjoined* or *remove* from the mother country, and may be made by private adventurers or the public; but in both cases the Colonists are entitled to as *ample* rights, liberties and priviledges as the subjects of the mother country are, and in some respects *to more.*" More because "If I were to define the *modern* Colonists, I should say, *they are the noble discoverers and settlers of a new world.*" He added that "Our fore-fathers" had secured their natural rights to American land by the "hard labour on their little plantations, and in war with the Savages." And he later elaborated: "The New England Colonies in particular, were not only settled without the least expence to the mother country, but they have all along defended themselves against the frequent incursions of the most inhuman Salvages, perhaps on the face of the whole earth, at *their own* cost." This settler-imperial history might have led him to a Jeffersonian "league & amity" imperial constitutionalism, yet he ultimately conceded Parliament's "supreme sacred and uncontroullable" power "not only in the realm, but thro' the dominions."[22]

It was thus the Virginian Richard Bland who made the first revolutionary-era case for a free state theory of settler imperialism and constitutionalism together. As "the Laws of the Kingdom" were "founded upon the Principles of the Law of Nature," as described in "Vattels Law of Nature. Locke on Civil Govern. Wollaston's Rel. of Nat.," Bland argued that people "retain so much of their natural Freedom . . . as to have a Right to retire from the Society, to renounce the Benefits of it, to enter into another Society, and to settle in another Country; for their Engagements to the Society, and their Submission to the publick Authority of the State, do not oblige them to continue in it longer than they find it will conduce to their Happiness, which they have a natural Right to promote." And "when Men exercise this Right . . . and withdraw themselves from their Country, they recover their natural Freedom and Independence: The Jurisdiction and Sovereignty of the State they have quitted ceases; and if they unite, and by common Consent take Possession of a new Country, and form themselves into a political Society, they become a sovereign State, independent of the State from which they separated."[23]

Bland gave this theory and practice of expatriation the same antiquity that Jefferson would. It "is a Fact as certain as History can make it," he wrote, "that the present civil Constitution of *England* derives its Original from those *Saxons* who, coming over to the Assistance of the *Britons* in the Time of their King *Vortigern*, made themselves Masters of the Kingdom, and established a Form of Government in it similar to that they had been accustomed to live under in their native Country," one that "was founded upon Principles of the most perfect Liberty." The "Lands were divided among the Individuals in Proportion to the Rank they held in the Nation," he continued, "and . . . every Freeholder, was a Member of their Wittinagemot, or Parliament." Bland further argued that America was a "new Country" and "no Part of the Kingdom of *England*" but instead "possessed by a savage People, scattered through the Country, who were not subject to the *English* Dominion, nor owed Obedience to its Laws." Colonies were then "founded by *Englishmen;* who, becoming private Adventurers, established themselves, without any Expense to the Nation, in this uncultivated and almost uninhabited Country."[24]

Yet, even while arguing that "This independent Country was settled by *Englishmen* at their own Expense," Bland admitted they had arrived "under Charters from the Crown" and "under particular Stipulations" that constituted "the sacred Band of Union between England and her Colonies, and cannot be infringed without Injustice." He resolved the apparent anomaly with a remarkably detailed history of the mutation of charters, beginning with Roanoke. "The first of these Charters," he wrote, "was granted to Sir *Walter Raleigh* by Queen *Elizabeth* . . . and was confirmed by the Parliament of *England* in the Year 1584. By this Charter," he continued, "the whole Country" was "to be possessed by Sir *Walter Raleigh* . . . with full Power of Legislation, and to establish a civil Government in it as near as conveniently might be agreeable to the Form of the *English* Government and Policy thereof." And, using the term Jefferson would use in his draft Declaration's account of migration and settlement, "The Country was to be united to the Realm of *England* in perfect LEAGUE AND AMITY, was to be within the Allegiance of the Crown of *England,* and to be held by Homage, and the Payment of one Fifth of all Gold and Silver Ore." A "Variety of Accidents" meant that the Virginia Company later "obtained new Charters from King *Iames*" containing "an express Clause of Exemption for ever from all Taxes or Impositions upon their Import and Export Trade," so that "the Proprietors effectually prosecuted, and happily succeeded, in planting a Colony upon that Part of the Continent which is now called *Virginia,*" despite "immense Difficulties" and "without receiving the least Assistance from the *English* Government." The colony "attained to such a Degree of Perfection that . . . a General Assembly, or legislative Authority, was established in the Governour, Council, and House of Burgesses, who were elected by the Freeholders as their Representatives; and they have continued from that Time to exercise the Power of Legislation over the Colony."[25]

After the 1622 Jamestown massacre and subsequent bankruptcy of the Virginia Company, "King *Iames* dissolved the Company by Proclamation, and took the Colony under his immediate Dependence; which occasioned much Confusion, and created mighty Apprehensions in the Colony lest they should be deprived of the Rights and Privileges granted them by the Company." After James's death, "*Charles* the First . . . declared that *Virginia* should be immediately dependent upon the Crown," increasing colonists' fears that "their regular Constitution was to be destroyed, and a Prerogative Government established over them." Eventually, however, "a Letter from the Lords of the Privy Council, dated *Iuly* the 22d, 1634," contained "the Royal Assurance and Confirmation that all their Estates, Trade, Freedom, and Privileges, should be enjoyed by them in as extensive a Manner as" before, leaving them "in full Possession of the Rights and Privileges of *Englishmen,* which they esteemed more than their Lives."[26]

Civil war subsequently complicated matters. Virginia submitted to parliamentary rule after what Bland delicately called "the King's Death" in 1649, but the Virginian gave an "Abstract" of the "Articles of Surrender" that, he said, reflected "no small Honour upon this Infant Colony." Virginia shall "remain in due Subjection to the Commonwealth," Bland abstracted, "not as a conquered Country, but as a Country submitting by their own voluntary Act, and shall enjoy such Freedoms and Privileges as belong to the free People of *England*." Namely, "The General Assembly as formerly shall convene, and transact the Affairs of the Colony," and Virginians shall "have a free Trade, as the People of *England,* to all Places, and with all Nations" and "be free from all Taxes, Customs, and Impositions whatsoever; and none shall be imposed on them without Consent of the General Assembly." Bland was even prouder, however, of Virginia's preemptive restoration. In "*Ianuary* 1659," he wrote, "Sir *William Berkeley* was replaced at the Head of the Government by the People, who unanimously renounced their Obedience to the Parliament, and restored the Royal Authority by proclaiming *Charles* the 2d . . . so that he was King in *Virginia* some Time before" having "Assurance of being restored to his Throne in *England*." But the main point of Bland's "Detail of the Charters, and other Acts of the Crown, under which the first Colony in *North America* was established" was "that the Colonists . . . had a regular Government long before the first Act of Navigation, and were respected as a distinct State, independent, as to their *internal* Government, of the original Kingdom, but united with her, as to their *external* Polity, in the closest and most intimate LEAGUE AND AMITY, under the same Allegiance, and enjoying the Benefits of a reciprocal Intercourse."[27]

Bland's radical free state settler-imperial history and confederal idea of empire soon came under attack. John Dickinson most likely meant Bland when he wrote in the second of his *Farmer's Letters*: "He, who considers these provinces as states distinct from the *British Empire,* has very slender notions of *justice,* or of *their interests.*" For Dickinson, the British parliament "unquestionably possesses a legal authority to *regulate* the trade of *Great-Britain,* and all its colonies," and furthermore, a unitary sovereignty was essential "to the relation between a mother country and its colonies; and necessary for the common good of all. . . . We are but parts of *a whole,*" he continued, "and therefore there must exist a power somewhere, to preside, and preserve the connection in due order. This power is lodged in the parliament." And he justified this position on historical grounds, arguing that the colonies were "settled by the nations of Europe for the purposes of trade. These purposes were to be attained by the colonies raising for their mother country those things which she did not produce herself; and by supplying themselves from her with things they wanted. These were the national objects in the commencement of our colonies," he concluded, "and have been uniformly so in their promotion."[28]

Dickinson nevertheless subscribed to a version of settler imperialism that emphasized the efforts and expenses of colonization as arguments for inviolable property rights that required a degree of self-government, certainly over taxation. "To answer" the "grand purposes" of settlement, he reasoned, "perfect liberty was known to be necessary; all history proving, that trade and freedom are nearly related to each other. By a due regard to this wise and just plan, the infant colonies exposed in the unknown climates, and unexplored wildernesses of this new world, lived, grew, and flourished." The "difficulties and distresses" settlers faced "in fixing themselves" required "recompense" via 'A communication of her rights in general, and particularly of that great one, the foundation of all the rest—that their property, acquired with so much pain and hazard, should not be disposed of by any one but themselves." In his 1775 *Essay on the Constitutional Power of Great-Britain*, Dickinson made his case more strongly, although he never fully converted to Blandian and by then Jeffersonian radicalism: "IN our provincial legislatures," he wrote, "the best judges in all cases what suits us ... is vested the *exclusive right of internal legislation*" and "A PARLIAMENTARY power of *internal legislation* over these colonies, appears therefore to us, equally contradictory to humanity and the constitution, and illegal." He also noted that "The colonies have no other head than the king of *England*," and his case for that assertion was again historical, based on a charter theory that implicitly evoked the idea of an inviolable contract: "To be subordinately connected with *England*, the colonies *have contracted*. To be subject to the general legislative authority of that kingdom, they *never contracted*." He would soon return, however, to his more moderate charter theory in his draft Declaration of the Causes and Necessity of Taking Up Arms, as shown below.[29]

It is possible that Dickinson's "He who" in his second farmer's letter was New Yorker William Hicks, who authored *The Nature and Extent of Parliamentary Power Considered* during the Stamp Act crisis but published it following the Townshend Acts. He also advanced a radical history of colonial emigration and settlement. "When the emigrants from Great-Britain crossed the Atlantic to settle the deserts of America," Hicks wrote, "they bro't with them the spirit of the English government," specifically, that is, "the same duties to their sovereign, which the freemen of England at that time acknowledged; and they very naturally supposed, that, under his direction, they should be allowed to make such regulations as might answer the purposes of their emigration." They thus "naturally applied to their Prince for such protection and assistance as might raise them to an equality with their brethren of England." But "Removed at an immense distance from the seat of government, they could no longer join the national council" and would therefore "totally disclaim all subordination to, and dependence upon, the two inferior estates of their mother country."[30]

James Wilson endorsed a free state theory of settler-imperialism even more emphatically. Although he rejected the right of expatriation because of the debt owed for protection in earlier life, he nevertheless argued that emigration and settlement determined that the colonies were separate states as they were dominions of the crown independently of Parliament. He began his argument "that the Colonies are not bound by the Acts of the British Parliament; because they have no share in the British legislature" by comparing the situation with medieval Ireland's relationship to England, citing a case "adjudged in the 2d year of Richard IId" when "all the Judges of England, met in the exchequer chamber, to consider whether the people in Ireland were bound by an Act of Parliament made in England." The judges ruled, he wrote, that Ireland "has a Parliament, who make laws; and our statutes do not bind them; BECAUSE THEY DO NOT SEND KNIGHTS TO PARLIAMENT: But their persons are the subjects of the King." And "if the inhabitants of Ireland are not bound by Acts of Parliament made in England; *a fortiori*, the inhabitants of the American Colonies are not bound by them." Wilson explained Poyning's Law of 1494 via "the title of conquest." But, he asked, "How come the Colonists to be a conquered people?" And "By whom was the conquest over them obtained? By the House of Commons? By the constituents of that House? If the idea of conquest must be taken into consideration when we examine into the title by which America is held, that idea, so far as it can operate, will operate in favour of the Colonists, and not against them."[31]

Rather, Wilson argued, "Permitted and commissioned by the crown," migrants "undertook, at their own expense, expeditions to this distant country, took possession of it, planted it, and cultivated it. Secure under the protection of their king, they grew and multiplied, and diffused British freedom and British spirit." In America they were then "Happy in the enjoyment of liberty, and in reaping the fruits of their toils" and "still more happy in the joyful prospect of transmitting their liberty and their fortunes to the latest posterity." The colonies were, therefore, "DISTINCT STATES, INDEPENDENT OF EACH OTHER, BUT CONNECTED TOGETHER UNDER THE SAME SOVEREIGN IN RIGHT OF THE SAME CROWN." Regarding later parliamentary usurpations, Wilson asked, "Is this the return made us for leaving our friends and our country—for braving the danger of the deep—for planting a wilderness, inhabited only by savage men and savage beasts—for extending the dominions of the British crown—for increasing the trade of the British merchants—for augmenting the rents of the British landlords—for heightening the wages of the British artificers?"[32]

Wilson also cited "MY Lord Bacon's sentiments" on this subject. "His immense genius, his universal learning, his deep insight into the laws and constitution of England are well known and much admired," he noted, and "he lived at that time when settling and improving the American Plantations began seriously to be attended to, and successfully to be carried into execution." The "settlement of Colonies, says he, must proceed from the option of those, who will settle them.... They must be raised by the *leave*, and not by the *command* of the *King*. At their setting out, they must have their commission, or letters patents from the *King*, that so they may acknowledge their DEPENDENCY UPON THE CROWN of England, and under his protection.'" However, Wilson continued, "my Lord Bacon had no conception, that the Parliament *would* or *ought* to interpose—either in the settlement or the government of the Colonies" and "The only dependency, which they ought to acknowledge, is ... on the Crown."[33]

Wilson wrote his *Considerations* in 1768 but published them in 1774, and early the next year John Adams made a case for a largely Blandian-Jeffersonian version of emigration and settlement that he would approve as a member of the drafting committee for the Declaration of Independence. Writing as *Novanglus*, Adams, like Wilson, began his case in medieval England, where there was no provision for colonization "at common law" or in "that system of customs, written and unwritten, which was known and in force in England, in the time of king Richard the first" or "the reign of Elizabeth and king James the first." The "laws of England were" therefore then "confined to the realm, and within the four seas," with "no provision ... for governing colonies, beyond the Atlantic ... by authority of parliament."

There was not even provision "for the king to grant charters to subjects to settle in foreign countries," merely "the king's prerogative to prohibit" or "permit his subjects to leave the kingdom." If permission was granted, however, the circumstances of emigration and settlement overseas were at the discretion of those leaving.[34]

Like Jefferson, Adams identified errors that caused people to believe in the king's right to dominium and imperium overseas, "one derived from the feudal, the other from the cannon law." Even if "the king of England was considered . . . Sovereign Lord of all the land within the realm," Adams reasoned, none had conquered "king Massachusetts," and "there was no rule of the common law, that made the discovery of a country by a subject, a title to that country in the prince" or "annexed the country to the realm" and therefore to Parliament. On canon law, Adams argued that popes had "claimed a sovereign propriety in, as well as authority over the whole earth . . . in order to propagate the catholic faith." However, "When king Henry the eighth . . . threw off the authority of the pope . . . and invested it in himself by an act of parliament, he and his courtiers seemed to think that all the right of the holy see, were transferred to him." And it was "a union of these two the most impertinent and fantastical ideas that ever got into an human pericranium, viz. that as feudal sovereign and supream head of the church together, a king of England had a right to all the land their subjects could find, not possessed by any Christian state or prince, tho' possessed by heathen or infidel nations, which seems to have deluded the nation about the time of the settlement of the colonies." Even then, Adams, argued, "none of these ideas gave or inferred any right in parliament, over the new countries conquered or discovered." In fact, Adams pointed out, "America was no more within the allegiance of those princes, by the common law of England, or by the law of nature, than France and Spain were." Nor did "Discovery" give "title to the English king, by common law, or by the law of nature, to the lands, tenements and hereditaments of the native Indians here." And so "Our ancestors . . . honestly purchased their lands of the natives" or won them in war, thereby securing exclusive title.[35]

Unlike Wales and Ireland, then, America "was not a conquered, but a discovered country," Adams wrote. And "came not to the king by descent, but was explored by the settlers. It came not by marriage to the king," he expanded, "but was purchased by the settlers of the savages. It was not granted of the king by his grace, but was dearly, very dearly earned by the planters, in the labor, blood, and treasure which they expended to subdue it by cultivation." Finally, Adams asked, "How then do we New Englandmen derive our laws? I say, not from parliament, not from common law, but from the law of nature and the compact made with the king in our charters. Our ancestors were intitled to the common law of England, when they emigrated, that is, to just so much of it as they pleased to adopt, and no more."[36]

Adams gave specific instances of colonies being founded as independent states. "The first planters of Plymouth," he claimed, "had no charter or patent for the land they took possession of, and derived no authority from the English Parliament or Crown, to set up their government." Rather, "They purchased land of the Indians, and set up a government of their own, on the simple principle of nature, and afterwards purchased a patent for the land of the council at Plymouth, but never purchased any charter for government of the Crown, or the King." They then "continued to exercise all the powers of government, legislative, executive and judicial, upon the plain ground of an original contract among independent individuals for 68 years, i.e. until their incorporation with Massachusetts by our present charter." It was the same, he claimed, for "Sea-Brook, New-Haven, and other Parts of Connecticut." Indeed, the "Secretary of Connecticut has now in his possession, an original Letter from Charles 2d. to that colony, in which he considers them rather as friendly allies, than as subjects to his English Parliament."[37]

Adams even delved into the Blandian territory of the history of Virginia, stating that "the charter to the treasurer and company of Virginia, 23 March 1609, grants ample powers of government, legislative, executive and judicial, and then contains an express covenant 'to and with the said treasurer and company, their successors, factors and assigns, that they, and every of them, shall be free from all taxes and impositions forever.'" James I later rescinded "this patent, but this was never regarded" and, anyway, following "a remonstrance from Virginia," Charles I issued "a letter from the lords of the privy council, 22d July 1634, containing the royal assurance that 'all their estates, trade, freedom, and privileges should be enjoyed by them, in as extensive a manner, as they enjoyed them before those proclamations.'" In sum, then, "the ancient Massachusettensians and Virginians, had precisely the same sense of the authority of parliament, viz. that it had none at all." Indeed, "American governments and constitutions were never erected by parliament, their regalia and jurisdiction were not given by parliament, and therefore parliament have no authority to take them away." And so, "if the colonies are feudatory to the kings of England, and subject to the government of the king's laws, it is only to such laws as are made in their general assemblies, their provincial legislatures."³⁸

The Boston Massacre Orations of the early 1770s popularized this history of emigration and settlement, and they pushed more and more toward a free state theory of settler imperialism and the idea of a confederal empire, some even disparaging John Dickinson. As James Lovell's 1771 oration noted, "Our fathers left their native land, risqued all the dangers of the sea, and came to this then-savage desart, with that true undaunted courage which is excited by a confidence in GOD. They came that they might here enjoy themselves, and leave to their posterity the best of earthly portions, full *English Liberty*." Oddly, but conveniently in keeping with the idea of a royal America, Lovell posited that the first migrants to Massachusetts were escaping parliamentary rather than royal oppression, arguing that "our *English Ancestors* disgusted in their native country at a *Legislation*, which they saw was sacrificing all their rights, left its Jurisdiction, and sought . . . some happier climate" where "The King of *England* was said to be the royal landlord of this territory." It was thus "with him they entered into mutual sacred compact, by which the price of tenure and the *rules of management* were fairly stated." And "It is in this compact that we find OUR ONLY TRUE LEGISLATIVE AUTHORITY." Lovell thus refuted the claims of "Chatham, Camden . . . and the Farmer" who "have owned that England has right to exercise every power over us, but that of taking money out of our pockets without our consent."³⁹

Joseph Warren's 1772 Oration repeated some of Lovell's argument, but without Parliament as the oppressor or the king as "landlord." It was, he said, "attachment to a constitution, founded on free and benevolent principles, which inspired the first settlers of this country:—who saw with grief the daring outrages committed on the free constitution of their native land." Knowing "that nothing but a civil war could at that time restore its pristine purity," and unwilling "to embrue their hands in the *blood* of their brethren . . . they choose rather to quit their fair possessions, and seek another habitation in a distant clime." And, he added, "When they came to this new world, which they fairly purchased of the Indian natives, the only rightful proprietors, they cultivated the then barren soil by their incessant labor, and defended their dear bought possessions with the fortitude of the christian, and the bravery of the hero." Warren focused the rest of his 1772 oration on the British and imperial constitutions and the matter of standing armies, but returned in greater detail to emigration and settlement in his 1775 offering. Indeed, in the wake of the Coercive Acts, further British intransigence, and with the war that broke out the following month already looking likely, he took "a retrospective view of the first settlement of our country" with even greater drama than before. "Our fathers," he said, "having nobly resolved never to wear the yoke of despotism, and seeing the European world, at the time, thro' indolence and cowardice, falling a prey to tyranny; bravely threw themselves upon the bosom of the ocean; determined to find a place in which they might enjoy their freedom, or perish in the glorious attempt. Approving heaven," he believed, "beheld the favourite ark dancing upon the waves, and graciously preserved it untill . . . the chosen families were brought in safety to these western regions."[40]

Warren had already further popularized this history by writing it into the Suffolk Resolves of September 6, 1774, and there he drew a direct line between the historically notorious misrule of Charles I and the misdeeds of the British Parliaments since 1764 and thus between the Pilgrim and Puritan refugees and their descendants:

> Whereas the power but not the justice, the vengeance but not the wisdom, of Great Britain, which of old persecuted, scourged and exiled our fugitive parents from their native shores, now pursues us, their guiltless children, with unrelenting severity; and whereas, this then savage and uncultivated desert was purchased by the toil and treasure, or acquired by the valor and blood, of those our venerable progenitors, who bequeathed to us the dear-bought inheritance, who consigned it to our care and protection,—the most sacred obligations are upon us to transmit the glorious purchase, unfettered by power, unclogged with shackles, to our innocent and beloved offspring.[41]

The Fairfax Resolves had made similar statements a few months earlier, asserting that Virginia was not "a conquered Country; and if it was, that the present Inhabitants are the Descendants not of the Conquered, but of the Conquerors." It was also "not setled at the national Expence of England, but at the private Expence of the Adventurers, our Ancestors, by solemn Compact with, and under the Auspices and Protection of the British Crown; upon which We are in every Respect as dependant, as the People of

Great Britain, and in the same Manner subject to all his Majesty's just, legal, and constitutional Prerogatives." And so "our Ancestors, when they left their native Land, and setled in America, brought with them ... the Civil-Constitution and Form of Government of the Country they came from; and were by the Laws of Nature and Nations, entitled to all it's Privileges, Immunities and Advantages; which have descended to Us their Posterity, and ought of Right to be as fully enjoyed, as if We had still continued within the Realm of England." The most significant public responses to the Coercive Acts thus based their cases on the circumstances of emigration and settlement that would be alluded to in the Declaration of Independence.[42]

Other official and quasi-official bodies from the beginning of the revolutionary era also relayed settler-imperial histories, although, as authors of public documents needing to appeal to as many people as possible, they avoided debating whether the colonies originated under crown charters or as free states. A New York Assembly petition to the House of Commons of October 1764 asserted that the colony's first settlers had endured the "Misfortune, to be always most exposed to the Incursions of the *Canadians,* and the more barbarous Irruptions of the Savages of the Desert ... and in many Wars we have suffered an immense Loss both of Blood and Treasure." Rights should not be denied to those who "submitted to Poverty, Barbarian Wars, Loss of Blood, Loss of Money, personal Fatigues, and ten Thousand unutterable Hardships, to enlarge the Trade, Wealth, and Domination of the Nation." A Virginia Assembly "Remonstrance to the House of Commons" that December asserted that a right not be taxed without consent was "inherent in the Persons who discovered and settled these Regions" and "could not be renounced or forfeited by their Removal hither, not as Vagabonds or Fugitives, but licensed and encouraged by their Prince and animated with a laudable Desire of enlarging the *British* Dominion, and extending its Commerce." Indeed, that right had been "secured to them and their Descendants, with all the other Rights and Immunities of *British* subjects, by a Royal Charter."[43]

The Stamp Act Congress the following year expanded on these themes in its Petition to the King and, as an intercolonial body, helped provide the basis for a shared American history resting on common experiences of colonization (explored further in chapter 5). It argued:

That these Colonies were Originally Planted by Subjects of the *British* Crown, who, animated with the Spirit of Liberty, encouraged by your Majesty's Royal Predecessors, and confiding in the Public Faith for the Enjoyment of all the Rights and Liberties essential to Freedom, emigrated from their Native Country to this Continent, and by their successful Perseverance in the midst of innumerable Dangers and Difficulties, together with a Profusion of their Blood and Treasure, have happily added these vast and valuable Dominions to the Empire of *Great-Britain.* That for the Enjoyment of these Rights and Liberties, several Governments were early formed in the said Colonies, with full Power of Legislation, agreeable to the Principles of the *English Constitution.*

The Congress added that "under those Governments, these Liberties, thus vested in their Ancestors, and transmitted to their Posterity, have been exercised and enjoyed, and by the inestimable Blessings thereof (under the Favour of Almighty GOD), the inhospitable Desarts of *America* have been converted into Flourishing Countries" where "Science, Humanity and the Knowledge of Divine Truths, diffused through Remote Regions of Ignorance, Infidelity, Barbarism; the Number of *British* Subjects wonderfully Increased, and the Wealth and Power of *Great-Britain* proportionally Augmented."[44]

Various colonies recounted similar histories in their own Stamp Act resolutions. The Connecticut Resolves of October 25, 1765, stated that "this Colony or the greatest Part thereof, was purchased and obtained for great and valuable Considerations, and some other Part thereof gained by Conquest, with much Difficulty, and" with the exclusive "Endeavours, expences and Charges, of our fore-Fathers, And that thereby considerable Addition was made to his Majesty's Dominion and Interest." The Massachusetts Resolves of October 29 noted that colonists' rights to taxation by consent and to trial by jury, "which are founded in the Law of God and Nature, and are the common Rights of Mankind," as well as "all the Rights, Liberties, and Immunities of free and natural Subjects of *Great-Britain,*" were secured in "the Royal Charter" and so "belong to the Inhabitants of this Province, upon Principles of *common Justice;* their ancestors having settled this Country at their *sole Expence;* and *their* Posterity, having consistently approved themselves most loyal and faithful subjects of *Great-Britain.*" The New York

Resolves of December 18 asserted that "the Colonists did not forfeit" their "essential Rights by Emigration; because *this* was by the Permission and Encouragement of the Crown; and that they rather merit Favour, than a Deprivation of those Rights, by giving an almost boundless Extent to the *British* Empire, expanding its Trade, increasing its Wealth, and augmenting that Power which renders it so formidable to all *Europe*."[45]

The nature of emigration and settlement remained controversial, however. Thomas Jefferson and John Dickinson went head-to-head on the issue in their drafts of the 1775 Declaration of the Causes and Necessity of Taking Up Arms, offering clues to the kinds of arguments that may have taken place in the Continental Congress the following year over how to represent "the circumstances of our emigration and settlement here" in the Declaration of Independence. The 1775 debates resulted in victory for Dickinsonian moderation, perhaps because there was still hope of reconciliation with Britain, although those of 1776 would yield a different result.

Thomas Jefferson's draft of the 1775 Declaration of the Causes of Taking Up Arms included an account of free emigration and of settlers forging new states before forming compacts with the crown and constituting a confederal empire:

> our forefathers, inhabitants of the island of Gr. Britn. having long endeavored to bear up against the evils of misrule, left their native land to seek on these shores a residence for civil & religious freedom. at the expence of their blood to the ruin of their fortunes, with the relinquishment of every thing quiet & comfortable in life, they effected settlements in the inhospitable wilds of America; they there established civil societies with various forms of constitution but possessing all, what is inherent in all, the full & perfect powers of legislation. to continue their connection with the friends whom they had left they arranged themselves by charters of compact under one common king who thus became the link of union between the several parts of the empire.

The copy that Jefferson submitted to Congress said the same. Dickinson's draft also argued that the efforts and expenses of conquest and colonization gave the colonists rights to self-government, using almost exactly the same words as Jefferson's, although it added that "the distant & inhospitable wilds of America" were "then fill'd with numerous & warlike Nations of Barbarians." Dickinson wrote next, though, that "Societies or Governments, vested with perfect legislatures were formed under Charters from the Crown, and an harmonious Intercourse was established between the colonies & the Kingdom from which they derived their origin." On July 6, 1775, the Continental Congress credited Dickinson's charter theory of emigration and settlement in its final Declaration of the Causes and Necessity of Taking Up Arms.[46]

Two days later, furthermore, Congress issued its petition "to the Inhabitants of Great Britain," one of the last of their "attentions to our Brittish brethren" later mentioned in the Declaration of Independence. The 1775 petition focused on what the delegates agreed on, stating that colonists would not "tamely submit" to "the wanton Exercise of arbitrary Power," for "while we revere the Memory of our gallant and virtuous Ancestors, we never can surrender those glorious Privileges, for which they fought, bled, and conquered." But the petition endorsed Dickinson's history of colonies and empire in its complaint about the annulment of "those Charters, which encouraged our Predecessors to brave Death and Danger in every Shape, on unknown Seas, in Deserts unexplored, amidst barbarous and inhospitable Nations."[47]

It is possible that Thomas Jefferson was still smarting from these rejections when he appended the words "if history may be credited" to his more radical account of emigration and settlement in the draft Declaration of Independence that he wrote a year later. Even so, in 1776 Congress again declined to give Jefferson's history of the colonies and empire the credit he felt it merited, cutting his explanation thereof to the strategically ambiguous reference to "the circumstances of our emigration and settlement here." This time, however, it did not replace Jefferson's account with a Dickinsonian alternative. In fact, notwithstanding the elision of Jefferson's explicit explanation, the document otherwise hinted at his interpretation of events, not least by retaining the word "emigration" to describe the movement of people from Britain to America. The *Oxford English Dictionary* indicates that contemporaries defined "migration" as movement within or out of a territory, but emigration as always outwards, as in "migrating or departing out of a particular place or set of surroundings," and "from one country, usually their native land, to settle permanently in another." It also defines "emigrate" as "To remove out of a country for the purpose of settling in another" and "emigrant" as "One who removes from his own land to settle (permanently) in another," citing "1754 . . . A Memorial of the Case of the German Emigrants settled in . . . Pensilvania" as an example.

Other parts of the Declaration also hinted at free state theory. The securing of liberty and property via emigration and settlement, for example, was likely what Jefferson meant when he wrote the words "the pursuit of Happiness" into the Declaration of Independence. As the Declaration also stated, people have a right "to institute new Government, laying its foundation on such principles and organizing its powers in such form, as to them shall seem most likely to effect their Safety and Happiness." In the context of the Declaration, therefore, "happiness" appears to be the security of people in their lives, liberty, and property under a government to which they have consented. Emigration was another means of pursuing happiness, as colonial promotional literature had long stressed regarding the benefits of moving to the colonies and as revolutionary writers had argued, notably in Jefferson's reference in his *Summary View* to settlers "establishing new societies, under such laws and regulations as to them shall seem most likely to promote public happiness."[48]

In a later letter to Dr. John Manners, furthermore, Jefferson associated the exact phrase "the pursuit of happiness" with property, liberty, and safety acquired through expatriation. Though written in 1817, the letter recollected Jefferson's own thoughts and actions from four decades before. "My opinion on the right of Expatriation has been," he wrote:

> so long ago as 1776, consigned to the record in the act of the Virginia code, drawn by myself, recognizing the right expressly, and prescribing the mode of exercising it. The evidence of this natural right, like that of our right to life, liberty, the use of our faculties, the pursuit of happiness, is not left to the feeble and sophistical investigations of reason, but is impressed on the sense of every man. We do not claim these under the charters of kings or legislators, but under the King of kings. If he has made a law in the nature of man to pursue his own happiness, he has left him free in the choice of place as well as mode; and we may safely call on the whole body of English jurists to produce the map on which Nature had traced, for each individual, the geographical line which she forbids him to cross in pursuit of happiness.[49]

The "code" that Jefferson referred to was Virginia's "Revisal of the Laws" of 1776 to 1786. When Jefferson's original proposal to recognize the "natural right" of moving to and repopulating a new country failed, he drafted a 1779 "Act Declaring Who Shall be Deemed Citizens of This Commonwealth" to the same effect. "And in order to preserve to the citizens of this commonwealth that natural right, which all men have of relinquishing the country, in which birth, or other accident may have thrown them, and seeking subsistence and happiness wheresoever they may be able, or may hope to find them," the draft act stated, "it is hereby enacted and declared [that when a citizen relinquishes his citizenship and departs] such person shall be considered as having exercised his natural right of expatriating himself."[50]

The seventh of the Declaration's grievances—"He has endeavoured to prevent the population of these States; for that purpose obstructing the Laws for Naturalization of Foreigners; refusing to pass others to encourage their migrations hither, and raising the conditions of new Appropriations of Lands"—further implied a tendency toward Jefferson's version of the origins of the colonies and empire. Restricting naturalization and free movement stood in the way of the natural right to emigration, although here the Declaration deployed the more general term "migration," perhaps to account for internal migration as well as transatlantic emigration. The reference to "these States" may have been a grammatical present or future applying to the moment of and the time after independence, but it could equally have been read as applying to a past condition of the colonies as "states," as Jefferson had called them throughout *A Summary View*. That seems most likely, given that the grievance referred to the king's actions in the past, and that the Declaration's preamble had accused the king of attempting to establish "an absolute Tyranny over these States." The seventh grievance also referenced the king "raising the conditions of new Appropriations of Lands," an action that colonists might find irksomely expensive but that, as Jefferson made clear in his revisionist history in *A Summary View*, could have counted as one of the Declaration's usurpations or injuries only if the crown had no original claim to American property or territory.

The Congress also added a grievance to Jefferson's list that again implied statehood before independence. The seventeenth grievance read, "He has constrained our fellow Citizens taken Captive on the high Seas to bear Arms against their Country, to become the executioners of their friends and Brethren, or to fall themselves by their Hands." It may have referred only to the period after the king had "abdicated Government here, by declaring us out of his Protection and waging War against us" from April 1775, though even that indicated an independence that predated the Declaration by over a year. It may equally have referred, however, to the idea that colonists had been distinct peoples, "Citizens" of separate states, since "our emigration and settlement here."

Another way in which Congress implied support for the idea of the empire as a league and amity was by eliminating the two uses of the word "parliament" that had been in both Jefferson's and the committee's draft declarations. Even while deploying the euphemistic "others" and "jurisdiction foreign to our constitutions" in the grievance about the king's collaboration with the British legislature, and "jurisdiction" and "unwarrantable jurisdiction" in their respective conclusions, both drafts stated that "submission to their parliament was no part of our constitution" and that "we utterly dissolve & break off all political connection which may have heretofore subsisted between us & the people or parliament of Great Britain." Congress edited the first reference out when it removed Jefferson's explanation of the circumstances of emigration and settlement. It eliminated the second by inserting the text of Richard Henry Lee's original resolution of independence, stating that colonists "are Absolved from all Allegiance to the British Crown, and that all political connection between them and the State of Great Britain, is and ought to be totally dissolved." It thereby left the final Declaration without a single explicit mention of Parliament and thus without any implied acknowledgment of its authority.

It was perhaps apt and even necessary in 1776 that the Continental Congress would abandon the charter theory of the origins of colonies and empire that it had advanced in the Declaration on the Causes and Necessity of Taking Up Arms. The 1775 Declaration was written when Congress still aimed at reconciliation, but declaring independence was a different matter, one that entailed diplomatic and legal complications. Charter theory's admission of an original crown title to American dominium and imperium would have made an American national claim to that property and territory difficult to establish "among the powers of the Earth" from whom the colonists needed approval to form an independent nation. And it opened the possibility of compensation, or at least legal vexation, to establish American title. By contrast, free state theory posited that original title belonged to emigrants and settlers, who had consented to royal rule later, implying that independence represented nothing more than a resumption of an original American independence with full entitlement to property and territory—an entitlement, as the Declaration's introduction put it, deriving from "the Laws of Nature and of Nature's God."

Yet, as necessary as it may have been to abandon charter theory, or at least not explicitly endorse it anymore, it was politically difficult openly to approve free state theory and its "league & amity" constitutionalism. John Dickinson had set himself against it. Though consequently excoriated by some, he was popular with others and an influential figure whose support was important and perhaps even necessary for independence to succeed. Dickinson held out for reconciliation longer than many fellow delegates did, declining to vote for independence in July or to sign the Declaration later, though he would serve in a Delaware militia regiment in the war against Britain before resuming a political career that included serving as president of Delaware in 1781–1783 and of Pennsylvania in 1782–1785, and participation in the Constitutional Convention of 1787. Other supporters of charter theory faced the same dilemmas. Some eventually chose loyalism, but the fact that many, like Dickinson, reconciled themselves to independence suggests that the Declaration succeeded in not alienating all. For reasons of harmonizing the divided sentiments of the day, therefore, the final Declaration of Independence only equivocally endorsed Jefferson's history of colonies and empire, in the strategic ambiguities of the unelaborated reference to emigration and settlement and its cognate phrases throughout the rest of the text. If the Declaration leaned toward free state theory, it did so gently, and left enough interpretative space to accommodate those who did not.[51]

The Declaration's mention of emigration and settlement may have been brief and buried in the document's conclusion, but it nevertheless evoked a well-known past in which the colonists' pursuits of happiness were believed to have been codified in colonial constitutions that guaranteed their inherent rights as men, their inherited rights as Englishmen, and their acquired rights as Americans. Whether that was by a Jeffersonian free-state version of settler imperialism or by a Dickinsonian charter theory version of settler imperialism was a vexing question, but it was resolved for the purposes of the Declaration by a strategic elision that allowed readers to interpret the circumstances of emigration and settlement as they pleased.

Whatever colonists' differences on this matter, though, they agreed that their forebears had earned entitlements to property and self-government by natural right, which passed on to their descendants also by natural right but inscribed as civil rights in their charters. Indeed, the possessive term "our" emigration and settlement here is interesting in this regard. Few members of the Continental Congress and only a minority of colonists generally had personally emigrated, and none of either group had been among the original settlers of any of the colonies except perhaps for a few survivors of the 1733 settlement of Georgia. The reference to "our" emigration and settlement therefore really referred to that of their ancestors. But the intergenerational elision implied a connectedness between the national founders and their colonial forebears that had two important meanings. First and most obviously, it meant a continuity of rights to self-government, property, and other liberties. That continuity of colonists' rights is the subject of chapter 3 and the king's violations of them is the subject of chapter 4. The other implication of "our" was in the idea of a creation of peoples, first of thirteen colonial peoples but then of an American "one people" identified in the introduction of the Declaration of Independence—one of the subjects of chapters 5, along with other reformulations of government in the new nation. But "our" is not only an inclusive word but also an exclusive one—and the fact that "our" emigration and settlement here excluded Native Americans and African Americans from the Declaration's "one people" and therefore from the equality and liberties of the new nation is the main subject of chapter 6. What the rest of this book therefore shows is that the Declaration's past, from God's creation of the laws of nature through "the circumstances of our emigration and settlement here," would profoundly shape America's revolutionary present and its national future.

PART II

The Past and the Present
The History of the Present King of Great Britain

3

Unfit to Be the Ruler of a Free People

A Prince whose character is thus marked by every act which may define a Tyrant, is unfit to be the ruler of a free people.

The preamble of the Declaration of Independence culminates in the claim that "The history of the present King of Great Britain is a history of repeated injuries and usurpations, all having in direct object the establishment of an absolute Tyranny over these States." That was just the beginning of a litany of blame aimed at George III. Each of the eighteen sets of grievances that follow begins with "He has" (or, in one case, "He is")—a striking visual reminder of the king's alleged culpability. The sheer length of the charge sheet forms a formidable indictment by itself, even more so its contents. The grievances eventually conclude by reminding readers that "in every stage of these Oppressions" the colonists had "Petitioned for Redress in the most humble terms" but found their "repeated Petitions . . . answered only by repeated injury," exonerating themselves from blame, affirming the singular responsibility of the king, and proving that he had acted knowingly and therefore intentionally. He was therefore "A Prince whose character is . . . marked by every act which may define a Tyrant" and thus "unfit to be the ruler of a free people."

The authors' determination to blame independence on the king was so complete that their Declaration avoided directly identifying the institution that had in fact initiated many of the oppressions that aggrieved them: the

British Parliament. The document refers to the institution only twice, and only implicitly even then. The thirteenth grievance denotes its members as "others" with whom the king had "combined . . . to subject us to a jurisdiction foreign to our constitution, and unacknowledged by our laws; giving his Assent to their Acts of pretended Legislation." The nine complaints that follow begin with "For," subsuming each under the general grievance against the king. The other reference was the conclusion's allusion to the failure of the British people to arrest the various "attempts by their legislature to extend an unwarrantable jurisdiction over us."[1]

The drafting committee's and the Continental Congress's changes to Thomas Jefferson's draft reinforced his original emphasis on the fundamental role of the king and the merely incidental role of the British Parliament in the Declaration's account of the causes of independence. The committee replaced Jefferson's possibly sarcastic reference in the preamble to "his present majesty" with "the present King of Great Britain," a more factual description that aligned more obviously with their opinions of his reign. Jefferson had also claimed at the end of his grievances that "future ages will scarce believe that the hardiness of one man, adventured within the short compass of 12 years only, on so many acts of tyranny without a mask, over a people fostered & fixed in principles of liberty." The committee replaced "acts of tyranny without a mask" with a more explanatory "to build a foundation, so broad and undisguised for tyranny," a clearer indication that the king's plans had not yet been fulfilled and resistance thus remained possible. But Congress deleted the entire passage, and some historians have speculated that delegates decided that it was excessively emotional. The formulation that Congress approved, however—that the king's character was "marked by every act which may define a Tyrant" and "is unfit to be the ruler of a free people"—certainly retained a sense of outrage, as did the retention of such terms as "evils," "absolute Despotism," and "absolute Tyranny," all of which underlined the "necessity" of revolution, a concept explored in chapter 4. Delegates may have therefore made the deletions simply for the sake of concision. And possibly for historical consistency too, as that elision had the further effect of eliminating the reference to "12 years only," which would have dated the beginning of the revolutionary era to the Sugar Act of 1764, and thus to acts of Parliament, rather than to 1760 and the accession to the throne of "the present King of Great Britain."[2]

Congress even eliminated the two uses of the word "parliament" that had been in previous drafts of the Declaration, which stated that "submission to their parliament was no part of our constitution" and that the colonists were breaking connections with "the people or parliament of Great Britain." The first usage disappeared with Congress's deletion of Jefferson's explanation of the circumstances of emigration and settlement, the second with the reappearance of Richard Henry Lee's original resolution of independence from June 7 stating that colonists "are Absolved from all Allegiance to the British Crown, and that all political connection between them and the State of Great Britain, is and ought to be totally dissolved." Congress thereby emphasized the absence of any constitutional authority of the British Parliament in the American colonies with a resounding silence.

In contrast to the Declaration's blaming of the king, however, almost all histories of the American Revolution written since the event have begun with the Sugar Act of 1764 or the Stamp Act of 1765, rather than with the accession of George III as king in 1760. Almost all the subsequent major moments those histories depict also begin with parliamentary legislation—the Declaratory Act of 1766, the Townshend Acts of 1767, the Tea Act of 1773, the Coercive Acts of 1774, and the Prohibitory Act of 1775. Even the royal proclamations of 1763, limiting British settlement to east of the Appalachians, and of 1775, declaring the colonies to be in rebellion and out of the king's protection, aligned with parliamentary policy. Britain was, after all, a constitutional monarchy, certainly since the Glorious Revolution of 1688–1689, which worked according to a principle of coordination whereby most executive prerogative operated through the legislature. Sovereignty thus lay with the "crown-in-Parliament," meaning Parliament. If Parliament had appropriated most of the crown's prerogative, that included its prerogatives in the colonies. In turn, it was supposedly constitutionally impossible for the king to cause grievances or to be blamed for them. If the king could "do no wrong," it was not because of the doctrine of "sovereign immunity" but because he had no substantive sovereignty. Yet blame the king is emphatically what the authors of the Declaration did in their official account of "the causes of the separation." They also presented their case to "a candid world" and "to the Supreme Judge of the World" and rested it on the laws of nature and God and thus on international law as well, seemingly confident that all the major players in the universe at the time would take their blaming of the king seriously. It therefore makes sense for us to take it seriously too, and that is what this and the next chapter aim to do.[3]

The previous chapter has already explained that the circumstances of emigration and settlement had established the colonists' rights to property and self-government under their own assemblies and the king, with little or no constitutional role for Parliament. This chapter begins by showing how, for most Britons, the Glorious Revolution established a limited monarchy under the crown-in-Parliament that they believed was also, in the words of the Declaratory Act of 1766, an "imperial crown and Parliament." Colonists rejected the idea that constitutional change in Britain applied in the colonies, however, as their charters were effectively social contracts and thus unchangeable without the colonists' consent. Colonists therefore believed that the imperial relations established by the circumstances of emigration and settlement continued to apply. The king thus retained separate authority and powers in his other dominions independently of the British Parliament, with parliamentary authority extending at most to the shores of those other dominions. Indeed, it was the crown's role to mediate disputes between his different dominions and to protect the lives, liberty, property, and pursuits of happiness of each of his peoples from encroachments by any of the others, even by using his veto if needed. It therefore made sense for the colonists to appeal to the king for protection, as they did before 1776, and to blame him for any calamities resulting from his exercising his independent powers tyrannously or combining with others to do so, as the colonists charged in the Declaration of Independence. The next chapter shows how another element of the Declaration that seems mysterious to many of us today—what the document blamed the king for in the grievances—also made sense to contemporaries in the context of the Declaration's history and historical consciousness.

Contemporaries, even critical ones, understood why the Declaration of Independence blamed the king for the colonists' grievances, even while denying the accuracy of the specific accusations and denouncing the colonists' rejection of parliamentary authority. Loyalist former governor of Massachusetts Thomas Hutchinson, for example, focused on the contents of the grievances in his *Strictures upon the Declaration of the Congress at Philadelphia*, rather than on the fact that they were directed at George III. Unofficial British government spokesman John Lind's *Answer to the Declaration* did the same, and added an attack on the natural rights element of its natural law theory. All Lind said about the blaming of the king, however, was that it was "*not the separate interests of his Majesty, but those of his British subjects*

[that] *are involved*. If the Americans insult him . . . it is because he asserted our rights:—if they have dared to renounce all allegiance to his Crown, it is because he *determined not to give up our rights*."[4]

What Lind hinted at here was the connection many post–Glorious Revolution Britons made between the crown and Parliament and in turn the people that both bodies represented in coordination through the sovereignty of the crown-in-Parliament. The Declaratory Act of 1766—the starkest statement the British made about the authority of Parliament over the colonies—was emphatic about the inseparability of the crown and Parliament, and indeed that parliamentary authority directly derived from the concept of the crown-in-Parliament. It stated first that the colonists' claims to "the sole and exclusive right of imposing duties and taxes upon His Majesty's subjects" in the colonies and that their "votes, resolutions, and orders derogatory to the legislative authority of Parliament" were "inconsistent with the dependency of the said colonies and plantations upon the crown of Great Britain." It said instead that the colonies "have been, are, and of right ought to be, subordinate unto, and dependent upon the imperial crown and Parliament of Great Britain." That portentous term—"imperial crown and Parliament"—was certainly an extension to Parliament of the principle of the Act of Restraint of Appeals of 1533, which declared that "England is an empire" and thus independent of Rome and papal authority, and the king of England was therefore the ultimate power within the realm. The context of the 1766 Declaratory Act, however, gave it a new implication if not a new meaning: of the crown-in-Parliament as the ultimate power throughout all British territories. Indeed, as the act continued, it may therefore be "declared by the king's Most Excellent Majesty, by and with the advice and consent of the Lords Spiritual and Temporal, and Commons, of Great Britain, in Parliament assembled" that the British Parliament "had, hath, and of right ought to have, full power and authority to make laws and statutes of sufficient force and validity to bind the colonies and people of America, subjects of the crown of Great Britain, in all cases whatsoever." Members of Parliament may have initiated most of the actions that aggrieved the colonists, then, but they did so by authority of "the imperial crown and Parliament of Great Britain" and because the colonists were "subjects of the crown of Great Britain" and therefore of its Parliament, too.

The Declaratory Act also twice insisted that the colonies' subordination to Parliament as well as to the crown was historical: that the colonies "have been" as well as "are, and of right ought to be subordinate . . . and dependent" on "the imperial crown and Parliament," and that Parliament "had" as well as "hath and ought to have full power to bind" them. It is true that, beginning with Elizabeth I, queens and kings had issued colonial charters, whether to private companies or to proprietors, and had eventually converted most of the originally private colonies into royal ones. Yet those territories had historically come under parliamentary authority in one way or another. Even before the Glorious Revolution, Parliament had exercised imperial power through the Navigation Ordinance of 1651 and through other navigation acts and trade regulations after the 1660 Restoration. The bodies charged with administering the colonies and empire, the Lords of Trade from 1676 and the Board of Trade from 1696, were committees of the Privy Council and thus advisers to the crown, but they took directions from the crown's ministers in Parliament as well.[5]

Appreciating contemporary historical perspectives also allows us to see how Britons at the time saw parliamentary supremacy as absolute and yet also benign and therefore rightful. For all the social strife and widespread accusations of political corruption in eighteenth-century Britain, many Britons believed that the Glorious Revolution of 1688 had made England, and Britain after the 1707 Act of Union, the freest nation on earth, possibly ever, even restoring a supposed Anglo-Saxon "Ancient Constitution" that had established the rights of freeborn Englishmen to freehold property and conciliar kingship that had existed before the Norman Conquest. In the process, 1688 had finally ended the often bloody conflict over royal prerogative versus parliamentary privilege that had afflicted England since 1066. The Glorious Revolution, at least according to British historical memory at the time of the American Revolution, created instead a constitutional balance of monarchy, aristocracy, and democracy that supposedly secured the lives, liberty, and property of king, lords, and commoners alike. One historian has even written of an eighteenth-century "cult" of Parliament, and British vanity on the matter was unhurt by praise lavished on British constitutionalism by foreign commentators such as Montesquieu.[6]

Although Parliament had exercised authority in the empire, in wartime and in regulating trade at all times from the 1650s, it rarely if ever did so within the colonies themselves before 1764. At the end of the hugely successful but vastly expensive Seven Years' War, however, influential Britons began arguing that Parliament ought to exercise its presumed powers to tax and otherwise govern the American colonies more effectively. Former colonial administrator William Knox, for example, argued for taxes and other reforms, and, crucially, that the "interposition of Parliament is absolutely necessary for all these purposes" as "no other Authority than that of the British Parliament will be regarded by the Colonys, or be able to awe them into acquiescence." Prime Minister George Grenville shared Knox's presumptions, hoping that "the power and sovereignty of Parliament, over every part of the British dominions, for the purpose of raising or collecting any tax, would never be disputed." When colonists did dispute that power and authority, many Britons reacted with a mix of bewilderment and outrage. Lord Hillsborough, Secretary of State for the Colonies from 1768 to 1772, went so far as to recommend that defiance of Parliament be treated as treason.[7]

Even colonial sympathizers such as Edmund Burke were seduced by the mystique of the crown-in-Parliament. Burke urged fellow members of Parliament to return to the days of "wise and salutary neglect" that preceded the Sugar Act and that had irrevocably accustomed colonists to self-government. Yet he also believed that the Glorious Revolution had transformed "a mere representative of the people into a mighty sovereign" and that Parliament thus had "the clearest right imaginable not only to bind" the colonies "with every Law, but with every mode of Legislative Taxation," even if MPs should be wise enough not to enforce the right. William Pitt similarly argued that it was impolitic but still constitutional to legislate for the colonists in almost all areas. "I maintain," he orated, "that the parliament has a right to bind, to restrain America. Our legislative power over the colonies is sovereign and supreme." So "we may bind their trade, confine their manufactures, and exercise every power whatsoever," he said, "except that of taking their money out of their pockets without their consent."[8]

Fervent British belief in the authority of Parliament explains the relentlessness of British actions in the face of repeated and escalating colonial resistance from 1764. Though forced to repeal the Stamp Act by a combination of petitions, pamphlets, economic boycott, and popular protests that compelled the resignation of Stamp officials in all thirteen colonies except Georgia, Parliament immediately passed the Declaratory Act to prevent that repeal being perceived as an admission of the unconstitutionality of parliamentary taxation of the colonists then and for the future. Indeed, a year later Parliament passed the Townshend Acts, imposing new duties on the colonies and creating a new Board of Customs Commissioners to collect them. When forced to repeal those taxes after the 1770 Boston Massacre, and in the face of an ongoing economic boycott, Parliament kept the commissioners in office and retained the tax on tea "to keep up the right," in the words of George III, who was, in his own British way, a scrupulous constitutional monarch. After the Boston Tea Party, Parliament reacted with the Coercive Acts, which closed Boston Harbor in lieu of compensation, provided for trials in England or in other colonies for those accused of crimes in Massachusetts, made unoccupied buildings in Boston available as housing for troops, and annulled the 1691 Massachusetts charter and imposed in its place what amounted to military rule, with General Thomas Gage, the commander in chief of British troops in America since 1763, appointed governor. For most Britons, the appropriate response to resistance to parliamentary authority was always an escalation in the assertion of parliamentary power.[9]

Britons knew that the colonists disagreed with their views on the imperial crown and Parliament, as countless pamphlets and petitions repeatedly explained the limits of British legislative authority. Some colonial pamphleteers even lived among them. An American resident in London in 1774, undoubtedly familiar with the cult of Parliament, anonymously warned British readers that parliamentary measures over the previous decade were not a logical outcome of 1688 but were in fact "A total contradiction to every principle laid down at the time of the Revolution." And he reminded them of the circumstances of American emigration and settlement, arguing that emigrants "left their mother country" and "crossed the unfrequented ocean, and entered into the wilderness of America." For their "fatigue and dangers" in doing so, he continued, they had the "consolation, that the fruit of their labour was their own" and "their toil was sweeten'd by reflection—Here is my charter... that says my property is my own and my heirs for ever." And colonists were also certain that "the King was their supreme governor," not Parliament, "for it was him with whom their compact was made." He also related colonial rights back to natural law, citing "Mr Locke... a man to whom every subject of the laws of England at this day, is in no small degree indebted," in support of his social contract theory of the nature of colonial charters.[10]

Yet Britons remained deaf to such voices "of justice and consanguinity." Even armed resistance failed at first to shake British constitutional convictions. When the Continental Congress offered its Olive Branch Petition to the king, following the April 19 outbreak of war at Lexington and Concord and the spread of violence afterward, he refused to reply and instead passed the petition on to Parliament, which in his view was the proper constitutional recipient. Parliament did not respond either, however. Nor did the Declaration of Independence itself diminish British determination to enforce its interpretation of constitutional law. It was only after the shock of the British surrender at Saratoga in October 1777 that Britons conceded anything on the matter of parliamentary supremacy. Even then, it was merely a proposed cessation of the practice without an admission of its unconstitutionality. It was only with the recognition of American independence in the Treaty of Paris of 1783 that Britons finally fully acknowledged that their Parliament had no authority in its now former colonies.[11]

Britons thus maintained that the king or crown-in-Parliament had always been supreme in the colonies and therefore had the right to change imperial arrangements whenever Parliament saw fit. Yet colonists believed that arrangements supposedly arising from "the circumstances of our emigration and settlement here" continued to pertain, notwithstanding occasional conflicts over temporary royal impositions, especially during the Restoration era, and more permanent changes such as the abolition and replacement of numerous colonial charters and the impositions of the Navigation Acts and other trade regulations. Some colonists expressed regret over these more permanent changes but, with some notable exceptions, rationalized them by hewing to the principles of precedence and tacit consent. Otherwise, however, colonists agreed that the fundamentals of the imperial constitution as established by emigration and settlement remained in place throughout the colonial era, and they were as determined as Britons were to uphold their version of the imperial constitution. Colonists had appealed repeatedly to kings against extensions of royal power even before 1764. They continued to do so afterward, and added appeals to him to protect them against novel parliamentary injuries and usurpations. When those appeals "were answered only with repeated injuries," including his abdication of government "by declaring us out of his Protection and waging War against us," it made sense for the colonists to blame him for the necessity of independence.

Thomas Jefferson's *A Summary View of the Rights of British America* was one of those appeals to the king for redress that the Declaration of Independence mentioned, although it did not use "the most humble terms" that the Continental Congress adopted in its more formal petitions. Jefferson addressed the king directly in the latter's role as protector of his subjects. Hence the pamphlet's Ciceronian epigraph, which, along with Cicero's strictures on natural law, cited in chapter 1, helps explain why Jefferson later included the Roman statesman, lawyer, philosopher, and rhetorician alongside "Aristotle, . . . Locke, Sidney Etc." as among the authors of "the books of public right" that helped constitute the "common sense of the subject" and the "harmonising sentiments of the day" that his letter claimed the Declaration aimed to express. The epigraph read: "It is the indispensible duty of the supreme magistrate to consider himself as acting for the whole community, and obliged to support its dignity, and assign to the people, with justice their various rights, as he would be faithful to the great trust reposed in him."[12] Toward the end of *A Summary View*, Jefferson wrote of having explained "our grievances . . . with that freedom of language and sentiment which becomes a free people claiming their rights, as derived from the laws of nature, and not as the gift of their chief magistrate," adding that "kings are the servants, not the proprietors of the people." He thus urged the king "to think and to act for yourself and your people" and "No longer persevere in sacrificing the rights of one part of the empire to the inordinate desires of another; but deal out to all equal and impartial right." And so, in language he would recycle in the Declaration, he urged the king "to interpose" against "acts of power, assumed by a body of men, foreign to our constitutions, and unacknowledged by our laws . . . on behalf of the inhabitants of British America."[13]

Sometimes the proposed interpositions would involve nothing more than offering advice to members of Parliament. We "earnestly entreat his majesty," Jefferson wrote, "as yet the only mediatory power between the several states of the British empire, to recommend to his parliament of Great Britain the total revocation of these acts." If such recommendations did not work, however, Jefferson urged the king to "Let no act be passed by any one legislature, which may infringe on the rights and liberties of another. This is the important post," Jefferson added, "in which fortune has placed you, holding the balance of a great, if a well poised empire." Jefferson's suggestion of a royal veto over Parliament was of course anathema to

Britons. The last use of a royal negative over nonprerogative legislation was Queen Anne's veto of a Scottish militia bill in 1708, and that was accepted only because of fears that such a militia might be disloyal in the event of a French invasion. Jefferson conceded that George III "and his ancestors, conscious of the impropriety of opposing their single opinion to the united wisdom of two houses of parliament . . . for several ages past have modestly declined the exercise of this power in that part of his empire called Great Britain"—a phrase that signified that the empire comprised dominions of the British king and that the British state was just one among many realms of equal standing under his authority. That, however, prefaced a description of historical developments that, for Jefferson, justified a restoration of the royal veto. The "addition of new states to the British empire," he wrote, "has produced an addition of new, and sometimes opposite interests. It is now, therefore, the great office of his majesty, to resume the exercise of his negative power, and to prevent the passage of laws by any one legislature of the empire, which might bear injuriously on the rights and interests of another." The first grievance in the Declaration of Independence would complain of the king vetoing colonial assembly legislation that was "wholesome and necessary for the public good," but that did not mean that vetoes were unconstitutional or always bad. Indeed, both colonial governors and the Privy Council had continued to veto and suspend assembly legislation, and even to prorogue and dissolve assemblies, for better and for worse but as a matter of course. It therefore made sense, from a colonial perspective, for Jefferson to write that "By the constitution of Great Britain, as well as of the several American states," his "majesty possesses the power of refusing to pass into a law any bill which has already passed the other two branches of legislature."[14]

For Jefferson, then, in both Britain and the colonies, the crown remained what it could not be for post–Glorious Revolution Britons—a separate branch of government with independent powers of its own. But Americans had a different historical experience and memory than Britons of the Glorious Revolution's causes and legacies. Jefferson wrote of England's seventeenth-century revolutions that "A family of princes" had been "on the British throne, whose treasonable crimes against their people brought on them afterwards the exertion of those sacred and sovereign rights of punishment reserved in the hands of the people"—a general enough appraisal that was acceptable to all but Jacobites. But the Stuarts' specific crimes in

America were that lands and territories "which had been acquired by the lives, the labours, and the fortunes of individual adventurers, was by these princes, at several times, parted out and distributed among the favourites and followers" under "an assumed right of the crown." Jefferson otherwise said little specifically about the Glorious Revolution or its settlement, however, perhaps because, unlike in Massachusetts, New York, and nearby Maryland, there had been no overthrow of James II's minions in Virginia. But his idea that the empire remained a "league & amity" of states indicates a belief that the accession of William III and Mary II simply restored the colonists' original rights to property and self-government under royal protection rather than augured the constitutional changes that it did in Britain.[15]

Or it may be that Jefferson had little specific to say about the Glorious Revolution because, for him, it had restored some but not all of those rights. Jefferson argued that "a free trade with all parts of the world" had originally been "possessed by the American colonists, as of natural right," and which "no law of their own had taken away or abridged." He thus described the Navigation Ordinance of 1651 as an "unjust encroachment" by which "the Parliament for the commonwealth . . . assumed upon themselves the power of prohibiting their trade with all other parts of the world, except the island of Great-Britain." Parliament annulled this "arbitrary act," however, "and by solemn treaty, entered into on the 12th day of March, 1651, between the said common wealth [England] . . . and the colony of Virginia by their house of burgesses, it was expressly stipulated . . . that they should have 'free trade as the people of England do enjoy to all places and with all nations, according to the laws of that common wealth.'" However, "upon the restoration" of Charles II, the colonists' "rights of free commerce fell once more a victim to arbitrary power; and by several acts of his reign, as well as of some of his successors, the trade of the colonies was laid under such restrictions as shew what hopes they might form from the justice of a British parliament, were its uncontrouled power admitted over these states." These laws not only continued to be in force after the Glorious Revolution but were reinforced by the new Navigation Act and the creation of the Board of Trade in place of the defunct Lords of Trade in 1696.[16]

Jefferson thus depicted trade regulations not to contrast the legality of trade regulation with the illegality of raising revenue after 1764, as John Dickinson and others did, but as a more general rebuke of parliamentary power. "History has informed us that bodies of men, as well as individuals, are susceptible of the spirit of tyranny," he famously wrote on this very point. He also identified "certain other acts of the British parliament, by which they would prohibit us from manufacturing for our own use the articles we raise on our own lands with our own labour." Those acts began with the Hat Act of 1732, whereby "an American subject is forbidden to make a hat for himself of the fur which he has taken perhaps on his own soil," which Jefferson described as "an instance of despotism to which no parrallel can be produced in the most arbitrary ages of British history." That description may seem rather overblown, but the point was that such restrictions violated the colonists' natural rights to property and local representation as inscribed in the colonial charters and imperial constitution they had consented to be governed by.[17]

Jefferson added that, besides "these exercises of usurped power," Parliament had "also intermeddled with the regulation of the internal affairs of the colonies. The act of the 9th of Anne for establishing a post office in America," he explained, "seems to have had little connexion with British convenience, except that of accommodating his majesty's ministers and favourites with the sale of a lucrative and easy office." But his main point was not the cost of such actions or the corruption they entailed but that "experience confirms the propriety of those political principles which exempt us from the jurisdiction of the British parliament." And, he starkly added, "The true ground on which we declare these acts void is, that the British parliament has no right to exercise authority over us."[18]

Jefferson thus argued that George III's predecessors had, as the Declaration of Independence would put it, "combined with others to subject us to a jurisdiction foreign to our constitution, and unacknowledged by our laws; giving his Assent to their Acts of pretended Legislation." The "abuses and usurpations" the Declaration described therefore, for Jefferson, predated "the history of the present King of Great Britain." He nevertheless wrote that in the "reigns which preceded his majesty's, the violations of our right were less alarming, because repeated at more distant intervals than that rapid and bold succession of injuries which is likely to distinguish the present from all other periods of American history." Indeed, he continued, "Scarcely have our minds been able to emerge from the astonishment into which one stroke of parliamentary thunder has involved us, before another more heavy, and more alarming, is fallen on us." But the main point of his historical evidence here was that, again in sentiments repeated in the

Declaration, "Single acts of tyranny may be ascribed to the accidental opinion of a day; but a series of oppressions begun at a distinguished period, and pursued, unalterably through every change of ministers, too plainly prove a deliberate and systematical plan of reducing us to slavery"—a point about the nature of the course of human events I return to in the next chapter. In any case, some colonists accepted the idea that trade regulation was a legitimate exercise of parliamentary power, and so Jefferson's focus in the Declaration of Independence on the reign of George III perhaps represented a concession to the "common sense of the subject" that he later wrote about.[19]

As with emigration and settlement, Jefferson's views on the development of colonies and empire were influenced by those of his friend and fellow Virginian Richard Bland. Bland claimed he did "not dispute the Authority of the Parliament, which is without Doubt supreme within the Body of the Kingdom, and cannot be abridged by any other Power; but" he wrote—before questioning the very basis of that power as Britons understood it—"may not the King have Prerogatives which he has a Right to exercise without the Consent of Parliament?" For Bland, with Parliament's authority limited "within the Body of the Kingdom," one such prerogative was that of "granting License to his Subjects to remove into a *new* Country, and to settle therein upon particular Conditions." And "If he has no such Prerogative," Bland insisted, "I cannot discover how the Royal Engagements can be made good, that the Freedom and other Benefits of the *British* Constitution shall be secured to those People who shall settle in a new Country under such Engagements." Indeed, they "cannot be secured to a People" unless "they are exempted from being taxed by any Authority but that of their Representatives, chosen by themselves." And "if the King cannot grant such an Exemption, in Right of his Prerogative, the Royal Promises cannot be fulfilled; and all Charters which have been granted by our former Kings, for this Purpose, must be Deceptions upon the Subjects who accepted them."[20]

Bland even gave an example of such prerogative exemption, pointedly comparing the historically ill-reputed Charles II favorably to George III. "Even in the Reign of *Charles* the Second, a Time by no Means favourable to Liberty," he noted, "these Rights of the Colonies were maintained inviolate; for when it was thought necessary to establish a permanent Revenue for the Support of Government in *Virginia*, the King did not apply to the *English* Parliament, but to the General Assembly, and sent over an Act, under the

Great Seal of *England*, by which it was enacted by the King's Most Excellent Majesty, by and with the Consent of the General Assembly" that a tax be raised for the "Support of the Government in the Colony." Even Charles II, then, acknowledged the colonists' exclusive right of taxation. Bland added that later, "Agents sent from *Virginia* . . . obtained a Declaration from *Charles 2d* the 19th of *April* 1676, under his Privy Seal, that Impositions or Taxes ought not to be laid upon the Inhabitants and Proprietors of the Colony but by the common Consent of the General Assembly." And, again contrasting the past favorably with his present, Bland noted that Charles II had "ordered a Charter to be made out, and to pass the Great Seal, for securing this Right, among others, to the Colony." By contrast, under the Stamp Act, "to serve a Purpose destructive of their Rights, and to introduce Principles of Despotism unknown to a free Constitution, the Legislature of the Colonies are degraded even below the Corporation of a petty Borough in *England*."[21]

Bland argued, then, as Jefferson would, that whatever arrangements pertained in Britain after the Glorious Revolution, an independent crown with separate powers remained essential to the maintenance of colonial rights to property and self-government as established at the founding of the colonies. In one of his most striking passages, Bland acknowledged that "Parliament is the sovereign legislative Power of the *British* Nation," but "by what *Right* is it that the Parliament can exercise such a Power over the Colonists, who have as natural a Right to the Liberties and Privileges of *Englishmen* as if they were actually resident within the Kingdom?" Parliament, in short, "cannot, constitutionally, deprive the People of their *natural* Rights; nor, in Virtue of the same Principle, can it deprive them of their *civil* Rights, which are founded in Compact, without their own Consent." Both natural law and civil history thus directed that no circumstance since emigration and settlement had altered the civil rights of colonists.[22]

And that, for Bland, as for Jefferson, included rights to free trade. "It must be admitted," he wrote, "that after the Restoration the Colonies lost that Liberty of Commerce with foreign Nations they had enjoyed before that Time." The Navigations Acts and other trade regulations, he said, "not only circumscribed the Trade of the Colonies with foreign Nations within very narrow Limits, but imposed Duties upon several Articles of their own Manufactory exported from one Colony to another." They thus "deprived the Colonies . . . of the Privileges of *English* Subjects, and constituted an unnatural Difference between Men under the same Allegiance, born equally free, and entitled to the same civil Rights." Nor did Bland believe that such trade restrictions were validated by precedent or tacit consent. In a passage directed against the Stamp Act but based on principles that could apply to any legislation before or after, he argued that as "the Colonies are not represented in Parliament . . . no new Law can bind them that is made without the Concurrence of their Representatives." Hence "every Act of Parliament that imposes *internal* Taxes upon the Colonies is an Act of *Power*, and not of *Right*," and "*Power* abstracted from *Right* cannot give a just Title to Dominion" because "If a Man invades my Property, he becomes an Aggressor, and puts himself into a State of War with me." Continuing in this ominous tone, Bland stated, "I have a Right to oppose this Invader; If I have not Strength to repel him, I must submit, but he acquires no Right to my Estate which he has usurped." And "Whenever I recover Strength I may renew my Claim, and attempt to regain my Possession; if I am never strong enough, my Son, or his Son, may, when able, recover the natural Right of his Ancestor which has been unjustly taken from him."[23]

Not everybody opposed trade regulations or denied the validity of precedent or tacit consent. As noted in the previous chapter, John Dickinson argued, apparently in response to Bland, that the British Parliament "possesses a legal authority to *regulate* the trade of *Great-Britain*, and all its colonies." That right was historical and original, since the American colonies had been "settled by the nations of Europe for the purposes of trade" and for "raising for their mother country those things which she did not produce herself; and by supplying themselves from her with things they wanted." Dickinson nevertheless used colonial acceptance of certain commercial laws as a cautionary tale against giving passive consent to internal taxation. "*Great-Britain* has prohibited the manufacturing iron and steel in these colonies, without any objection being made to her right of doing it," he warned. "The like right she must have to prohibit any manufacturing among us. Thus she is possessed of an undisputed *precedent* on this point." He therefore counseled his "countrymen" to "ROUSE yourselves, and behold the ruin hanging over your heads. If you ONCE admit, that Great-Britain may lay duties upon her exportations to us, *for the purpose of levying money on us only*, she then will have nothing to do, but to lay those duties on the articles which she prohibits us to manufacture—and the tragedy of American liberty is finished."[24]

Dickinson also saw a distinction between crown and parliamentary powers within the colonies, thus rejecting the idea that the principle of the crown-in-Parliament applied to the colonies. In the first of his *Farmer's Letters*, he argued forcefully against the New York Restraining Act, which required the governor to suspend all assembly legislation until its members agreed to provision British soldiers fully, as per the Quartering Act of 1765. "It was not *necessary* that this suspension should be caused by an act of parliament," Dickinson specified, as "The crown might have restrained the governor of *New-York*, even from calling the assembly together, by its prerogative in the royal governments." That step might have been taken "if the conduct of the assembly of *New-York* had been regarded as an act of disobedience *to the crown alone*." But, he pointed out, "it is regarded as an act of disobedience to the authority of the BRITISH LEGISLATURE." That made the act "vastly more affecting," as it "is a parliamentary assertion of the *supreme authority* of the *British legislature* over these colonies, in *the point of taxation*, and is intended to compel *New York* into a submission to that authority."²⁵

Though he would to be a reluctant revolutionary in 1776, Dickinson invoked the Glorious Revolution as a warning against parliamentary usurpation. He published the first of his *Farmer's Letters* in the *Pennsylvania Gazette* on November 5, 1767, the anniversary of the landing at Torbay of William of Orange, eventually leading to the overthrow of James II. In case anyone missed the point, he dated the letter "Nov. 5" and added the words, "The day of King WILLIAM the Third's landing." The thrust of his argument, however, was against the parliamentary supremacy that Britons believed the events of 1688–1689 had established. Although the Glorious Revolution had not seen the overthrow of Pennsylvania's proprietary regime or of any particular measures or minions imposed by James II, as occurred in Maryland, Massachusetts, and New York, Dickinson clearly saw it as a reassertion of the traditions of colonial rights to property and self-government first established, as he saw them, by the circumstances of colonial emigration and settlement.²⁶

William Hicks, though a free state theorist, accepted Parliament's right to regulate trade and even colonial manufacturing, but, like Dickinson, he came to see it as dangerous in light of parliamentary actions since 1764. "I am not so great a stickler for the independence of the colonies," he wrote, and "I am ready to acknowledge the *necessity* of lodging in some part of the community a *restraining* power, for the regulating and limiting the trade and manufactures of each particular county or colony, in such a manner as might most effectually promote the good of the whole." However, he continued, "I should not obstinately object to the vesting this power in the parliament of Great-Britain, if the violent measures which have lately been carried into execution, did not afford me too much reason to believe, that every concession which might at this time be made from a *principle of necessity,* and a regard to the public utility, would be immediately considered as an acknowledgment of such a *subordination,* as is totally inconsistent with the nature of our constitution." Hicks even noted that an older cult of Parliament encouraged many Britons to regard its power as absolute. "The friends of parliamentary power lose themselves," he alleged, "in contemplating the idol they have raised; and to confirm the veneration which they have entertained, they annex to it the idea of omnipotence and infallibility."[27]

Hicks therefore raised some penetrating questions about parliamentary authority. "When the parliament of *Great-Britain* arrogate to themselves this sovereign jurisdiction over the colonies, I should be glad to know on what principles they found their claim. Do they ground their pretensions on the excellent principles of their own constitution," he asked, "or is this supremacy a power *virtually inherent* in the name of parliament?" The House of "Lords indeed may, with some appearance of reason, assert a supreme jurisdiction over the whole body of the nation, as the highest court of judicature," he conceded, "But when an aspiring member of the Commons House confidently declares that he has a power to bind our trade, and restrain our manufactures, I should be glad to know whether he derived this power from the honest freemen his constituents, or whether he acquired it by virtue of his office? From his constituents he could receive no more power than they *naturally possessed,*" he explained, but "from his office he cannot reasonably be supposed vested with any other authority, than that of deciding upon the formalities, and punctilios annexed to it."[28]

For Hicks as for Jefferson, it was the king's duty to interpose against injustices perpetrated against the colonies by Parliament. In order that laws "may not interfere with the general welfare of the whole," Hicks argued, "the restraining power lodged in the Crown will always be able to insure; since we cannot suppose that a wise and just Prince would ever consent to sacrifice the interest and happiness of any one part to the selfish views of another." The king was therefore ultimately responsible for any injustice he allowed. "It is a received maxim of the law—'that the king can do no wrong,'" Hicks noted, "and yet our brave forefathers were not so deluded by this royal dogma as to suffer themselves to be stripped of their invaluable rights and privileges by the arbitrary fiat of a wicked prince." Colonists' allegiance was therefore to the king, but it was always provisional.[29]

James Wilson was even more emphatic about the limits of Parliament and the protective role of monarchy. "NO question can be more important to Great-Britain, and to the Colonies, than this," he asserted, "—*Does the legislative authority of the British Parliament extend over them?*" Part of his case against rested on principles of political economy—that the colonists were not and could not be represented in Parliament in London as it was too distant from the colonies, and MPs who passed laws for the colonies would not themselves be subject to those laws. In any case, like Jefferson, Wilson saw the authority and roles of the king and Parliament as historically and constitutionally distinct. "Allegiance to the King and obedience to the Parliament are founded on very different principles," he explained. "The former is founded on protection: The latter, on representation. An inattention to this difference has produced, I apprehend, much uncertainty and confusion in our ideas concerning the connexion, which ought to subsist between Great-Britain and the American Colonies."[30]

For Wilson, nothing had changed to alter the connections between the colonies and the crown since they were first established by emigration and settlement. "THE original and true ground of the superiority of Great Britain over the American Colonies," he wrote, "is not shewn in any book of the law, unless, as I have already observed, it be derived from the right of conquest," which he considered "inapplicable to the Colonists." Certainly, the Glorious Revolution had changed nothing, as colonists remained "dependent on the King, because they have hitherto enjoyed, and still continue to enjoy his protection. Allegiance is the faith and obedience, which every subject owes to his Prince." However: "obedience is founded on the protection derived from government: For protection and allegiance are the reciprocal bonds, which connect the Prince and his subjects." For Wilson, that protective role meant that the king retained prerogatives, included a veto power. "To the King is entrusted the direction and management of the great machine of government," Wilson concluded, as the king

> is fittest to adjust the different wheels, and, to regulate their motions in such a manner as to co-operate in the same general designs. He makes war: He concludes peace: He forms alliances: He regulates domestic trade by his prerogative; and directs foreign commerce by his treaties, with those nations, with whom it is carried on. He names the officers of government; so what he can check every jarring movement in the administration. He has a negative in the different legislatures

throughout his dominions, so that he can prevent any repugnancy in their different laws."[31]

It was harder to argue for continuity in the history of colonial New England, insofar as the original Massachusetts charter was replaced by a royal one in 1692 and Plymouth Plantation disappeared altogether. Even so, in his *Novanglus* letters of early 1775, John Adams maintained that the disruptions of the Restoration Era and the aftermath of the Glorious Revolution had altered elements but not the essence of the inheritance of the circumstances and emigration and settlement. Addressing the "great dispute whether charters granted within the realm, can be forfeited," Adams looked back to the royalization of 1684 and the subsequent Dominion of New England, when the "charter of Massachusetts was declared forfeited," along with "other American charters." He regretted that "Massachusetts alone, were tame enough to give it up. But," he declared, "no American charter will ever be decreed forfeited again." Adams also regretted the ultimate abandonment of the original Massachusetts charter in favor of the one implemented in 1692. "The passivity of this colony in receiving the present charter in lieu of the first, is in the opinion of some the deepest stain upon its character," he complained, even adding that there was "less excuse" for that than for "the witchcraft, or hanging the quakers." Adams nevertheless put his personal preferences aside and accepted the validity of the 1692 charter on the grounds of the consent of the governed. Adams conceded that the charter "was granted by king William and queen Mary, three years after the revolution," and, crucially, that "the oaths of allegiance are established by a law of the province." But allegiance was therefore "not due by virtue of any act of a British parliament, but by our own charter and province laws" through "an original, express contract with king William, as well as the people of England." Parliament had therefore gained no new authority over the colonies "excepting to regulate their trade, and this" too was "not by any principle of common law, but merely by the consent of the colonies, founded on the obvious necessity of a case."[32]

Yet Adams again had mixed feelings about Parliament's role in regulating trade, similarly deeming it initially unconstitutional but ultimately legitimized by consent. After initial protests about and disobedience of the Navigation Acts because colonists "were not represented in parliament," they finally "thought it just and necessary" that Parliament "should regulate the trade which their power protected." Adams nevertheless denied that parliamentary authority rested on the idea, advanced by his epistolary opponent, *Massachusettensis* (thought by Adams to be Jonathan Sewall but now believed to be Daniel Leonard) that it "protected and defended the colonies against the maritime powers of Europe from their first settlement to this day." Britain protected the colonies, he observed, only "for her own interest, because all the profits of our trade centered in her lap." Adams added, as Jefferson also argued, neither "her purse, nor her fleets and armies, ever protected us, untill the last war." Nor was parliamentary authority based on "any principle of common or statute law" or "original principle of the English constitution," and certainly not on "the principle that parliament is the supream and sovereign legislature over them in all cases whatsoever." Rather, the legitimacy of parliamentary trade regulation was based solely on the "compact and consent of the colonies." "We have by our own express consent contracted to observe the navigation act," he insisted, "and by our implied consent, by long usage and uninterrupted acquiescence, have submitted to the other acts of trade, however grievous some of them may be." This arrangement therefore "may be compared to a treaty of commerce, by which those distinct states are cemented together, in perpetual league and amity."[33]

Consent to parliamentary trade regulation did not extend to regulating other economic activities, however. The "hatter's act" that caused Jefferson such consternation was, for Adams, "never regarded." The "act against slitting mills, and tilt-hammers, never was executed here." The "act to destroy the Land Bank Scheme raised a greater ferment in this province, than the Stamp-Act did" and therefore offered no precedent of consent. The 1710 Post Office Act was, he said sarcastically, "so useful a regulation" that "few persons paid it, and they found such a benefit by it, that little opposition was made to it: yet every man who thought about it, call'd it an usurpation." And, he added, no "duties for a revenue . . . were ever laid by parliament for that purpose until 1764." And since then "its authority to do it has been constantly denied." For Adams, then, "the authority of parliament was never generally acknowledged in America."[34]

"I would ask," Adams therefore asked, "by what law the parliament has authority over America?" And he answered his question with a set of historical counterfactuals that invalidated parliamentary pretensions. "By the law of GOD in the Old and New Testament," he wrote, it has none. By the law of nature and nations, it has none. By the common law of England it has none. For the common law, and the authority of parliament founded on it, never extended beyond the four seas. By statute law it has none, for no statute was made before the settlement of the colonies for this purpose; and the declaratory act made in 1766, was made without our consent, by a parliament which had no authority beyond the four seas. What religious, moral or political obligation then are we under, to submit to parliament as a supreme legislative? None at all.[35]

Adams made clear that no new circumstance had arisen to alter the arrangements made at the time of original emigration and settlement. Will "any man soberly contend," Adams asked, "that America was ever annexed to the realm?" And if so, "To what realm? When New-England was settled, there was a realm of England, a realm of Scotland, and a realm of Ireland. To which of these three realms was New England annexed?" If to England, "by what law? . . . Acts of parliament have been passed to annex Wales, &c. &c. to the realm. But none ever passed to annex America." And "if New-England was annexed to the realm of England, how came she annexed to the realm of or kingdom of Great-Britain? The two realms of England and Scotland were by the act of union incorporated into one kingdom by the name of Great-Britain: But there is not one word about America in that act." In addition, "if America was annexed to the realm . . . every act of parliament that is made, would extend to it." Yet "every act of parliament, and every other record, constantly distinguishes between this kingdom, and his Majesty's other dominions." Even "Ireland is a distinct kingdom or realm by itself," he said, despite Poynings' Law. And so "Massachusetts is a realm, New-York is a realm, Pennsylvania another realm . . . as much as Ireland is, or England or Scotland ever were." And only "The king of Great Britain is the sovereign of all these realms." Ultimately, then, the colonies were not "a part of the British kingdom, realm or state; and therefore the supreme power of the kingdom, realm or state is not . . . the supreme power over us." And the idea "That 'supreme power over America is vested in the estates in parliament,' is an affront to us; for there is not an acre of American land represented there—there are no American estates in parliament."[36]

Adams also addressed the frequently repeated argument that sovereignty is indivisible and thus must reside in Parliament, and he agreed "that 'two supreme and independent authorities cannot exist in the same state,' any more than two supream beings in one universe." But, he argued "our provincial legislatures are the only supream authorities in our colonies. Parliament," he admitted, "may be allowed an authority supreme and sovereign over the ocean, which may be limited by the banks of the ocean, or the bounds of our charters" as "our charters give us no authority over the high seas," though only because it "has our consent to assume a jurisdiction over them." He also denied the claim that different states would work against each other, using historical evidence to make his point. In "fact and experience," he said, "it has not been found so," pointing to cooperation during the French and Indian War and concluding therefore that "Distinct states may be united under one king," as indeed England, Ireland, Scotland, and Wales had in previous times been.[37]

As for the Declaratory Act's assertions of parliamentary supremacy, Adams described the "language of 'the imperial crown of Great-Britain'" as "not the stile of the common law but of court sycophants." The act "was introduced," he claimed, "in allusion to the Roman empire, and intended to insinuate, that the prerogative of the imperial crown of England, was like that of the Roman emperor . . . and so far from including the two houses of parliament in the idea of this imperial crown, it was intended to insinuate that the crown was absolute, and had no need of lords or commons to make or dispense with laws." The act, seen from a British perspective, actually stressed the power of the crown-in-Parliament rather than the absolute power of the crown. Yet Adams's fears made sense from a colonial historical perspective that rejected the British idea that the Glorious Revolution settlement had subsumed royal power within a sovereign and supreme Parliament and instead that saw the crown as a separate power with its own prerogatives in America that sometimes conflicted with the privileges of the colonial assemblies. Colonies thus retained the separation of the executive and legislative branches of government and the prerogative-versus-privilege antagonisms that went with it. And the fears that arose from those antagonisms were not instances of "conspiracy theory" in American politics but perfectly reasonable apprehensions of reprises of the conflicts of the past, not least the civil wars of the thirteenth and seventeenth centuries.[38]

Writers from Massachusetts memorialized the American history of the Glorious Revolution more than those from other colonies, perhaps because the traditions of religious and political autonomy were originally stronger there than elsewhere and because the actions of the Dominion of New England were more disruptive there than elsewhere. While Adams regretted the loss of the colony's original charter in 1692 in the wake of that revolution, others were less sanguine about liberties under the original charter and more so about their liberties under that of 1692. In 1764, James Otis, for example, echoed Edward Rawson and other Massachusetts revolutionaries from eight decades earlier, listing writs of *quo warranto* in the 1670s, the abolition of the original Massachusetts charter and the colony's royalization in 1684, and the subsequent creation and absolutist administration of the Dominion of New England as among the "wicked proceedings of the Stuarts." Happily, however, "the form and mode of government is to be settled by *compact,* as it was rightfully done by the convention after the abdication of *James* II."[39]

Once again, Joseph Warren popularized this history of Massachusetts, and he also generalized it as a history of other colonies. "AFTER various struggles, which, during the tyrannic reigns of the House of STUART, were constantly kept up between right and wrong, between liberty and slavery," he orated in 1772, "the connection between Great-Britain and this colony, was settled in the reign of King William and Queen Mary, by a Compact, the conditions of which were expressed in a charter; by which all the liberties and immunities of BRITISH SUBJECTS, were confined to this province, as fully and as absolutely as they possibly could be by any human instrument which can be devised." Warren went into more detail in his Boston Massacre Oration in 1775, after the Coercive Acts and in the midst of an escalating crisis. After "an infinite expense of toil and blood, this widely extended continent had been cultivated and defended," he explained. This "country was then thought worthy the attention of the British ministry," however; and so followed the ruptures of the Restoration Era and the Dominion of New England. After the Glorious Revolution, though, there followed an "intercourse of friendly offices" and "the two countries became so united in affection that they thought not of any distinct or separate interests: they found both countries flourishing and happy." Britain "saw her commerce extended, and her wealth increased; her lands raised to an immense value, her fleets riding triumphant on the ocean, the terror of her arms spreading to every quarter of the globe." Meanwhile, "The colonist found himself free, and thought himself secure." Warren painted a picture of an archetypal Massachusetts colonist who "dwelt *under his own vine, and under his own fig tree and had none to make him afraid,*" evoking a bucolic theme derived from the biblical Book of Micah and often adopted in earlier colonial promotional literature. That colonist "saw, or thought he saw, the British nation risen to a pitch of grandeur which cast a veil over the Roman glory, and ravished with the praeview, boasted a race of British kings, whose names should eccho thro' those realms where Cyrus, Alexander, and the Caesars were unknown." However, he concluded, "unhappily for us, unhappily for Britain, the madness of an avaricious minister of state has drawn a sable curtain over the charming scene, and in its stead has brought upon the stage discord, envy, hatred and revenge, with civil war close in their rear." The more that Parliament asserted its assumed authority over the colonies, then, the more the colonists insisted on their historical autonomy.[40]

These settler-imperial versions of colonial history since emigration and settlement were also the official doctrines of colonial assemblies and intercolonial congresses. The Stamp Act Congress did not mention the Glorious Revolution directly but clearly rejected the British idea of a post-1688 crown-in-Parliament arrangement that extended to the colonies. The first clause of its 1765 Declaration of Rights and Grievances stated that "his Majesty's Subjects in these Colonies, owe the same allegiance to the Crown of *Great-Britain* that is owing from his Subjects born within the Realm, and all due Subordination to that August Body, the Parliament of *Great-Britain*," thereby indicating a differing connection between the colonies and the crown and the colonies and Parliament. The former, based on the concept of allegiance, implied the protective role of the monarchy that inhered in social contract theory. If subordination implied representation, however, then "due Subordination" may have meant little or none. The colonists were, of course, represented in their own assemblies rather than in London, as suggested by the first resolve's distinction between "these Colonies" and the implicitly separate "Realm" of Great Britain. The fourth resolve clarified that "the People of these Colonies are not, and from their local Circumstances cannot be, represented in the House of Commons in *Great-Britain*," and the fifth that "the only Representatives of the People of these Colonies, are Persons chosen therein, by themselves, and that no Taxes ever have been or can be Constitutionally imposed on them but by their respective Legislatures." With John Dickinson present in New York, however, the document left room for an interpretation that allowed for obedience to parliamentary trade regulation.⁴¹

The final clause of the 1765 Declaration stated that "it is the Right of the *British* Subjects in these Colonies, to Petition the King, or either House of Parliament," and the conclusion claimed that "it is the indispensable Duty of these Colonies, to the best of Sovereigns, to the Mother Country, and to themselves, to endeavor by a loyal and dutiful address to his Majesty, and humble Applications to both Houses of Parliament, to procure the Repeal" of the Stamp Act and "any other Acts of Parliament, whereby the Jurisdiction of the Admiralty is extended as aforesaid, and of the other late Acts for the Restriction of the *American* commerce." The Congress duly petitioned the king to state that "under those Governments, these Liberties, thus vested in their Ancestors, and transmitted to their Posterity, have been exercised and enjoyed, and by the inestimable Blessings thereof (under the Favour of Almighty GOD), the inhospitable Desarts of *America* have been converted into Flourishing Countries; Science, Humanity, and the Knowledge of Divine Truths, diffused through Remote Regions of Ignorance, Infidelity, and Barbarism; the Number of *British* Subjects wonderfully Increased, and the Wealth and Power of *Great-Britain* proportionally Augmented." The Congress also petitioned both houses of Parliament to the same effect.⁴²

From the Declaratory Act onward, however, colonial petitions and other publications addressed themselves to the king alone, as to address Parliament would have implicitly acknowledged its authority "in all cases whatsoever," as asserted by that act. The 1774 Declaration and Resolves of the First Continental Congress was clear on this matter. It first observed that colonists "are entitled to the benefit of such of the English statutes, as existed at the time of their colonization; and which they have, by experience, respectively found to be applicable to their several local and other circumstances." It also observed that "these, *his Majesty's colonies*, are likewise entitled to all the immunities and privileges granted and confirmed to them by royal charters, or secured by their several codes of provincial laws" (emphasis added), and that they thus "have a right peaceably to assemble, consider of their grievances, and petition the king." The document said nothing about petitioning Parliament. The closest it came to lobbying Parliament was through its members' constituents. The colonists' attentions to their British brethren comprised the Declaration and Resolves of October 1774 and a petition of July 1775 by the Second Continental Congress, after the outbreak of war and at the same time as the Olive Branch Petition the Congress sent to the king. Two weeks before its Declaration and Resolves, the First Continental Congress had already agreed on the following: "That a loyal address to his Majesty be prepared, dutifully requesting the royal attention to the grievances that alarm and distress his Majesty's faithful subjects in North-America, and," as was constitutionally impossible for Britons but constitutionally imperative for Americans, "entreating his Majesty's gracious interposition for the removal of such grievances." Five days later, Congress appointed a committee of five, including John Adams, Richard Henry Lee, and Patrick Henry, "to prepare an Address to his Majesty" to that effect.

The petition they produced began with a list of fourteen grievances, with eleven other complaints about specific acts of Parliament subsumed under two of them. Most of the grievances were similar to those of the later Declaration of Independence, and so was their form, except that the complaints, though addressed to the king, were aimed at parliamentary actions as Congress still hoped for reconciliation by means of royal intercession. The document rested its constitutional assumptions on the natural law and social contract theories that were familiar from previous literature. It expressed confidence, for example, that the king "rejoices that your title to the crown is . . . founded on the title of your people to liberty," which "teaches your subjects anxiously to guard the blessing they received from divine providence, and thereby to prove the performance of that compact which elevated the illustrious house of Brunswick to the imperial dignity it now possesses." "Duty to your majesty," it continued, "and regard for the preservation of ourselves and our posterity—the primary obligations of nature and of society—command us to entreat your royal attention." The petition's authors hoped that the king's "royal indignation" would fall not on the colonists but "on those designing and dangerous men who, daringly interposing themselves between your royal person and your faithful subjects, and for several years past incessantly employed to dissolve the bonds of society by abusing your majesty's authority, misrepresenting your American subjects, and prosecuting the most desperate and irritating projects of oppression."

Blaming the king's ministers was of course a traditional way to display loyalty while expressing dissent. Yet the petition also followed the logic of colonial history and the historical consciousness through which the authors understood that history. "Had we been permitted to enjoy . . . the inheritance left us by our forefathers," it stated, there would be no need of dissent. Dissent was caused only by the colonists being "exposed to unexpected and unnatural scenes of distress by a contention with that Nation in whose parental guidance" they had hitherto trusted. In any case, the petitioners warned that they answered to a higher authority than the king, asserting that "the purity of our intention, and the integrity of our conduct, will justify us at that grand tribunal before which all mankind must submit to judgement." In the meantime, the petitioners expected the king to justify himself to them, "for your glory, which can be advanced only by rendering your subjects happy, and keeping them united . . . though dwelling in various countries." It thus concluded by beseeching "that your royal authority and interposition may be used for our relief, and that a gracious answer may be given to this petition."[43]

Yet no such answer arrived. The king received but refused to respond to the petition as he viewed its contents as a matter for Parliament. It was submitted instead to the House of Commons by the king's prime minister, Lord North, on January 19, 1775, and to the House of Lords the following day. Benjamin Franklin observed that it was not received in the Commons with respect, arriving "among a great Heap of letters of Intelligence from Governors and officers in America, Newspapers, Pamphlets, Handbills, etc., from that Country, the last in the List, and was laid upon the Table with them, undistinguished by any particular Recommendation of it to the Notice of either House." And, he concluded, "I do not find that it has had any further notice taken of it as yet." That insult was among the incidents later recorded in the Second Continental Congress's 1775 Declaration on the Causes and Necessity of Taking Up Arms. "A Congress of Delegates from the United Colonies was assembled at Philadelphia, on the fifth Day of last September," when, it said, "We resolved again to offer an humble and dutiful Petition to the King, and also addressed our Fellow Subjects of Great-Britain." And "we were told," not entirely truthfully, "that his Majesty had been pleased to receive it graciously, and to promise laying it before his Parliament," but as Franklin had related, it "was huddled into both Houses among a Bundle of American Papers, and there neglected."[44]

As the Declaration of Independence noted, if the 1774 petition was answered at all, it was only by "repeated injury" in the form of military escalation after Lexington and Concord, by the king's Proclamation of Rebellion of August 23, and by the December 22 Prohibitory Act, which cut the colonies off from all trade and confirmed the removal of royal protection. Even so, the Second Continental Congress attempted to make peace with the Olive Branch Petition of July 1775. After briefly alluding to the previously stated grievances, it reiterated the colonists' natural, sacred, and civil right and duty to demand royal intervention, noting that "we think ourselves required by indispensable obligations to Almighty God, to your Majesty, to our fellow subjects, and to ourselves, immediately to use all the means in our power not incompatible with our safety, for stopping the further effusion of blood" and, the petition added ominously, "for averting the impending calamities that threaten the British Empire." Once again, it appealed to the king to use an authority over his ministers that his ministers would not have accepted. "We, therefore, beseech your Majesty," it said, "that your royal authority and influence may be graciously interposed to procure us relief from our afflicting fears and jealousies, occasioned by the system before mentioned, and to settle peace through every part of your dominions." As the next chapter shows, these petitions, and the king answering them only "by repeated injury," would be essential to the Declaration's case that the king *intended* to impose tyranny and that independence was therefore necessary.[45]

It made perfectly good historical sense for the Declaration of Independence to portray the British Parliament as playing only a secondary role in the causes of the American Revolution. The colonists had never consented to the authority of Parliament within the colonies, granting it at most an authority to regulate trade, and some even disputed that. The authors of the Declaration obviously knew that Parliament had played a part in the king's injuries and usurpations after 1764, and many of them had previously been directly involved in petitioning the king about that problem. Ultimately, however, the problem was not the king's ministers but rather the king's failure to heed those petitions and restrain those ministers, and his colluding with his ministers as well as abusing his own prerogatives in committing "injuries and usurpations" against his colonial subjects. The structure of the Declaration's thirteenth grievance is thus very telling. It is headed by a statement that the king "has combined with others to subject us to a jurisdiction foreign to our constitution, and unacknowledged by our laws; giving his Assent to their Acts of pretended Legislation." That is then followed by nine examples, each beginning with the word "For." Each of the complaints represented a serious assault on the colonists' rights, and indeed, some had already been mentioned in previous grievances, but the structure confirms that the authors regarded Parliament's role in provoking independence to be as incidental as its role in governing the empire.

And it made equally good historical sense for the Declaration of Independence to blame that king for the necessity of separation. Colonial and revolutionary pamphlets, orations, newspapers, declarations, and petitions explained how the first settlers had earned rights to property and self-government by representation in their own colonial assemblies and under the protection of the crown. They also explained how that inheritance had remained in place throughout the colonial era, despite various challenges to colonists' rights that in some instances strengthened their attachment to them. It thus made sense to petition the king as the colonists' protector repeatedly for redress in the years preceding independence. And it made equal sense to blame him in the end for independence, once his "history of repeated injuries and usurpations" revealed themselves as "all having in direct object the establishment of an absolute Tyranny," as the Declaration's preamble put it, and having in "every stage of these Oppressions" answered "repeated Petitions . . . only by repeated injury," as the Declaration's conclusion put it.

Between the preamble and the conclusion lay the grievances, the "Facts" that the Declaration's authors "submitted to a candid world" and that constituted "the history of the present king of Great Britain" and proved it to be "a history of repeated injuries and usurpations, all having in direct object the establishment of an absolute Tyranny over these States." As the next chapter shows, each of the grievances referred to recognizable actions by the king, but they were framed in way that emphasized how those actions violated the colonists' historic rights derived first from nature, then from English inheritance, and finally from American emigration and settlement. It also shows how the preamble, grievances, and conclusions together made the case not only that the king was to blame but that he had made it *necessary* "for one people to dissolve the political bands which have connected them with another, and to assume among the powers of the earth, the separate and equal station to which the Laws of Nature and of Nature's God entitle them."

4

A History of Repeated Injuries and Usurpations

The history of the present King of Great Britain is a history of repeated injuries and usurpations, all having in direct object the establishment of an absolute Tyranny over these States. To prove this, let Facts be submitted to a candid world.

The authors of the Declaration of Independence announced in their opening words the historical moment they intended to address: "When in the Course of human events, it becomes necessary for one people to dissolve the political bands which have connected them with another, and to assume among the powers of the earth, the separate and equal station to which the Laws of Nature and of Nature's God entitle them. . . ." And the final words of the single-sentence opening paragraph state that "a decent respect to the opinions of mankind requires that they should declare the causes which impel them to the separation." The introduction thus makes clear that the Declaration's principal purpose is to explain the American Revolution that it is announcing.

The introduction thus prefaces the grievances—"the causes" of the Revolution—and the preamble frames them more fully, first by explaining the right to revolution inherent in natural law and human history, and then by introducing how the king's actions had caused the colonists to invoke that right. The preamble's general history of humankind shows how an equal creation and state of nature determined the conditions of civil government by consent and in order to secure "certain unalienable rights." The Declaration's preamble then enunciates a right to revolution based on these historical conditions: "That whenever any Form of Government becomes destructive of these ends, it is the Right of the People to alter or to abolish it, and to institute new Government" to facilitate "their Safety and Happiness." Immediately afterward, though, the preamble enunciates limits to the right to revolution: "Prudence . . . will dictate that Governments long established should not be changed for light and transient causes" and "all experience hath shewn, that mankind are more disposed to suffer, while evils are sufferable, than to right themselves by abolishing the forms to which they are accustomed." It is therefore only "when a long train of abuses and usurpations, pursuing invariably the same Object evinces a design to reduce" a people "under absolute Despotism" that it becomes their right and duty "to throw off such Government, and to provide new Guards for their future security."

The preamble's general justification of revolution then transitions into a justification of the American Revolution, based on the same rights and limits: "Such has been the patient sufferance of these Colonies; and such is now the necessity which constrains them to alter their former Systems of Government"—because "The history of the present King of Great Britain is a history of repeated injuries and usurpations, all having in direct object the establishment of an absolute Tyranny over these States." In its concluding sentence—"To prove this, let Facts be submitted to a candid world"—the preamble segues into its eighteen sets of grievances against the king, which are followed by a reference at the beginning of the conclusion to how "repeated Petitions have been answered only by repeated injury," concluding the argument that the king's "character is thus marked by every act which may define a Tyrant" and is therefore "unfit to be the ruler of a free people." The Declaration thus presents a powerful yet nuanced case for independence, laying out a course of human events, analyzed according to the laws of nature and God, that cautions against precipitous revolution but explains the circumstances in which revolution is necessary, and that provides copious evidence that those circumstances of necessity apply to the American colonies.

It is therefore strange that few historians have taken the Declaration of Independence seriously as an account of the causes of the American Revolution. One reason for this dismissal is the perception that the document is more concerned with setting an egalitarian agenda for the future than with dwelling on the past. If the Declaration is thought to have any relationship to the causes of the Revolution, it lies in the idea that the relative equality and extensive liberties of Americans rendered them unwilling to continue tolerating their status as colonial subjects. That idea is less popular now than it used to be, partly a result of the modern appreciation that colonists abandoned their attachment to Britain reluctantly and partly owing to modern appreciation that the inequalities that survived independence demonstrate that many of the founders were rather less committed to equality than previously believed. Indeed, the disparity between the Declaration's supposed ideals and the social realities of the time has become another reason why few take the Declaration seriously except as an augury of the future.[1]

Another reason for historians' dismissing the Declaration's account of the causes of the Revolution is its supposed historical inaccuracies and vagueness. One of the most significant purported faults is the blaming of the king for independence—the subject of the last chapter. Another, the subject of this chapter, is that the Declaration presented its "Facts" as general principles violated rather than as specific actions by the king, prompting some to dismiss the grievances as more designed to hide than to highlight the colonists' real reasons for revolution. The Declaration's complaints were described at the time by Thomas Hutchinson as "false and frivolous"—perhaps an unsurprising assessment from a former governor of Massachusetts and Loyalist in exile. Yet that judgment prevails today. One of the Declaration's most eminent recent historians, for example, described the grievances as so vague as to leave people then and since "scrambling to figure out" their meanings. In any case, she added, "the less said the better" as "there are two sides to every story, and the colonists weren't always clearly on the side of the angels."[2]

Yet the Declaration's authors were evidently more confident in their case than such criticisms suggest, whatever we may make of it today. They based that case on "the laws of Nature and of Nature's God" at the beginning and appealed "to the Supreme Judge of the world for the rectitude of our intentions" at the end. And, with "a firm reliance on the protection of divine Providence," they seemed to believe that God, and presumably therefore the angels too, would in fact be on their side. And they presented their "Facts" to a "candid world," by which they meant an impartial one that would consider their allegations fairly. Indeed, independence and even their own lives depended on the quality of the case they made for it. They needed people at home to fight a war against a formidable enemy, and they needed foreign aid to help win that war and to gain international recognition to secure the separate and equal station among the powers of the earth to which they aspired. They were unlikely to succeed in these imperatives by being false or frivolous or by leaving readers wondering what they were talking about.

It was thus essential that the Declaration's case for independence made sense, the grievances especially. The laws of nature and of God were eternal and therefore ahistorical. It is only in violations of those rights, in the course of human events, in history, that a people can experience grievances that justify revolution. And, though generalized, the events those grievances alluded to were identifiable to contemporaries who had lived through them, or read about them in the hundreds of pamphlets, broadsides, newspapers, resolutions, and petitions, or heard them aired in speeches, or discussed them in countless conversations. The Declaration's "history of the present King of Great Britain" had also been recounted in the numerous state constitutions and local declarations published in the months before independence. The First Continental Congress's Declaration of Rights and Grievances and its Petition to the King, the Second Continental Congress's Declaration on the Causes and Necessity of Taking Up Arms, and various state and local declarations of independence had all contained lists of grievances in the same brief and generalized form as would appear in the Declaration of Independence. And all these documents followed the model of the English Bill of Rights of 1689 in its generalized recounting of the crimes of James II. The listing of grievances in terms of general principles violated rather than in terms of specific actions was therefore a known and common practice. And the Declaration's authors could rely as well on readers' prior knowledge of the principles behind the facts of the grievances. Indeed, presenting those grievances as violations of general principles allowed them to be more easily placed in the context of American, British, and more general human history dating back through the events of the reign of king George to the origins of the colonies and empire, and then back to the origins of government, the state of nature, and Creation itself. Generalization thereby gave the grievances an awe-inspiring antiquity.[3]

Each of the individual injuries and usurpations alluded to in the grievances, then, was identifiable to contemporaries as one or more particular actions by the king, or by him in collusion with Parliament, and also as an assault on colonists' natural rights as men, their inherited rights as Englishmen, and their acquired rights as Americans, or two or all three of these related sets of rights together. And the violations could be interpreted according to the common method of analysis that measured human actions against the laws of nature and of God. Furthermore, the authors structured the grievances into three clearly demarcated sections. The first (grievances 1–12) concerned the king's actions before April 1775 in undermining colonial assemblies and judiciaries and his collaborations with customs officials and military forces. The second section (grievance 13, plus its nine clauses) covered the same period and some of the same events but addressed the king's collaborations with the British Parliament. And the third section (grievances 14–18) dealt with the Proclamation of Rebellion by the king and the war that spread across the colonies from April 1775 on.

That much is well known today, but what is less well appreciated is how the structure of the grievances was foreshadowed by the Declaration's preamble. First, the first thirteen grievances, plus the nine complaints about the king's collaborations with Parliament, represented direct assaults on people's rights to liberty and the pursuit of happiness. They also represented indirect threats to their other unalienable right, the right to life, by weakening legislative and judicial protection, undermining or threatening their property rights and thus their means of subsistence, and using military forces to restore order (a threat that was realized in the 1770 Boston Massacre). The final five grievances, however, addressed the war and therefore depicted *direct* attacks on people's lives. Armed resistance thus became a necessity of self-defense—the first law of nature and of God. Revolution became necessary when the king refused to heed colonial petitions and thereby revealed the intention to impose absolute tyranny that lay behind the actions that the grievances described. The preamble prefigured this two-stage process of revolution with its cautions about prudence and sufferance, followed by its evocation of a people's right and duty to throw off a government "when a long train of abuses and usurpations, pursuing invariably the same Object evinces a design to reduce them under absolute Despotism." It then repeats the two stages in reference to the American Revolution: "Such has been the patient sufferance of these Colonies; and such is now the necessity which constrains them to alter their former Systems of Government," before repeating them again in the facts submitted to a candid world that distinguished between the first thirteen grievances and the final five.

The first law of nature and God was thus key to the causes of American independence—triggering a revolutionary turning point. Yet the direct attacks on life were not quite enough on their own to justify independence, for they also had to be proven as deliberate. The Declaration's authors knew that actions may be evidence of intention but are not proof of intention. Hence the preamble's mentions of "a design" of absolute despotism and a "direct object" of absolute tyranny as necessary to the justification of revolution. And hence the statements that "In every stage of these Oppressions We have Petitioned for Redress" and that "Our repeated Petitions have been answered only by repeated injury." The petitions proved that the king had acted with knowledge and his answers to them proved that he had acted with intent. And it was only after providing that proof of intent that the founders could finally declare independence. The final five grievances and the first sections of the conclusions therefore together mark the moment when in the course of human events it became necessary for one people to dissolve the political bands that had connected them with another. Far from being false, frivolous, or incomprehensible, then, the Declaration provided a highly sophisticated, precise, and understandable account of "the causes of the separation" the Declaration's authors were announcing. And it is an account we should take seriously as an authoritative contemporary statement on the causes of the American Revolution.[4]

The Declaration's first grievance complained that the king "has refused his Assent to Laws, the most wholesome and necessary for the public good." Many contemporaries would have understood from numerous sources that it likely referred to royal vetoes of colonial attempts to limit the slave trade. Thomas Jefferson's *Summary View*, for example, had stated that the "abolition of domestic slavery is the great object of desire," but that it was necessary first "to exclude all further importations from Africa." However, Jefferson lamented, "our repeated attempts to effect this by prohibitions, and by imposing duties which might amount to a prohibition, have been hither to defeated by his majesty's negative." Others might have interpreted the grievance as referring to vetoes of colonial currency acts authorizing the use of paper money, or to vetoes of acts to create land banks, or to the veto of acts prohibiting the immigration of convicts, or, in Massachusetts, to the veto of an act of the assembly pardoning those involved in the Stamp Act protests of 1765. Whatever the case, though, the problem the Declaration identified was not that the king had "refused his Assent to Laws" but that the laws so vetoed were "wholesome and necessary for the public good."

As the last chapter showed, Americans were accustomed to vetoes of assembly bills as a working element of the imperial constitution, and Jefferson and others argued for royal vetoes of British parliamentary legislation that violated colonists' rights. He also stated in A *Summary View*, however, that lawful vetoes did not include "the wanton exercise of this power which we have seen his Majesty practise on the laws of the American legislatures," complaining that for "the most trifling reasons, and sometimes for no conceivable reason at all, his majesty has rejected laws of the most salutary tendency."[5]

As well as thereby being one of a number of identifiable actions by the king that were also identifiable as violations of historic English and American constitutional rights to laws for the public good, the first grievance also invoked the laws of nature and God. If people consented to civil government and law to secure their lives, liberties, property, safety, and happiness, then vetoing laws that were necessary for the public good was destructive of those ends. And not only did the grievance imply an undermining of the purpose of government itself, its use of the word "necessary" implied that the veto indirectly endangered the unalienable right to life. Certainly, as slavery was considered a state of war, the undermining of attempts to abolish it, or at least to ameliorate or diminish its significance by restricting slave trading, undermined public safety. That point would be made explicitly in the final grievance, which identified a direct and deliberate threat to colonists' lives, with the king inspiring "domestic insurrections amongst us." And Jefferson's *Summary View* made the additional point that vetoing legislation against the slave trade was as an offense against "the rights of human nature" of Africans, a point he would repeat at length in the final grievance of his draft declaration.[6]

If the first grievance depicted an identifiable action or actions by the king that violated colonists' constitutional and natural rights by undermining the purposes of civil law and governance, then so did all the others. The second grievance logically followed the first by stating that the king had undermined good government and law by forbidding "his Governors to pass Laws of immediate and pressing importance, unless suspended in their operation till his Assent should be obtained; and when so suspended, he has utterly neglected to attend to them." Such suspensions by governors and the Board of Trade, acting under the Privy Council and therefore royal authority, were common practice. But the most notorious instance was the New York Restraining Act of 1767, also known as the Suspending Act, which ordered the governor to annul assembly legislation pending full compliance with the Quartering Act, which ordered New York to house and feed British troops stationed in the colony and which additionally violated colonists' constitutional rights by being an act of Parliament. And its seriousness as a violation of the natural right to safety was highlighted at length not only in the first of John Dickinson's *Farmer's Letters* but also by New Yorker William Hicks, who observed that it was "passed to strip us of our legislative power, and render us unable to provide for ourselves in a situation of the most imminent danger." Jefferson also noted in *A Summary View* that by "inattention to the necessities of his people . . . his majesty permitted our laws to lie neglected in England for years," neither affirmed nor vetoed. Worse still, "his majesty by his instructions has laid his governors under such restrictions that they can pass no law of any moment" without a suspending clause, and "however immediate may be the call for legislative interposition, the law cannot be executed till it has twice crossed the Atlantic, by which time the evil may have spent it's whole force."[7]

This second grievance also recalled the first grievance and constitutional provision of the English Bill of Rights of 1689. This then revered document began by stating that "the late King James the Second, by the Assistance of diverse evill Councellors Judges and Ministers imployed by him did endeavour to subvert and extirpate the Protestant Religion and the Laws and Liberties of this Kingdome," before listing its grievances in much the same way the U.S. Declaration would—as a generalized list of offenses in principle. The first grievance of 1689 was that the king had abused his authority "By Assumeing and Exerciseing a Power of Dispensing with and Suspending of Lawes and the Execution of Lawes without Consent of Parlyament." The first of its constitutional assertions, listed after the grievances, similarly stated "That the pretended Power of Suspending of Laws or the Execution of Laws by Regall Authority without Consent of Parlyament is illegall." "Dispensing" referred mostly to exempting Catholics from oaths of allegiance to the Anglican Church, but "suspending" certainly applied to the second grievance of 1776—and certainly violated legislative freedoms guaranteed by the colonists' sense of constitutional law and the protections provided by statute law. And the second grievance thus most directly identified George III as a new James II, associated the American colonists with the English Whigs of the seventeenth century, and placed the American Revolution in the venerated tradition of the Glorious Revolution.[8]

The third grievance was specifically American and so had no direct precedent in the English Bill of Rights, though it called on similar constitutional and natural law principles of legislative freedom and the protection provided by civil law. It complained of the king's refusal to pass other "Laws for the accommodation of large districts of people, unless those people would relinquish the right of Representation in the Legislature, a right inestimable to them and formidable to tyrants only," referring to apportionment controversies in New Hampshire, New Jersey, New York, and Virginia. In the latter case, Jefferson had noted in his *Summary View* an "instruction to his majesty's governor, by which he is forbidden to assent to any law for the division of a county, unless the new county will consent to have no representative in assembly." With no fixed western boundary, some people had to travel "many hundred miles . . . in order to obtain justice for injuries, however great or small . . . , with all their witnesses, monthly, till their litigation be determined." Also, forbidding new representatives would "confine the legislative body to their present numbers, that they may be the cheaper bargain whenever they shall become worth a purchase"—a reference to colonial claims that the king regularly influenced legislators with emoluments, and something that affected not only individuals but everyone in a political community. Worse still, Jefferson pondered, it was possible that the king intended "that his subjects should give up the glorious right of representation . . . and submit themselves the absolute slaves of his sovereign will."[9]

The fourth grievance—"He has called together legislative bodies at places unusual, uncomfortable, and distant from the depository of their public Records, for the sole purpose of fatiguing them into compliance with his measures"—was not included in Jefferson's draft declaration but was considered important enough by the committee of five to be added to their draft and included by the Continental Congress in the final Declaration. It too addressed legislative process and freedom generally, and referred to Governor Francis Bernard's removal of the Massachusetts Assembly to Cambridge from Boston during the Liberty Riot of 1768, and to a later removal by Governor General Thomas Gage after the Boston Tea Party.

Moreover, fifth, "He has dissolved Representative Houses repeatedly, for opposing with manly firmness his invasions on the rights of the people." This grievance was originally included in Jefferson's draft, although Congress dropped "and continually" after "repeatedly" to reflect the fact that no assembly had been closed on a permanent basis, illustrating a scrupulous attention to accuracy and avoidance of the falsity and frivolity that Thomas Hutchinson would nevertheless allege. Jefferson might have had in mind the Massachusetts Assembly after the Coercive Acts, though that was technically an abolition of the assembly following from the replacement of the colony's charter and was in any case the subject of one of the clauses of the thirteenth grievance. But the matter of dissolution was important, whether permanent or temporary, and it was a regular occurrence. A notorious instance was Governor Cadwallader Colden's dissolution of the New York Assembly for failing to comply with the 1765 Quartering Act, followed by the New York Restraining (Suspending) Act of 1767, which ordered the governor to suspend all local legislation until the assembly complied with the former act (also alluded to in the second grievance, discussed above, and the ninth clause of the thirteenth grievance, discussed below). Another major instance occurred after the Boston Tea Party of 1773 (which was followed by the Massachusetts Government Act of 1774, the subject of clause eight of grievance thirteen). And Jefferson will certainly have had in mind Governor Dunmore's dissolution of the Virginia Assembly for calling for support for Massachusetts after the Coercive Acts.

As with vetoes, dissolutions had long been constitutional practice in the American colonies. Some contemporary readers might therefore have believed that the real grievance was not the dissolutions themselves but the reasons for them, or the absence of good reasons for them. The dissolutions in this case represented violations of the colonists' constitutional right and a people's natural right to petition or otherwise protest against their rulers. Yet readers of *A Summary View* might have interpreted this grievance as a complaint against dissolution per se, a practice that had been disputed long before vetoes were finally abandoned in Britain. The pamphlet provided quite a history of the subject, stating first that "One of the articles of impeachment against Tresilian, and the other judges of Westminster-Hall, in the reign of Richard the second, for which they suffered death, as traitors to their country, was, that they had advised the king that he might dissolve his parliament at any time." While "succeeding kings have adopted the opinion of these unjust judges," Jefferson added, "Since the establishment . . . of the British constitution, at the glorious revolution, on its free and antient principles, neither his majesty, nor his ancestors, have exercised such a power of dissolution in the island of Great Britain." Yet, Jefferson noted, "how different their language and his practice here!" And "will it not appear strange to an unbiassed observer, that that of Great Britain was not dissolved, while those of the colonies have repeatedly incurred that sentence?" Vetoes too had long been practiced, and indeed, Jefferson wanted an imperial veto to be revived for the purpose of protecting the rights of one realm from another. But the closing down of legislatures altogether seems to him to have been a graver matter, an act of power that protected no one but the king and at great cost to his subjects. Indeed, the sixth grievance explained the meaning of such government shut-downs, stating that "He has refused for a long time, after such dissolutions, to cause others to be elected; whereby the Legislative powers, incapable of Annihilation, have returned to the People at large for their exercise; the State remaining in the mean time exposed to all the dangers of invasion from without, and convulsions within"—once again raising the matter of a people's natural and civil right to safety. That grievance clearly referred to the same events as the previous one, but it also recalled the prorogations of the English Parliament by Charles I during the "Eleven Years' Tyranny" of 1629 to 1640 and of James II throughout most of his reign from 1685 to 1688.[10]

This sixth grievance also made the most explicit allusion in all the facts submitted to a candid world to natural law and rights. Its idea that legislative power cannot be annihilated but instead returns to the people indicates that such a power exists in nature, irrespective of civil governance, and that ultimate sovereignty therefore inheres in the people. Furthermore, the reference to the dangers of invasion and convulsions (no doubt including slave rebellions) alludes to the natural rights to safety that government is entrusted to secure. And if anyone was still unsure about how these actions violated colonists' natural rights, *A Summary View* was once again available for reference. "After dissolving one house of representatives," Jefferson wrote, governors "have refused to call another, so that for a great length of time, the legislature provided by the laws has been out of existence," explaining that "From the nature of things, every society must at all times possess within itself the sovereign powers of legislation." And, he added, "The feelings of human nature revolt against the supposition of a state so situated as that it may not in any emergency provide against dangers which perhaps threaten immediate ruin. While those bodies are in existence to whom the people have delegated the powers of legislation, they alone possess and may exercise those powers," although "when they are dissolved by the lopping off one or more of their branches, the power reverts to the people."[11]

The seventh grievance referred to various violations of historic and natural rights. "He has endeavoured," it says, "to prevent the population of these States; for that purpose obstructing the Laws for Naturalization of Foreigners; refusing to pass others to encourage their migrations hither, and raising the conditions of new Appropriations of Lands." Those accusations referred to actions discouraging emigration from Britain and elsewhere in Europe, the raising of quitrents, and restrictions on American westward expansion, most obviously the Proclamation Line of 1763 and a 1773 Privy Council order forbidding governors from issuing new land patents. The Plantation Act of 1740 had allowed for naturalization of foreigners who had been resident in the colonies for seven years (if absent for no more than two months), but certificates had to be approved in British or Irish courts and those so naturalized were considered British Americans rather than subjects of individual colonies. New York, Pennsylvania, and South Carolina had nonetheless naturalized people more permissively, especially foreign Protestants, but in 1773 the Privy Council ordered governors to veto all colonial naturalization bills, and in 1774 Parliament legislated that no one could be naturalized for the sake of receiving trade privileges (thereby evading the spirit if not the letter of British trade laws). As well as referring to the undermining of legislative rights, this grievance thus supported Jefferson's idea of free immigration in pursuit of happiness as a natural right, as detailed in chapter 2. It also subtly supported his free state theory of the origins of colonies and empire by denying the crown's right to raise quitrents and restrict settlement, negating the idea of an original crown property or jurisdiction in America.[12]

The eighth grievance similarly concerned the liberty of colonial assemblies and protection of the law, but it also transitioned into injuries committed against colonial judiciaries and their administration of civil law. It states that the king "has obstructed the Administration of Justice, by refusing his Assent to Laws for establishing Judiciary powers," referring to the closure of the superior courts of North Carolina because an assembly court bill had allowed the attachment of nonresidents' property in prosecutions for debt. The issue was thus highly localized and specific. Yet, like the third grievance, it addressed an issue of principle that could potentially affect every colony if allowed in one, namely, people's ability to seek justice and protection of their unalienable rights to life, liberty, and property. It is notable that once again, Congress modified a Jeffersonian overstatement that the committee had submitted unedited, changing the original "he has suffered the administration of justice totally to cease in some of these colonies" to the more accurate "obstructed the Administration of Justice" in certain places and at certain times.

Grievance number nine states, "He has made Judges dependent on his Will alone, for the tenure of their offices, and the amount and payment of their salaries." It thus referred to an order of December 1761 making colonial judges serve "at the pleasure of the crown" rather than on "good behaviour," and to suggestions from 1767 and the reality in Massachusetts from 1774 of making judges financially dependent on British rather than on local authorities. It also may have included the extension of Vice Admiralty Courts' jurisdiction under the 1764 Sugar Act. Again, as courts had authority to punish people by execution, imprisonment, and fines, they had power over people's lives, liberties, and property. The principle of judicial independence was thus increasingly considered a guard against tyrannical government. The right to trial by jury had long been part of English common law and had been included in the Magna Carta in 1215. Since 1701, though, the principle of judicial independence had been extended in England to the practice of appointing judges on good behavior. In the colonies, however, judges continued to serve at the pleasure of the crown, and their salaries remained a source of possible corruption of judicial impartiality.

The tenth grievance referred to another branch of government—tax collectors. "He has erected a multitude of New Offices," it said, "and sent hither swarms of Officers to harrass our people, and eat out their substance," alluding to the Board of Customs Commissioners, created under the Townshend Acts of 1767. Two-thirds of the value of the taxes and fines that commissioners collected went to the British treasury and colonial governors, the latter fact undermining the colonial assemblies' power of the purse strings, though this was not specified in the grievance. The grievance itself referred to the fact that the remaining one-third of revenues collected were to pay the commissioners, encouraging lucratively assiduous prosecution of their duties in imposing taxation without representation, which violated the colonists' natural and constitutional property rights. Historians have questioned the use of the word "swarms," given the small number of commissioners. On the other hand, the commissioners were entitled to employ deputies if they chose, and in any case the grievance might also have been referring to Admiralty Court judges and the fact that from 1764, all ships' captains were required to take the customs house oath. Whatever the case, the word's meaning, or at least its intended impact, may have derived from scripture. The word often referred biblically to locusts, whose proverbial ravenousness caused famines, with various examples cited in the Old Testament, especially in Exodus and Jeremiah. Locusts were also one of the augurs of the end times detailed in Revelation. Rather dramatic, perhaps, but historically informed and impactful nonetheless.[13]

The next two grievances also referred to other branches of government. The eleventh states, "He has kept among us, in times of peace, Standing Armies without the Consent of our legislatures," referring to the stationing of the regular army in New York from 1763 and Boston from 1768 to 1770, following the Liberty Riot, and from 1774 to 1776, following the Tea Party and then the outbreak of war. Congress declined to approve Jefferson's and the committee's inclusion of the king keeping "among us . . . ships of war," probably because of a historically acknowledged jurisdiction of Parliament over the seas for the purposes of trade regulation and naval protection of colonial coasts and shipping. The complaint certainly counted for land forces, however, as it had been a maxim since at least the reign of Charles I that a standing army in peacetime was a threat to people's lives, liberties, and property unless approved by the people's representatives. Otherwise, armed forces should consist only of local civilian militias. In line with their respective historical and constitutional perspectives, Britons claimed that approval for a peacetime standing army in America had been granted by Parliament, while colonists complained that it had indeed been granted by Parliament, rather than by their own assemblies. As Jefferson said in *A Summary View*, "That in order to enforce the arbitrary measures before complained of, his majesty has from time to time sent among us large bodies of armed forces, not made up of the people here, nor raised by the authority of our laws." He further claimed that "his majesty has no right to land a single armed man on our shores, and those whom he sends here are liable to our laws made for the suppression and punishment of riots, routs, and unlawful assemblies; or are hostile bodies, invading us in defiance of law."[14]

Jefferson added in *A Summary View* that "To render these proceedings still more criminal against our laws, instead of subjecting the military to the civil powers, his majesty has expressly made the civil subordinate to the military," thereby placing "all law under his feet." Correspondingly, the twelfth grievance noted that "He has affected to render the Military independent of and superior to the Civil power," referring to the appointment of General Thomas Gage as governor of Massachusetts and to the Massachusetts Government Act of 1774. That annulled the colony's charter, in defiance of the natural right of consent to be governed. It also gave the military governor even greater powers, not least to appoint members of the upper house of the assembly, as formerly appointed by the lower house, and to refuse permission to hold town meetings, annulling the ancient political freedoms and the natural right of representation and self-government of the people of Massachusetts.[15]

The thirteenth grievance returned to injuries inflicted on colonial legislative rights, but this time also to usurpations of their rights by the British parliament. The grievance maintained the focus of blame on the king by not naming Parliament and by stating, "He has combined with others to subject us to a jurisdiction foreign to our constitution, and unacknowledged by our laws; giving his Assent to their Acts of pretended Legislation." This passage is often depicted as merely a heading for the nine that follow, each beginning with "For," but the fact that the king had "combined with others" was the grievance itself, and the nine clauses that follow are examples of that combining (some of them repeating previous grievances). Indeed, the king's collusion with Parliament was fundamental to the American Revolution. As earlier chapters have shown, colonists believed their ancestors had by natural right earned chartered and constitutional rights to property and self-government under the crown through the circumstances of their emigration and settlement, and that later generations inherited these rights by natural right. The king arbitrarily changing these constitutional arrangements therefore represented an attack on all those natural and constitutional rights, on the legislative freedoms and security they secured, and therefore on the principle of government by consent. As John Locke explained, "THE great end of Mens entring into Society, being the enjoyment of their Properties in Peace and Safety, and the great instrument and means of that being the Laws establish'd in that Society; the *first and fundamental positive Law of all Commonwealths, is the establishing of the Legislative* Power." For the colonists, that "*Legislative* Power," at least within the borders of the colonies themselves, lay with their assemblies in conjunction with the British crown. And, as Locke further explained, "This *Legislative* is not only the *supream power* of the Common-wealth, but sacred and unalterable in the hands where the Community have once placed it." The king's altering of the colonists' legislative by collaborating with the British parliament thus violated "*the first and fundamental*" laws of commonwealths, as well as the particular rights of American colonists.[16]

It is notable too that the committee, in its submission of the draft Declaration of Independence to Congress on June 28, included the heading and the nine clauses in one paragraph, as if the committee considered it a single grievance. Congress individualized the clauses line by line, making them more visible, even while maintaining the "For . . ." and thereby retaining the focus of blame on the king. Some of the nine subgrievances were also repetitions of previous grievances, rather than standing on their own, and indeed they were ordered so that the first two clauses addressed the same subject as the immediately preceding eleventh and twelfth grievances—the abuse of military power. It therefore seems apt to classify the nine together as a single grievance against the king's combining with a foreign jurisdiction to impose laws. Even so, each of the nine clauses also represented serious offenses against natural and civil rights that helped make the case for independence, and are thus worth considering individually.

The first act of combination between crown and Parliament was "For Quartering large bodies of armed troops among us," referring to the quartering acts of 1765 and 1774 and possibly the restoration of troops in Boston after the Tea Party. It thus followed thematically from the eleventh and twelfth grievances. And the second clause of the thirteenth grievance did the same by accusing the two bodies of protecting those soldiers "by a mock Trial, from punishment for any Murders which they should commit on the Inhabitants of these States"—a reference to the trial following the Boston Massacre of 1770, which failed to produce a murder conviction, and to the Administration of Justice Act of 1774, which would have offered further protections to soldiers accused of crimes against civilians in Massachusetts. These two clauses thus alluded to the same English civil war history and natural rights violations that the twelfth grievance did, and it also recalled previous grievances concerning the undermining of the judicial system and therefore of access to protection of such rights as life, liberty, property, and happiness.

The third clause accused the king with Parliament of "cutting off our Trade with all parts of the world," referring to the New England Restraining

Act of 1774 and the Prohibitory Act of 1775, which made American ships and goods subject to seizure and confiscation. As the last chapter showed, views on the legitimacy of parliamentary trade regulation varied. Richard Bland and Thomas Jefferson opposed the Navigation Acts and other trade laws on the grounds that they violated the colonists' constitutional and natural and therefore inviolable rights to free trade. John Adams agreed that they initially violated these rights but were later legitimized by colonial consent. On the other hand, John Dickinson believed that, while Parliament had no right to raise revenue directly from the colonists by taxation, it did have the right to regulate trade because advancing the economic interests of the mother country had been one of the original purposes of colonization. All agreed, however, that the New England Restraining Act and the Prohibitory Act were oppressive as they were a form of political coercion rather than part of an economic policy supposedly for the benefit of the whole imperial community.[17]

All agreed, too, on the injustice of Parliament's "imposing Taxes on us without our Consent," the fourth clause of the thirteenth grievance—easily identifiable as referring to the Sugar Act, Stamp Act, and Townshend Duties, although some may also have seen it as including the Tea Act of 1773, though that legislated an East India Company exemption from the tea tax that survived the repeal of the other Townshend Duties. Many colonists would have believed also that protection from taxation without representation dated to England's Ancient Constitution and that the right was resurrected with the Magna Carta. It then had to be fought for in the Barons' Wars of the thirteenth century, which saw the institutionalization of Parliament itself via the Provisions of Oxford in 1258, before being legislated in the *Statutum de Tallagio non concedendo* of 1297. It was fought for again in the civil wars of the seventeenth century before the 1689 English Bill of Rights stated that "levying Money for or to the Use of the Crowne by pretence of Prerogative without Grant of Parlyament for longer time or in other manner than the same is or shall be granted is Illegall." It was also a specific provision of various charters and later petitions that colonists would not be taxed without the consent of their own representatives. Taxation by consent was thus a long-established English and American civil right.[18]

It was also long conceived of as a natural right on numerous grounds. First, property was an original right in the state of nature and based on the right to subsistence that followed from the right to life—as argued by John

Locke in opposition to Robert Filmer's case for feudal proprietorship by divine right. Hence, as detailed in chapter 1, all were created with equal rights to the earth and its produce either as "the common stock of mankind" or as private property. Locke also argued that private property was originally the product of labor and therefore the body and was thus unalienably personal, whether in the state of nature or under civil government and law. Every "Man has a *Property* in his own *Person*," Locke wrote. "This no Body has any Right to but himself. The *Labour* of his Body, and the *Work* of his Hands, we may say, are properly his. Whatsoever then he removes out of the State that Nature hath provided, and left it in, he hath mixed his *Labour* with, and joyned to it something that is his own, and thereby makes it his *Property*." It thus followed that no one could take anyone's property without their consent, either given personally or by their representatives. Nor could anyone tax the surplus created by property without consent because it is "*Labour* . . . that *puts the difference of value* on every thing; and let any one consider, what the difference is between an Acre of Land planted with Tobacco, or Sugar, sown with Wheat or Barley; and an Acre of the same Land lying in common, without any Husbandry upon it, and he will find, that the improvement of *labour makes* the far greater part of *the value.*"[19]

Natural rights to property also underlay the complaint that the king had combined with Parliament in "depriving us in many cases, of the benefits of Trial by Jury" by replacing civil courts with Vice-Admiralty Courts for trials for smuggling under the 1764 Sugar Act. Indeed, this fifth clause represented a twofold attack on property rights. Besides such rights being violated by the sugar tax, the use of military courts for its enforcement meant a greater danger of fines being imposed without the protection of juries. The fifth clause thus segued into another one about due process of law, the sixth clause complaining that the 1774 Administration of Justice Act and a proposed resurrection of an act of Henry VIII for trials within England for treason committed outside the realm entailed "transporting us beyond Seas to be tried for pretended offences," again placing people's lives, liberty, and property under arbitrary power. No one had yet been tried in this way, but the law asserted that it was constitutionally possible and therefore could be done.

The seventh clause, not included in Jefferson's draft but added into the draft submitted by the committee, accused the king and Parliament of "abolishing the free System of English Laws in a neighbouring Province, establishing therein an Arbitrary government, and enlarging its Boundaries so as to render it at once an example and fit instrument for introducing the same absolute rule into these Colonies." This clause appears initially to focus on the arbitrary nature of the new government established by the 1774 Quebec Act, which represented a threat to the liberties of the older colonies, both as a model of governance and as a possible base for military invasion. Its provision of toleration of Catholicism also threatened what some colonists, especially in New England, saw as their specifically Protestant religious liberties. As important as all that was, contemporaries may have also perceived it as a direct attack on colonists' existing political and property rights as it altered jurisdictional boundaries. That both violated the principles of self-government and threatened the property rights of land speculators who had made their purchases from older colonial governments that, according to the Quebec Act, now had no jurisdiction in the relevant regions.

The seventh clause of the thirteenth grievance thus segued into the eighth—"For taking away our Charters, abolishing our most valuable Laws, and altering fundamentally the Forms of our Governments"—an unmistakable reference to the 1774 Massachusetts Government Act that abolished the 1692 charter and replaced it with something close to martial law. This was thus an even more direct attack on self-government—indeed, a total negation of what colonists saw as a historical right based on social contract that was an inviolable inheritance by natural right. In this context it is notable that the committee added "abolishing our most valuable laws," and Timothy Matlack added the uppercase to "Laws." They may have done so to appeal to those in the candid world who did not agree that colonial charters were social contracts or otherwise inviolable. Those people may nevertheless have taken the point that abolishing the colonists' most valuable laws violated legislative prerogative and a people's natural right to protection under civil law.

The final clause in the grievance against the king's collaborations with Parliament—"For suspending our own Legislatures, and declaring themselves invested with power to legislate for us in all cases whatsoever"—was certainly, once again, a violation of colonists' rights to representation and protection under law. As well as numerous prorogations and dissolutions of colonial assemblies, that accusation referred to the Declaratory Act of 1766 that so emphatically pronounced the power of the "imperial crown and Parliament" over the colonies. Of that act, the Declaration on the Causes and Necessity of Taking Up Arms had already asked: "why should we enumerate our Injuries in detail? By one Statute it is declared, that Parliament can 'of right make Laws to bind us in all Cases whatsoever.' What is to defend us against so enormous, so unlimited a Power?" This last clause thus returned the reader to the fundamentals of the thirteenth grievance—that the king, by extending the specifically British concept of the sovereignty of the crown-in-Parliament to the colonies, had "combined with others to subject us to a jurisdiction foreign to our constitution" and thereby violated Locke's "*first and fundamental positive Law* of all Commonwealths" and therefore the natural right of government by consent itself.[20]

Thomas Jefferson's draft declaration stated in its preamble that in the "history of unremitting injuries and usurpations" the colonists had suffered, there "appears no one fact to contradict the uniform tenor of the rest." The committee of five validated the phrases (except for changing "one fact" to "solitary fact"), but the Continental Congress replaced "unremitting injuries and usurpations" with "repeated injuries and usurpations," which aligned the phrase with the "repeated injuries" of the conclusion and more accurately reflected temporary remissions in the history of injuries and usurpations, such as the year or so between the repeal of the Stamp Act in March 1766 and the imposition of the Townshend Acts beginning in June 1767, and the period of quiescence between the Boston Massacre of 1770 and the Tea Act of 1773, another instance of scrupulous accuracy and avoidance of falsity and frivolity (although taxes on sugar and tea remained in place all that time, as did the overarching threat of the Declaratory Act from 1766).

More important, though, Congress deleted the implication of uniformity altogether, probably because delegates decided that there was in fact a change of content and tone, as the final five grievances described the king's abdication and his war against the colonies. That change did not contradict the "tenor" of the previous thirteen grievances, in that all eighteen together, plus the nine offenses listed under the thirteenth grievance, had "in direct object the establishment of an absolute tyranny over these States." But, paradoxically, the different content and tone of the final five grievances, together with the king's and the British people's rejections of the colonists' final petitions, were necessary to demonstrate that essential continuity in the Declaration's revolutionary narrative, as they collectively constituted proof that the king had intended to establish an absolute tyranny all along. The final five grievances and the beginning of the conclusion thus signaled a revolutionary turning point that was also part of a historical continuity: the moment when a long train of abuses and usurpations finally evinced a preexisting design to reduce the colonists under absolute despotism. This in turn signaled the moment when prudence and patient sufferance had to be abandoned and it became the colonists' "right" and "duty, to throw off their former government": the "when" it was "in the course of human events" that it became "necessary for one people to dissolve the political bands" that had "connected them with another."

The first of the final five grievances stated that the king "has abdicated Government here, by declaring us out of his Protection and waging War against us"—direct and deliberate attacks on the right to life. Jefferson had included a clause stating that the king had withdrawn his governors, which underlined the absence of executive protection, but the committee edited it out as some governors remained in place, and in any case, the point about the king abdicating government already made the point about an abandonment of protection. The grievance referred, of course, to the king's proclamation of August 23, 1775, declaring that the colonies were in "open and avowed rebellion" and out of his protection, authorizing the expansion of war that began at Lexington and Concord the previous April and that the grievance also alluded to. It also referred to the Prohibitory Act of December 22, which not only cut off American trade from the world but gave parliamentary affirmation that the colonists were outside royal protection. Indeed, John Adams wrote in March 1776 that placing the "colonies out of the royal protection . . . makes us independent in spite of our supplications and entreaties." The complaint also recalled Congress's resolution of May 15, 1776, written by Adams, that Parliament had "excluded these United Colonies from the protection of the crown" and the individual colonies should therefore "adopt such Government as shall in the opinion of the Representatives of the People best conduce to the happiness and safety of their Constituents in particular, and America in general." Adams promoted the resolution in part to coerce the Pennsylvania Assembly into declaring independence and adopting a new constitution, but it still rested on the natural right and sacred duty of people to throw off a tyrannical government and adopt a new one for their safety and happiness.[21]

The Declaration's specific use of the word "abdicated" had historical resonance too, as that was how the English Convention and subsequent Parliament justified abandonment of allegiance to James II in 1688–1689. The word had been used then, though, in deference to English Tory objections that an overthrow of the king represented a violation of divine right and thus an offense against God. The overthrow therefore had to be presented as the king's own doing. In 1775–1776, abdication also signaled permission to abandon allegiance, but this time in accord with Whig and Lockean precepts rather than a Tory and Filmerian interpretation of the laws of nature and God. The Declaration's "abdicated" meant the disappearance of the protection the king was entrusted to provide for the colonists' lives, liberties, property, and pursuit of happiness. As that was his primary purpose as chief magistrate, George III had effectively overthrown his own authority. Yet he continued to exercise power. And, of course, his waging war against the colonies was a direct assault on all those unalienable rights as well. Indeed, the king was now assaulting the most fundamental of natural rights—the right to life—thereby invoking the colonists' right of self-protection—the first law of nature and God.[22]

Although the Declaration thus presented a possible dissolution of royal government in 1775–1776, it did not represent it as a return to a state of nature via a breakdown of society or even of all government. It had noted in the sixth grievance that "the Legislative powers" are "incapable of Annihilation," and that during previous long dissolutions of assemblies those powers had "returned to the People at large for their exercise," indicating that "the People" and therefore a society continued to exist even while the state was inoperative. In late 1775 and early 1776, however, not only society but even a state continued to exist in the form of the Continental Congress, which was, as the breakdown of royal government progressed, taking on more and more governmental responsibilities to itself and authorizing committees to administer its policies, and in the form of colonial and state governments, which were also in the process of reforming their own constitutions to cope with new exigencies and protect their peoples. With representatives of the peoples and the colonies or states still sitting, therefore, legislative power had not reverted to the people at large during the crisis of 1775–1776 as it had done previously. Hence perhaps another seemingly small alteration of the Declaration's text. Where the draft versions had written of the necessity for colonists "to expunge their former systems of government," Congress deleted "expunge" in favor of "alter."

In the next grievance, the fifteenth, the Declaration began detailing the war, confirming that colonists' lives were in direct danger, noting first that the king "has plundered our seas, ravaged our Coasts, burnt our towns, and destroyed the lives of our people"—and there was no shortage of examples that all colonists were only too well aware of. The remaining three grievances referred to various allies the king had co-opted in that war, each one describing their depredations in lurid tones that highlighted that the king was attacking the very lives of his subjects or former subjects. "He is at this time transporting large Armies of foreign Mercenaries to compleat the works of death, desolation and tyranny, already begun with circumstances of Cruelty & perfidy scarcely paralleled in the most barbarous ages, and totally unworthy the Head of a civilized nation," as the sixteenth grievance put it in reference to the British use of Hessian mercenaries. "He has constrained our fellow Citizens taken Captive on the high Seas to bear Arms against their Country," the Declaration observed next, "to become the executioners of their friends and Brethren, or to fall themselves by their Hands." This grievance was absent in Jefferson's draft but added by the committee. Congress also inserted "our fellow Citizens" in place of "others" because it also deleted a grievance that had preceded it in the version submitted by the committee that had designated Loyalists as "fellow-citizens" (identified below), so Congress then needed to specify who those "others" were in the grievance they retained.

The grievances concluded by complaining that the king "has excited domestic insurrections amongst us, and has endeavoured to bring on the inhabitants of our frontiers, the merciless Indian Savages, whose known rule of warfare, is an undistinguished destruction of all ages, sexes and conditions." That eighteenth and final grievance was an abbreviated amalgamation of three distinct ones originally drafted by Jefferson and submitted by the committee; two well-known today, one less so. The one that preceded the complaint about the impressment of "fellow-citizens" on the high seas had stated that the king "has incited treasonable insurrections in our fellow-subjects, with the allurements of forfeiture & confiscation of our property," which the committee submitted with the word "citizens" in place of Jefferson's "subjects." Loyalists were thus among the domestic insurrectionaries that the final Declaration noted in its final grievance. That final grievance of course also referred to widespread and numerous incitements to slave rebellion, most notoriously Governor Dunmore's November 1775 proclamation inviting adult male slaves of Virginia rebels to join him in fighting against his enemies and theirs. The grievance was, however, shorn of the attack on British conduct of the slave trade that had preceded it in Jefferson's original and in the committee's submission. And the king and his agents had indeed recruited Native Americans to their cause as well.

As Robert Parkinson and others have shown, that grievance, as least as it pertained to Native Americans and African Americans, added a racist dimension to the Declaration's appeal for independence, the present and future implications of which are explored further in chapter 6. It is worth noting here, though, that the final grievance should also be seen in the context of the more general attack on the unalienable right to life that the final five grievances collectively represented. The Declaration's call for revolution was based on the notion that the colonists had a natural right and sacred duty to defend their lives according to the laws of nature and God. However effective the dog-whistling of the final grievance was, the fundamental ideological justification for it—the law of nature and God that it rested on—was the threat to the first and most fundamental of unalienable rights, the right to life, whether that threat came from the king directly or from his other agents: British soldiers and seamen, Hessian mercenaries, coerced fellow patriots, Loyalists, enslaved people, and Native Americans alike.[23]

Yet the series of oppressions depicted in the Declaration's grievances was not quite enough to justify revolution. The claims made at the beginnings of the conclusion were also essential to proving to a candid world that the laws of nature and God entitled Americans to independence. Those laws required two more things: proof that a people had attempted to resolve matters without resort to revolution, and proof of intent on the part of their oppressors. Immediately after the grievances, therefore, the Declaration stated that "In every stage of these Oppressions We have Petitioned for Redress in the most humble terms" but "Our repeated Petitions have been answered only by repeated injury." After that, the document noted that the colonists had not been wanting "in attentions to our Brittish brethren. We have warned them from time to time of attempts by their legislature to extend an unwarrantable jurisdiction over us" and "reminded them of the circumstances of our emigration and settlement here," adding, "We have appealed to their native justice and magnanimity, and . . . conjured them by the ties of our common kindred to disavow these usurpations, which, would inevitably interrupt our connections and correspondence," but they too proved "deaf to the voice of justice and of consanguinity."

These petitions and warnings demonstrated that the colonists had undertaken due diligence in attempting to prevent revolution. Moreover, the king's receipt and rejection of the colonists' petitions proved that he had subsequently acted with knowledge and therefore intent—or with "a design" and "direct object," as the Declaration's preamble had indicated. They thus demonstrated that colonists had observed the strictures of John Locke, who had written that tyranny may appear in "*a long Train of Actings*," but "People . . . are more disposed to suffer, than to right themselves by Resistance." However, as Locke continued, "if a long train of Abuses, Prevarications, and Artifices, all tending in the same way, make a design visible," a people "have a Right to resume their original Liberty." And, he added, people will revolt only "if they universally have a perswasion, grounded upon manifest evidence, that designs are carrying on against their Liberties, and the general course and tendency of things cannot but give them strong suspicions of the evil intention of their Governors."[24]

The Declaration of Independence thus portrays two narratives of the American Revolution and, in the process, two historical stages that should, according to the laws of nature and God, feature in all rightful revolutions. One narrative arises from retrospective knowledge and portrays the king's actions as a single series of injuries and usurpations all having in direct object the establishment of an absolute tyranny. The other is contemporaneous with events and shows the colonists suffering "while evils are sufferable" and acting to overthrow the king only when a "direct object the establishment of an absolute Tyranny" is proven. This presentation of the Revolution as a process of awakening in turn reveals other elements of the authors' historical consciousness and methodology. Those authors were clearly aware that correlation is not causation and that action does not prove intention. A train of events may happen by accident rather than design, so there needs to be other proof of the latter. The authors thus acknowledged the difference between the circumstantial evidence of the king's actions and the written and therefore more certain evidence of his intentions in the form of the petitions he ignored and the subsequent speeches and proclamations he made and legislation he signed. And it was only after all of the above—the framing of arguments based on the course of human events seen in the light of the laws of nature and God, the presentation of the facts of the reign of George III in the light of natural and civil laws broken, the evidence of the colonists' efforts at resolution, and the proofs of intention on the part of the king—that the Declaration could finally state, "We must, therefore, acquiesce in the necessity, which denounces our Separation, and hold" the British people "as we hold the rest of mankind, Enemies in War, in Peace Friends."[25]

Even then, though, there was still one more authority to appeal to for the rightness of the decision for revolution: the original lawmaker and ultimate judge of human affairs Himself. John Locke had asked, "*Who shall be Judge* whether the Prince or Legislative act contrary to their Trust?," given that "ill-affected and factious Men may spread amongst the People, when the Prince only makes use of his due Prerogative." He answered: "*The People shall be Judge,* for who shall be *Judge* whether his Trustee or Deputy acts well, and according to the Trust reposed in him, but he who deputes him?" Yet he also argued that, as a guard against the "ill-affected and factious," people must look to a higher authority while making such judgments. "For where there is no Judicature on Earth to decide Controversies amongst Men," Locke reasoned, "God in heaven is judge. He alone, it is true, is judge of the right." Hence "*every Man* is Judge for himself . . . whether another hath put himself into a State of War with him, and whether he should appeal to the Supreme Judge, as *Jephtha* did."

The Declaration's final paragraph correspondingly begins with an appeal "to the Supreme Judge of the world for the rectitude of our intentions" before declaring that the "Colonies are, and of Right ought to be Free and Independent States." And, in the document's final sentence, "for the support of this Declaration," the authors asserted their "firm reliance on the protection of divine Providence" before pledging to each other their lives, fortunes, and sacred honor. This reliance was no surrender to fate or a fickle deity, however; nor was it an empty piety. It represented, rather, a solemn commitment, as the authors saw it, to doing things the right way. They had assessed the course of human events for themselves according to the laws of nature and of God, and they had decided, as they thought a people must, on the necessity of separation, which they then thought it proper to explain to mankind. And finally, demonstrating their faith that they were not merely "ill-affected or factious" men, they appealed to the supreme judge to validate their decision, just as Locke said Jephthah had done almost three-thousand years before.[26]

What the colonists ultimately needed to demonstrate to God as well to mankind was the *necessity* of revolution. The Declaration is thus replete with imperative language that reflected the intersecting of the course of human events and natural and sacred law. The introduction refers to a moment in the course of human events when "it becomes *necessary*" for one people to separate from another and promised to declare the causes that "*impel* them to the separation." The preamble describes revolution not only as a people's right but also as "their *duty*," and refers to "the *necessity* which constrains" the colonists to alter their government. The first grievance complains of vetoes of laws "wholesome and *necessary* for the public good." And, in the conclusion: "We *must*, therefore, acquiesce in the *necessity*, which denounces our Separation"—the use of the word "acquiesce" signifying that, at least under the first law of nature and God, there is no other rightful choice. Also, the colonies "are, and *of Right ought to be* Free and Independent States;" their political connection to Britain "is and *ought to be* totally dissolved." This imperative language should be understood in the light of the final five grievances and their invocation of the first law of nature and God, and the king's intention as proven by his dismissal of colonial petitions. They show that the Declaration's authors did not declare independence for "light and transient causes," but did so because the course of human events in conjunction with laws of nature and God told them that they must.[27]

As much as John Adams feared disorder, he nevertheless agreed that resistance, rebellion, and even revolution were sometimes necessary. Indeed, Adams's combination of caution and certitude on the matter perhaps best represents the Declaration's own careful but ultimately decisive argument for independence. On February 27, 1775, for example, Adams, writing as *Novanglus*, quoted Daniel Leonard quoting John Locke's lessons on prudence, but then quoted Locke back at Leonard on the necessity of revolution. "If it is objected, that the people being ignorant, and always discontented, to lay the foundation of government in the unsteady opinion and the uncertain humour of the people, is to expose it to certain ruin," Adams wrote of Leonard's reading of Locke, "the same author will answer you, that on the contrary, people are not so easily got out of their old forms as some are apt to suggest. England, for instance, notwithstanding the many revolutions that have been seen in that kingdom, has always kept to its old legislative of king, lords and commons." And Adams also quoted "Grotius, Puffendorf, Barbeyrac, Lock, Sidney, and LeClerk" extensively to support his case that "If the laws of God and men, are therefore of no effect, when the magistracy is left at liberty to break them; and if the lusts of those who are too strong for the tribunals of justice, cannot be otherwise restrained than by sedition, tumults and war, those seditions, tumults and wars, are justified by the laws of God and man."[28]

Ultimately, the Declaration's concept of necessity was based on threats to life and the absence of any alternative means to defend life, as depicted in the final five grievances and the king answering repeated petitions with repeated injuries. The right to life, after all, was "the first principle of nature," as Jefferson himself and many others described it. Jefferson also wrote in his draft preamble that "We hold these truths to be sacred & undeniable; that all men are created equal & independant, that from that equal creation they derive rights inherent & inalienable, among which are the preservation of life, & liberty, & the pursuit of happiness." The committee of five edited out "the preservation of," presumably deciding that the right to life, as Locke frequently maintained, entailed the right to preserve and defend it. In other words, life was not something merely received but something to be preserved or at least defended as far as possible. And the imperative of self-preservation was for Jefferson not only an individual right but also belonged to a whole community in the form of "reasons of state," as based on the intersection between the laws of nature and those of nations. "A strict observance of the written laws is doubtless *one* of the highest duties of a good citizen, but it is not *the highest*," he wrote. "The laws of necessity," he continued, "of self-preservation, of saving our country when we are in danger, are of higher obligation." Hence such famous Jeffersonian aphorisms as "a little rebellion now and then is a good thing, and as necessary in the political world as storms in the physical," and "The tree of liberty must be refreshed from time to time with the blood of patriots and tyrants." These were not merely provocative slogans, then, but were political maxims that Jefferson wrote into the Declaration of Independence.[29]

Another alteration to Jefferson's draft concerned the laws of God and the necessity of obeying them. While editing out "sacred" from Jefferson's truths, the committee of five nevertheless subtly reinforced the Declaration's portrayal of the relationship between God and the right to life by replacing Jefferson's "from that equal creation they derive" certain rights with the more active "endowed by their creator with" certain rights. And Timothy Matlack capitalized "Creator" for Congress's final official version of the Declaration. These alterations reinforced the point a few lines later (a point originally made by Jefferson) that "when a long train of abuses and usurpations, pursuing invariably the same Object evinces a design to reduce" a people "under absolute Despotism, it is their right, it is their duty, to throw off such Government, and to provide new Guards for their future security." Revolution was therefore not only a natural right but also a sacred duty—not only a political act but a religious one. The idea that disobedience to tyrants is obedience to God, which Benjamin Franklin as well as Jefferson considered as possible family mottos, was not merely a catchy slogan, then, but a theological maxim that they wrote into the Declaration of Independence.

The stress on the necessity of revolution, though undoubtedly sincere, was one of many persuasive tactics the Declaration's authors used in presenting their case. They knew, of course, that independence depended in part on how effectively they fulfilled their main aim of explaining to humankind the causes of the separation of the American colonies from the British Empire. They also knew that their lives depended partly on the same. As Benjamin Franklin is reputed to have said during the debates over the Declaration, "We must, indeed, all hang together, or assuredly we shall all hang separately." Whether Franklin spoke those words or not, the authors knew that their Declaration had to be as persuasive as they could make it in order to maintain existing patriot support, persuade the undecided to join them, win over or demoralize Loyalists, and encourage foreign powers to recognize the United States and come to their aid, and that their lives depended on their Declaration succeeding in all these aims.[30]

This book has already highlighted many of the ways in which the authors made the Declaration as persuasive as possible—how their argument rested on the laws of nature and God as applied to the general history of humankind, the origins and development of the colonies, a history of abuses and usurpations, and proof of the king's design of absolute tyranny and therefore the necessity of revolution. It has also shown how orthography provided visual cues for readers, such as the hyphens and em-dashes that emphasized the logic of the preamble's arguments, and the addition of capital letters to highlight certain words and concepts, such as "the Course of human events" and "the Laws of Nature and of Nature's God"—all deployed to reinforce the Declaration's *logos*. And then there were the seventeen uses of "He has" and one of "He is"—an anaphorical onslaught depicting the king's injuries and usurpations in the face of the colonists' prudence and patient sufferance, and finally the depiction of the revolutionary turning point in light of natural and sacred law—*ethos*. And the authors deployed *pathos*, too, most especially when addressing their "Brittish brethren." After noting that the colonists had warned their British brethren against their legislature extending an unwarrantable jurisdiction, and reminding them of the circumstances of emigration and settlement, the Declaration stated, "We have appealed to their native justice and magnanimity" and "conjured them by the ties of our common kindred to disavow these usurpations." But they proved "deaf to the voice of justice and of consanguinity" and so "We must . . . acquiesce in the necessity, which denounces our Separation, and hold them, as we hold the rest of mankind, Enemies in War, in Peace Friends."[31]

But not too much pathos. Thomas Jefferson had originally elaborated that "when occasions have been given" to the British people "by the regular course of their laws, of removing from their councils the disturbers of our harmony, they have by their free election re-established them in power." And so, he said,

> at this very time too they are permitting their chief magistrate to send over not only soldiers of our common blood, but Scotch & foreign mercenaries to invade & deluge us in blood. these facts have given the last stab to agonizing affection, and manly spirit bids us to renounce for ever these unfeeling brethren. we must endeavor to forget our former love for them . . . and to hold them as we hold the rest of mankind, enemies in war, in peace friends. we might have been a free & great people together; but a communication of grandeur & of freedom it seems is below their dignity. be it so, since they will have it: the road to glory & happiness is open to us too; we will climb it in a separate state, and acquiesce in the necessity which pronounces our everlasting Adieu!

The committee toned the passage down slightly for the June 28 version submitted to Congress, with "Scotch and other foreign mercenaries" now sent "to destroy us" rather than "deluge us in blood," the climbing of the road to glory and happiness now "apart from" the British rather than "in a separate state," and with a necessity that now "denounces our eternal separation!" rather than "pronounces our everlasting Adieu!" The only part of the passage that survived Congress's scrutiny, however, was "They too have been deaf to the voice of justice and of consanguinity. We must, therefore, acquiesce in the necessity, which denounces our Separation, and hold them, as we hold the rest of mankind, Enemies in War, in Peace Friends." Jefferson later complained of what he called the "pusillanimous" idea of maintaining friendship with the British people, but Congress seems to have taken the view that it was best not to alienate Britons any more than necessary as they might yet turn against their government, eventually undermining its war effort. We can thus add another instance of *silentium* to the Declaration's authors' rhetoric. Just as they elided Jefferson's account of the circumstances of emigration and settlement and of the slave trade for reasons of internal politics, so they elided his attack on the British people for reasons of external diplomacy.[32]

Part of the reason for these silences, as this book has already shown, was to harmonize the sentiments of the day, if not to express its harmonizing sentiments, as Jefferson would later claim. And the Declaration's authors reinforced that impression of harmony by stressing and indeed exaggerating the extent of unity of opinion in favor of independence. One means was in the retitling of the final version of the Declaration issued on August 2. They had titled earlier versions "A Declaration by the representatives of the United states of America, in General Congress assembled," but designated the final one as "The unanimous Declaration of the thirteen united States of America." The switch from the indefinite to the definite article at the start of the later iteration was one signal of assertiveness, as was the transition of attribution from "the representatives of the United states . . . in General Congress" to the broader authority of "the thirteen united States." But the use of the word "unanimous" was perhaps the most significant change. That claim for unanimity had some basis in fact, in that on July 9 the New York Assembly finally authorized its delegates at the Continental Congress to vote for independence, bringing the tally of yes votes to thirteen of thirteen colonies or states. Ten days later, Congress ordered that the Declaration be "fairly engrossed on parchment, with the title and stile of 'The unanimous declaration of the thirteen United States of America.'" Yet not all the delegations were unanimous, with some abstaining on the vote for independence. Nor were all the local assemblymen who gave the delegates their orders, nor, by any means, were all the people of what the Congress's proceedings called the "United States" but which the final Declaration more cautiously called the "united States." "Unanimous" could and can mean "Exhibiting general agreement or consent" in the context "Of beliefs, statements, actions, etc.," rather than signaling the agreement of every individual, and that looser definition was appropriate enough in the circumstances. Even then, though, the word implied a formidable unity of opinion that may have had persuasive effects on the undecided and intimidating effects on those who opposed independence. Indeed, it implied that people who disagreed were not among the "one people" of the United States—a sobering prospect for those considering their futures, and one that might even make some of them reconsider their political alignment.[33]

In addition, the authors claimed in the Declaration's conclusion to be announcing independence on nothing less than "the Authority of the good People of these Colonies." As well as thus invoking the consent of the governed and the ultimate sovereignty of the people, this phrase further implied a unified support for independence, and also that those who disagreed were neither good nor among those people—the "one people" of the Declaration's introduction. And, at the very end of the document, the authors pledged to each other their lives, fortunes, and sacred honor. That pledge also indicated solidarity, aligning the document's authors with those whose lives were in more immediate danger, whether in the fields of battle or in homes under attack by British forces and their allies, as did the act of signing the Declaration, as most, though not all, delegates did from August 2 onward.[34]

The authors of the Declaration of Independence did what they said they were going to do in the document's first paragraph—explain why it was necessary in the course of human events for one people to dissolve the political bands that had connected them with another and thereby declare the causes that impelled them to the separation. They reached back to

Creation's laws of nature and of God as rules of human behavior and as measures for judging that behavior. They showed how the origins of English and British American colonial society and government reflected the origins of human society and government, and how the causes and course of the American Revolution reflected those of previous revolutions. They gave a precise account of the American Revolution as arising from the actions of a king whose behavior imperiled his subjects' liberty, property, pursuits of happiness, and finally their lives. They proved intention on the king's part, and appealed to the maker of the laws of nature for His approval of their actions. They aimed by these means to gain local and global support to help win the War of Independence. Their arguments may seem strange to us today—their laws of nature and of nature's God and their course of human events may seem alien or else are long forgotten, but they were well understood at the time. Even if some contemporaries disagreed with much of what the Declaration said, as was bound to be the case, the document made what for many was a profoundly persuasive argument for American independence.

After all their efforts in writing the Declaration, therefore, the authors ensured that they distributed the document as far and wide as possible as quickly as they could. On the evening of July 4, Congress authorized Philadelphia printer John Dunlap to publish a broadside version for quick and efficient distribution and display. It was reprinted in newspapers across the colonies. Marks on one of Jefferson's copies of the document indicate how the Declaration was meant to be read out loud. It was often received with boisterous celebration. Most famously, a crowd in Manhattan tore down a statue of George III and melted its lead into bullets to fire at British soldiers. These people evidently understood the Declaration's grievances and why they were aimed at the king. On July 5, the president of the Congress, John Hancock, sent a copy to the Philadelphia Committee of Safety and to the New Jersey Convention. The day after that, he informed General George Washington in New York that Congress had "judged it necessary to dissolve the Connection between Great Britain and the American Colonies, and to declare them free & independent States," enclosing a copy of the Declaration to be "proclaimed at the Head of the Army in the Way, you shall think most proper." Washington duly issued orders stating that "Congress, impelled by the dictates of duty, policy and necessity," had declared independence, and that "The several brigades are to be drawn up this evening on their respective Parades, at six OClock, when the declaration of Congress, shewing the grounds & reasons of this measure, is to be read with an audible voice." He added his hopes that "this important Event will serve as a fresh incentive to every officer, and soldier, to act with Fidelity and Courage, as knowing that now the peace and safety of his Country depends (under God) solely on the success of our arms: And that he is now in the service of a State, possessed of sufficient power to reward his merit, and advance him to the highest Honors of a free Country." Hancock also sent the same instructions to "To the States," adding, "The important Consequences to the American States from this Declaration of Independence, considered as the Ground & Foundation of a future Government, will naturally suggest the Propriety of proclaiming it in such a Manner, that the People may be universally informed of it."[35]

The Declaration thus played the part it was designed to play in influencing the present. It did not magic independence into being by means of some kind of "performance." As the sending of the document to the army and the states indicates, a long, hard slog of military sacrifice and political and diplomatic work lay ahead before its aims could be achieved. But it played a key part in that process, inspiring those who did that work and made those sacrifices. It also played a part in defining the new nation for the future. As Hancock asserted, the document was to be "considered as the Ground & Foundation of a future Government." It was not, to be sure, a new constitution, but it did enunciate certain principles of government. Those principles were ancient and had been the foundations of government since time immemorial, or so the Declaration's authors believed. As those authors looked to the future, then, they did not envision a *novus ordo seclorum* in the way we imagine today. Rather, they looked to a future that would be based on the eternal laws of nature and God, modeled on their general history of humankind, and shaped by their particular history of the American colonies and revolution. The founders did not intend that their Declaration of Independence make a break with history. Rather, they saw the future as inseparable from the past and the present.[36]

PART III

The Past, the Present, and the Future
To Institute New Government

5

The Right of the People

Whenever any Form of Government becomes destructive of these ends, it is the Right of the People to alter or to abolish it, and to institute new Government, laying its foundation on such principles and organizing its powers in such form, as to them shall seem most likely to effect their Safety and Happiness.

Part II of this book showed how "The history of the present King of Great Britain" was inscribed in the Declaration of Independence as "a history of repeated injuries and usurpations, all having in direct object the establishment of an absolute Tyranny over these States." Government under George III was therefore destructive of its ends of securing the colonists' lives, liberties, and pursuits of happiness. It thus became "the Right of the People," in this case the American people, "to alter or to abolish" that government. And the same imperatives that made people consent to government in the first place also impelled them "to institute new Government, laying its foundation on such principles and organizing its powers in such form, as to them shall seem most likely to effect their Safety and Happiness" and "provide new Guards for their future security." But what kind of "principles," "powers," and "Guards" did the authors of the document have in mind for the American people? What did John Hancock mean, for example, when he stated that the Declaration of Independence was to be "considered as the Ground & Foundation of a future Government"?

Today we tend to believe that the Declaration's authors founded a nation on the equality and unalienable rights of "all men," even if that amounted to little more than thoughts and prayers at that time. Yet we also know that few if any of the Declaration's authors believed that women, Black people, or even poor white men were the equals of themselves, or that such people were entitled to equal civil rights, whether in the past, the present, or the future. As discussed earlier, the authors' idea that "all men are created equal" referred to God granting individual sovereignty and the right to property for the sake of subsistence, as John Locke argued in opposition to Robert Filmer's case for God granting absolute power and proprietorship to Adam and succeeding kings. To be sure, the equality and liberty of the state of nature should translate into the founding of government on the consent of the people and for the securing of their unalienable rights, and should be manifest in a representative element in government and in the form of an ultimate sovereignty of the people who could resort to revolution if necessary. Yet all were required by the social contract to abandon their individual sovereignty for a collective one, and to obey their new government and its laws, thereby abandoning their natural equality. And some were required to abandon more of their equality and liberty than others. As the Declaration's authors' main intellectual forebear, John Locke, put it, "Though I have said . . . *That all Men by Nature are equal*, I cannot be supposed to understand all sorts of *Equality*." And, as he explained:

> *Age* or *Virtue* may give Men a just Precedency: *Excellency of Parts and Merit* may place others above the Common Level: *Birth* may subject some, and *Alliance* or *Benefits* others, to pay an Observance to those to whom Nature, Gratitude or other Respects may have made it due; and yet all this consists with the *Equality*, which all Men are in, in respect of Jurisdiction or Dominion one over another . . . that *equal Right* that every Man hath, *to his Natural Freedom*, without being subjected to the Will or Authority of any other Man.[1]

And that, for the founders, is how it had always been and always should be.

The Declaration of Independence certainly had implications for the future, but all were grounded in one way or another in the past and present as those were perceived in 1776. Most obviously, it helped remove thirteen colonies from the British Empire and reconstitute them as the United States of America—a "new Government," if not a new kind of government or society. And, as the last chapter showed, the Declaration helped to persuade people at home and abroad of the necessity of separation and thereby helped to win the war and achieve independence. In the process, it became the first founding text in history that explicitly justified the overthrow of one government and its replacement with another on the grounds of the laws of nature and God and in the course of human events, even as it argued that all new nations and governments had been implicitly founded on these principles and in this way. That discourse on government, however, provided what was perhaps the Declaration's unique contribution to the future. It was, in effect, a civics lesson, and one with all the authority of also being a nation's founding text. And, if its lessons were learned, it offered the prospect that a duly educated American people might preserve its liberties longer than any other people had ever done in the past. It might even break the cycles of history, the rise and fall of nations and empires that the Declaration itself depicted, and fashion instead a linear future. The novelty of the Declaration thus lay in its explication of ancient principles, rather than in their invention or unprecedented application, and consequently in the possibility of a new direction for the future course of human events.

But even that potential linear future would be grounded on the principles and facts of the past and the present—the eternal laws of nature and of God and the lessons learned from the course of human events. One of the laws of nature and God was that people would and should seek security of their lives, liberty, property, and happiness under government. And one of the lessons of the recent course of human events was that public safety was better secured by the colonies and states acting together. The process of creating an American union for the sake of security both predated and postdated the Declaration of Independence, but the document played an important part in that process. The Declaration articulated an antiquity of an American people—the "one people" of the document's introduction—through "the circumstances of our emigration and settlement here." Those circumstances originally created thirteen peoples, or more if one includes Britain's other colonies. Yet the common processes of migration, settlement, and colonial development, and then the common experience of the "history of the present King of Great Britain," allowed the Declaration to articulate the unity first formalized in the Articles of Association and later made "more perfect" by the Constitution's "We the People of the United States."[2]

Furthermore, the principle of government by consent necessitated that the new American nation be a republic, that is, that it should be a government of laws, not of men, and that those laws should be made at least in part by the representatives of the people. That did not necessitate, however, that the United States be a republic—a polity without a monarchy. The Declaration's history posited that past peoples, including American colonial peoples, had consented to and long lived freely under monarchs as their protectors in conjunction with elected assemblies as their representatives. If the Declaration led the nation toward a republican (nonmonarchical) government, then it did so through its cautionary "history of the present King of Britain" rather than through a supposedly egalitarian ideology. Nor did representation necessitate that the United States be a democracy, at least as we understand the term today. Certainly, ultimate sovereignty rested with the people, but only with the people collectively, and that sovereignty was only to be exercised in certain strictly defined exigencies, as described in the previous chapter. For routine purposes, there had to be representation of the people, but that did not mean voting by all the people. Indeed, for many of the founders, voting was a social and not a natural right, and only those who were supposedly personally independent and virtuous, possessing an incorruptible free will of their own, should be enfranchised. That idea, with rare exceptions, meant the disfranchisement of women and of men with little or no property. It also led, combined with racism, to increasing restrictions on the right of Black men to vote in the years after the Revolution.

In these respects, the original Declaration of Independence was more concerned with what its authors saw as "the Right of the People" collectively rather than with the rights of individuals. Indeed, the historical trajectory on which the Declaration's history was based led away from individualism and toward a form of "commonwealth," a word frequently used by John Locke. The movement from a state of nature to society and government meant abandoning individual sovereignty in favor of collective sovereignty, and, although some rights were unalienable, others were social—and the latter would be distributed unequally, the better to reflect natural and circumstantial inequalities and to secure the supposed happiness and safety of all. The Declaration's principle of "the Right of the People" was thus inimical to the equality of individuals, as this chapter shows. And, as the next chapter will show, it was also inimical to full inclusion, for the social contract took people out of the realm of "all men" and divided them into different peoples in distinct nations; and it was the purpose of a government to protect its own people from all dangers—from enemies without as well as within.[3]

The presumption that the Declaration of Independence promised a new kind of government and nation has been reinforced by a misinterpretation of the term affixed to the Great Seal of the United States, designed soon after independence: *Novus ordo seclorum*. Yet Charles Thomson, the Secretary of Congress, suggested this legend to signify "the beginning of the New American Era" rather than a more global or universal one. He borrowed the phrase from an ancient source, after all—the fourth poem of the *Eclogues* (or *Bucolics*) of the Roman poet Virgil: "Now is come the last age of the Cumaean prophecy: / The great cycle of ages is born anew. / Now returns the Maid, returns the reign of Saturn. . . ." Thomson's use of the term thus indicated a rebirth rather than a new birth, another turn in the cycles of history rather than a break with the past, and a return to an old regime rather than a journey into a new age.[4]

If the Declaration did one thing new, though, it was to raise the possibility of breaking this cyclical pattern of history and to augur a possibly more linear future by articulating the laws of nature and God and demonstrating how to use them to assess the course of human events. The Declaration thus inscribed the origins and principles of government and the right to revolution into the nation's founding text, providing a permanent and venerable reminder of them. In addition, the Declaration indicated examples of the cycles of the past and present, its history depicting a traditional story of the rise and fall of states and empires, in this case the British Empire, but in terms familiar from common knowledge of the Roman and other empires and city-states. But greater familiarity with the principles of government, with the grounds on which states and empires rise and fall, might obviate an American fall in the future.

Contemporaries were familiar with such ancient and Renaissance histories, as well as with the rise and fall of the Stuart kings of England and Scotland, a familiarity that helped them make sense of the Declaration's general history of humankind. And access to the illustrative qualities of ancient history was not limited to the highly educated. In his 1772 Boston

Massacre Oration, Joseph Warren first addressed the origins of government from states of nature by consent and for the purpose of protecting natural rights, as shown in chapter 1. He then continued:

> IT was *this* noble attachment to a free constitution, which raised ancient Rome from the smallest beginnings to that bright summit of happiness and glory to which she arrived; and it was the loss of *this* which plunged her from *that* summit into the black gulph of infamy and slavery. It was *this* attachment... which guarded her liberties, and extended her dominions, gave peace at home and commanded respect abroad: And when *this* decayed, her magistrates lost their reverence for justice and the laws, and degenerated into tyrants and oppressors.... Thus *this empress* of the world lost her dominions abroad, and her inhabitants dissolute in their manners, at length became contented *slaves;* and she stands to this day, the scorn and derision of nations, and a monument of this eternal truth, that PUBLIC HAPPINESS DEPENDS ON A VIRTUOUS AND UNSHAKEN ATTACHMENT TO A FREE CONSTITUTION.

After that, Warren explained how the same ideals inspired migrants to Massachusetts, as shown in chapter 2.[5]

Above all, though, the Declaration's authors were influenced by the Enlightenment and the more modern prospect of progress that might make future history different from past history, linear rather than cyclical. American revolutionaries, after all, called themselves Whigs, after those who had opposed the accession of James, duke of York, to the English throne during the Exclusion Crisis of 1679–1681, and who then overthrew him after nearly four years of tyrannical and pro-Catholic rule as King James II, albeit with Tories who accepted James's removal provided it was defined as an "abdication" and his daughter, Mary, was made queen regnant, rather than William's queen consort, in order to maintain the principle of succession by divine right. The Glorious Revolution settlement established the sovereignty of the crown-in-Parliament, at least according to eighteenth-century British historical memory, and for many Britons that form of limited monarchy represented the sine qua non of liberty itself. Yet the bloated powers of the crown-in-Parliament led in practice to the corrupt "Court Whig" regimes of eighteenth-century Britain and eventually to the extension of its "unwarrantable jurisdiction" over the colonies. The American revolutionary use of the term Whig also therefore recalled the English Opposition, County, Real, or True Whigs of the eighteenth century, including their philosophical forebear, John Locke, and his journalistic interpreters, John Trenchard and Thomas Gordon. Trenchard and Gordon's pseudonym for their famous *Cato's Letters* recalled Cato the Younger, the incorruptible republican opponent of the rise of the tyrannical Julius Caesar as Roman emperor. But the letters' contents provided judgments of political corruption in early eighteenth-century Britain based on Lockean standards of natural law. The Declaration of Independence did much the same, though obviously rather more briefly.[6]

But the Enlightenment and Whiggish promise of the Declaration for the future was that this cyclical process of instituting, abolishing, and reinstituting might be broken by the further diffusion of knowledge of historical process itself. The laws of nature and God had supposedly always existed, just as the laws of motion always had. It was, however, knowledge of those laws that might alter the course of human events. Just as Isaac Newton's *Principia* advanced scientific progress, Locke's *Two Treatises of Government* and their many exegeses might advance historical progress. Locke's own *Essay Concerning Human Understanding* showed how the laws of nature and God could be revealed by observation and then realized through the application of reason. As noted earlier, eighteenth-century "philosophical history" posited an idealized convergence of the constancy of absolute time, based on eternal laws, with historically contingent relative time, based on human behavior in all its volatility, as Enlightenment knowledge of natural law advanced to the point that its principles could be increasingly integrated into the constitutions and conduct of civil governance. History itself could reveal "the constant and universal principles of human nature," as David Hume claimed, and was thus a form of "philosophy teaching by examples," according to Henry Bolingbroke. Thomas Jefferson and other Americans were influenced by such thinking, although a more pessimistic view of governmental adherence to the laws of nature and God in the course of human events entered their thinking during the reign of George III. The experience of failure, however, and the prospect of a new American era made the project of public education all the more pressing.[7]

John Adams thus advocated wider public education in civics in his April 1776 "Thoughts on Government," stating that "LAWS for the liberal education of youth, especially of the lower class of people, are so extremely wise and useful, that to a humane and generous mind, no expence for this purpose would be thought extravagant." Thomas Jefferson actively supported public education; his Bill for the More General Diffusion of Knowledge, composed in 1778, eventually resulted in a 1796 Act to Establish Public Schools. The law's stated purpose was to enhance historical knowledge to preserve liberty. "Whereas it appeareth," the act said, "that however certain forms of government are better calculated than others to protect individuals in the free exercise of their natural rights, and are at the same time themselves better guarded against degeneracy . . . experience hath shewn, that even under the best forms, those entrusted with power have, in time . . . perverted it into tyranny." Thus "the most effectual means of preventing this would be, to illuminate . . . the minds of the people at large, and more especially to give them knowledge of those facts, which history exhibiteth, that . . . they may be enabled to know ambition under all its shapes, and prompt to exert their natural powers to defeat its purposes."[8]

Later in his life, furthermore, Jefferson extended the supposedly Baconian aphorism that "knoledge is power" by adding "that knowledge is safety, and that knowledge is happiness." He thus aligned knowledge with the ends of government earlier expressed in the Declaration of Independence: "to effect" a people's "Safety and Happiness."[9]

But how, according to the Declaration, could government best be structured to preserve as well as effect a people's safety and happiness? The first count, safety, was in fact the reason for being of the institution that issued the Declaration. The First Continental Congress had formed to provide a unified, intercolonial response to the Coercive Acts, and the Second sat as the revolutionary crisis escalated into war in the weeks before it convened. But the advantages of unifying in the face of danger had been apparent even earlier, first in the meeting of the Albany Congress of 1754, in response to French fort building on lands claimed by Britons. It was there that Benjamin Franklin produced a Plan of Union and a vivid illustration of the dangers of disunity and advantages of unity in the form of his segmented snake, each section of which bore the initials of a colony and under which were the words "JOIN, or DIE." That plan came to nothing at the time, but Franklin's serpent is perhaps so well remembered as a result of more unified responses to later events. The pleas of Massachusetts for a collective response to the Sugar Act went unheeded, but the Stamp Act inspired another intercolonial congress, this time in New York. The Stamp Act Congress issued its petitions and its Declaration of Rights and Grievances, but, with the repeal of the stamp tax, there was no apparent need for a permanent union or even a reunion, although committees of correspondence worked hard to maintain a sense that the colonies shared common problems and should respond collectively. In 1774, then, a continental congress met in response to the Coercive Acts and immediately created the conditions for the more permanent union that would evolve in subsequent years.

One of the first things the First Continental Congress did was agree to the Articles of Association of October 20, 1774. The articles were primarily a nonimportation pact, a form of collective action that colonists had previously engaged in to protest the Stamp Act and the Townshend Acts. But the articles also institutionalized the relationship between the colonies by authorizing local committees to enforce the boycott. They stated that the colonies, "for ourselves and the Inhabitants of the several colonies whom we represent, firmly agree and associate, under the sacred Ties of Virtue, Honour, and Love of our Country," and directed that "a Committee be chosen in every County, City, and Town, by those who are qualified to vote for representatives in the Legislature," thereby creating an intercolonial form of government. Without intending independence at this stage, the Congress nevertheless thereby began a process of state formation, with the peoples of the thirteen colonies acting as a single community "under the sacred Ties of Virtue, Honour and"—using another singular—"Love of our Country." The articles thus allowed the Declaration of Independence to posit its "one people" as a preexisting entity.[10]

But the Declaration of Independence did something more than posit a people unified in the face of temporary danger; it articulated something more historically grounded and potentially enduring—an origin story of the American people. As detailed in chapter 2, the document's "circumstances of our emigration and settlement here" depicted the creation of colonial American peoples but also implied the possibility of "one people." Thomas Jefferson's free state version posited that emigrants abandoned their subjecthood to the English or British crown and Parliament and then constituted themselves as new peoples in America. John Dickinson's more traditional charter theory did not posit an abandonment of subjecthood but still argued that the efforts and expenses of migration and settlement entitled Americans to property and self-government. Colonists thus became distinct if not separate peoples by dint of having their own polities, most especially their own legislatures, which represented them as peoples. Hence, in the very same passage in his *Farmer's Letters* in which Dickinson denied that the colonies were "states," he could still describe colonists as being "as much dependant on *Great-Britain,* as a perfectly free people can be on another."[11]

Of course, the process of emigration and settlement, under either interpretation of it, originally created thirteen peoples rather than one, or more than that, if we include Plymouth Colony, East and West Jersey, and the various British colonies, from Canada through Florida to the Caribbean, that did not join in declaring independence. The formation of American peoples was further complicated by the religious, ethnic, and racial identities of different emigrants, and then by migrations within the colonies, such as that of Scotch-Irish and others, into the backcountries, and of New Englanders into the Green Mountains region of New York, who eventually constituted themselves as the people of Vermont. Yet the common process of emigration and settlement also allowed for the development of the "one people" the Declaration of Independence identified.

Once again, it was Thomas Jefferson in 1774 who showed us how that process of emigration and settlement worked toward a possible union of American peoples. Jefferson referred in his *Summary View of the Rights of British America* to the colonies as "states," and he called his native Virginia his "country" all his life, and he retained a strong although often ambiguous commitment to states' rights, as manifest in his later Kentucky Resolutions and comments on the Missouri Controversy. Even so, he presented his 1774 pamphlet in proto-unionist terms, as an account of the history and politics of all the colonies, not just of Virginia. It was a summary view, after all, of the rights of British America, and it assumed that the colonies had enough in common to be considered together. The first words of the main text thus stated "RESOLVED, that it be an instruction to the said deputies" of Virginia that "when assembled in general congress with the deputies from the other states of British America, to propose to the said congress that an humble and dutiful address be presented to his Majesty, begging leave to lay before him, as Chief Magistrate of the British empire, the united complaints of his Majesty's subjects in America." These united complaints of America would thus be "a joint address" rather than the kind that "these his states have often individually made." Also, at the end of the pamphlet's first paragraph, Jefferson proposed to consider "our rights, as well as the invasions of them . . . from the origin and first settlement of these countries," with "countries" in the plural but "origin and first settlement" in the singular. And he duly addressed emigration, settlement, and the development of the colonies throughout the pamphlet as a single or at least generalizable process.[12]

That common experience of emigration and settlement might have eventuated in nothing more than the creation of thirteen independent peoples rather than one, but the Declaration's course of human events included, of course, a "history of the present King of Great Britain" as "a history of repeated injuries and usurpations, all having in direct object the establishment of an absolute Tyranny over these States." Indeed, as chapter 4 showed, the Declaration's grievances represented common complaints against violations of natural rights, English rights, and American rights that had been instituted in all the colonies as part of common circumstances of emigration and settlement. The history of the origins of the colonies and empire thus had direct bearing on the revolutionary era, as a source of colonists' rights. In addition, the imperative to resist violations of those common rights harnessed the unifying potentialities of the common inheritance, experiences, and memories of emigration, settlement, and development of the colonies, encouraging colonists to act collectively, to the point that the Declaration could describe Americans as "one people" and thereby foreshadow, though by no means predetermine, the "We the People of the United States" who formed "a more perfect Union."

Furthermore, in depicting this course of events, and then by playing its own part in history by arguing for independence, the Declaration invested its one people with even greater potential to develop as both an idea and a real phenomenon in the future. It showed indeed how such a thing was possible according to the laws of nature and God. Its advancement of the concept of popular sovereignty demonstrated that a people could "alter their former Systems of Government" in any way that "to them shall seem most likely to effect their Safety and Happiness." Although a people could only force such a change under the strict natural law confines that the Declaration detailed as the limits to revolution, they could certainly change their system of government in accord with their rulers, and could even alter the terms and scope of their own composition as a people or nation. And the American peoples did precisely that after independence, or at least their leaders depicted their actions that way. Not long after July 4, the Declaration's "one people" became a legendary *E Pluribus Unum* on the new nation's Great Seal. The Articles of Association were eventually replaced by the Articles of Confederation, and finally by the federal Constitution. It took a long and often tortuous course of human events to get from declaring independence to the Constitutional Convention of 1787, and the final conditions for creating a federal union were not in place until ratification of the Bill of Rights in December 1791. But without the common histories of emigration and settlement and the experiences of the reign of King George that the Declaration recounted, and without the "one people" it articulated, the "We the People of the United States" and the federal union they supposedly formed might never have come into existence.

Thomas Jefferson and James Madison exaggerated when they later described the Declaration of Independence as "the fundamental Act of Union of these States," partly because that statement failed to account for the formative history of the British American colonies or the Articles of Association that made the Declaration of Independence possible and to which the Declaration itself alluded—in Jefferson's own draft even more than in the final version. They were thus among the first of many to overinterpret the Declaration as a singular and isolated event rather than as part of a historical process. Furthermore, as they both knew, the nature of the union had been and remained deeply contested long after 1776. That was partly because, although the Declaration helped to enable the continuing development of the one people it identified, it also expressed the historical limitations of the concept. The fact that its circumstances of emigration and settlement originally entailed the creation of thirteen peoples was one of those limitations, and that multiple antiquity of American peoples made its way into the document's language. The final part of the preamble referred to the sufferance of "these Colonies" and the object of establishing an absolute tyranny over "these States," both plurals and beginning with capital letters in the final Declaration. The conclusion declared independence "by Authority of the good People of these Colonies," with "People" undefined as singular or plural but with "Colonies" in the plural. The document referred then to "these United Colonies," the formal title of the union under the Articles of Association—plural, though united. It then transitioned to a language signifying independence but still referred to multiple political entities, referring twice to "Free and Independent States" and once to

"Independent States." The authors also identified themselves as "the Representatives of the united States of America," the lowercase u contrasting with the consistent use of the uppercase S. The document's original July 4 title as written orthographically was "A DECLARATION BY THE REPRESENTATIVES OF THE UNITED STATES OF AMERICA IN GENERAL CONGRESS ASSEMBLED." The August 2 title—"The unanimous Declaration of the thirteen united States of America"—did more to signify the idea of a union, but it kept the lowercase for "united." Far from decisively creating a people and a nation, then, the Declaration's authors were studiously ambiguous, respecting old colonial and new state identities even while attempting to articulate a national identity, trying to forge a new future without getting too far ahead of the course of human events.[13]

This is not surprising as the institution that commissioned and crafted the Declaration saw itself as a product of an original state sovereignty. Both Continental Congresses represented the colonies and states, its members being appointed as delegates to express the will of their assemblies rather than elected as representatives of the people of the colonies or states, much less of the United States. The state sovereignty that was implicit under the Articles of Association was made explicit in the Articles of Confederation. The first article stated, "The Stile of this confederacy shall be, 'The United States of America.'" The union now had a capital U, but the meaning of "confederacy" is clear in the second article: "Each state retains its sovereignty, freedom and independence, and every Power, Jurisdiction and right, which is not by this confederation expressly delegated to the United States, in Congress assembled." And the third article described the nation in similar terms to those of Richard Bland and Thomas Jefferson in describing their confederal empire as a "firm league of friendship." Even then, conflict over the nature of the union as well as over particular issues, notably the matter of some states' western land claims, meant that it took until November 15, 1777, for Congress to agree on the articles, a year and four months after the committee of thirteen submitted its proposals on July 12, 1776: a long time, even considering the numerous moves that Congress had to make to avoid being caught up in the theaters of the War of Independence. It then took more than three more years before Maryland ratified on February 2, 1781, after Virginia offered to cede its western lands to the national government, meaning the articles could finally come into effect on March 1, almost five years after they were first proposed.

Another six years of financial crisis and political instability passed before delegates met to draft a federal constitution in the summer of 1787. Even then, the remit from the Confederation Congress was to revise rather than replace the Articles of Confederation, and the only way to justify defying that institution's representation of the sovereign will of the individual states or their peoples was to invoke a putatively higher sovereign will of the "People of the United States." Even then, the new constitution's national institutions were defined to a great extent by states' rights, especially in the case of the upper house of Congress, with its equal number of senators per state, which in turn affected the composition of the Electoral College and the outcomes of presidential elections. And, after four months of often rancorous debate and near failure, it took another year and a half before the Constitution was ratified by nine states and subsequently implemented, and it took even longer to be ratified by all the states. And ratification required the persuasive powers of the *Federalist Papers* and a promise of what became the Bill of Rights of 1791, including a Tenth Amendment stating that "The powers not delegated to the United States by the Constitution, nor prohibited by it to the States, are reserved to the States respectively, or to the people."

After all that, the question of where the authority of the federal government ended and that of the states began remained open in many areas. Opponents of the Washington and Adams administrations cited states' rights in attempts to forestall debt funding, the creation of a national bank, and the promotion of manufactures, culminating in the Virginia and Kentucky Resolutions in opposition to the Alien and Sedition Acts of 1798. And when northerners began disputing the expansion of slavery in the western territories, southerners increasingly questioned the nature of the supposedly federal union and sovereignty of "We the people of the United States." The state compact theory of John C. Calhoun, and secession itself, owed much to the Declaration's "circumstances of our emigration and settlement here," especially the free state theory, which posited an original sovereign independence of the colonies as states. On the other hand, the unionism of Daniel Webster and Abraham Lincoln also owed much to the Declaration's circumstances of emigration and settlement, but this time to the charter theory, which posited an original central authority over the colonies in the form of the British crown. But the argument begun by Richard Bland in 1766, that John Dickinson engaged with in 1767, and that raged through the literature of the revolutionary era, in the Continental Congresses, and in the Constitutional Convention and ratifying debates was only finally settled, after four years of war, at Appomattox Courthouse in Virginia in April 1865.[14]

While the Declaration of Independence did not advocate for a particular system of government, its principles certainly ruled some forms of government in and others out. Most obviously, the document's history of equality and liberty in a state of nature determined that governments must derive their "just powers from the consent of the governed" and their purpose must be to secure "unalienable Rights" to "Life, Liberty, and the pursuit of Happiness." If God had granted people equality and liberty in state of nature, no earthly power could rightly take them away. And in these laws of nature and God, especially in a people's unalienable rights, inhered an ultimate sovereignty of the people and therefore a right to revolution "whenever any Form of Government becomes destructive of these ends." As John Locke argued, no one "can transfer to another more power than he has in himself; and no Body has an absolute Arbitrary Power over himself, or over any other, to destroy his own Life, or take away the Life or Property of another." No one can therefore, at the point of consenting to government, "subject himself to the Arbitrary Power of another; and having in the State of Nature no Arbitrary Power over the Life, Liberty, or Possessions, of another, but only so much as the Law of Nature gave him for the preservation of himself, and the rest of Mankind; this is all he doth, or can give up to the Common-wealth." And this is "a Power," Locke concluded, "that hath no other end but preservation, and therefore can never have a right to destroy, enslave, or designedly to impoverish the Subjects." Because a government was formed by "the joynt power of every Member of the Society" and "given up to that person, or Assembly, which is Legislator, it can be no more than those persons had in a State of Nature before they enter'd into Society, and gave up to the Community." And government, therefore, "tho' it be the *Supream* Power in every Common-wealth" cannot be "absolutely *Arbitrary* over the Lives and Fortunes of the People."[15]

Popular sovereignty would lie latent during the normal course of events, however, and could only be invoked if and when a long train of abuses and usurpations evinced a ruler's intention to impose absolute despotism.

In ordinary times, though, the laws of nature and God directed, and ultimate sovereignty of the people required, a representative element in government, and so all legitimate governments, at least once they evolved beyond their supposedly typical origins in warrior kingship, had to be republics—including monarchies. But the Declaration's laws of nature and God did not rule out monarchy. As chapter 1 showed, the document's Lockean historiography depicted monarchs as elective, at least originally, and normally appointed by the people for their own protection. And Locke illustrated the ultimate benignity of elective monarchy with claims that it sometimes emerged from familial custom. In "the beginning of things," Locke wrote, "the Father's Government of the Childhood of those sprung from him, having accustomed them to the *Rule of one Man,* and taught them that where it was exercised with Care and Skill, with Affection and Love to those under it, it was sufficient to procure and preserve to Men all the Political Happiness they sought for, in Society." It was thus "no wonder, that they should . . . naturally run into that Form of Government, which from their Infancy they had been all accustomed to; and which, by experience they had found both easie and safe." That, though, being consensual, was no concession to Filmer's version of absolute patriarchy. Looking "back as far as Records give us any account of Peopling the World, and the History of Nations," Locke wrote, "we commonly find the *Government* to be in one hand, yet it destroys not that, which I affirm, (viz.) That the *beginning* of *Politick Society* depends upon the consent of the Individuals, to joyn into and make one Society" and "set up what form of Government they thought fit." It was thus a "mistake" to conclude "that by Nature Government was Monarchical," as "almost all *Monarchies,* near their Original, have been . . . Elective."[16]

The idea of a monarch as benign protector also appeared in the Declaration's general history of humankind and its particular history of British America, at least up to the reign of George III. Even colonial negativity about the house of Stuart really meant Charles I (1625–1649), Charles II (1660–1685), and James II (1685–1688), while William III (1689–1702), Mary II (1689–1694), George I (1714–1730), and George II (1730–1760) were widely celebrated as monarchs, Queen Anne (1702–1714) slightly less so owing to the enduringly controversial creation by Parliament of the colonial post office in 1706. Thomas Jefferson's depiction of the British Empire as a "league & amity" was based on an original Lockean social contract among the settlers and then a secondary one between the settlers' states and the crown as protector. The charter theory of John Dickinson also presumed that Americans enjoyed representation in colonial assemblies and protection under monarchs, or under proprietors in the cases of Pennsylvania and Maryland and under private charters in the cases of Connecticut and Rhode Island, though the private colonies too were ultimately under the authority and protection of the crown. As chapter 3 showed, furthermore, settler imperialism and constitutionalism posited that the crown remained a separate power and monarchs retained extensive powers in the colonies throughout the colonial era. The Declaration's authors, even in the midst of war against George III, edited out any original inference of monarchy being incompatible with liberty. Thomas Jefferson's draft, for example, opened with the necessity for "a people to advance from that subordination in which they have hitherto remained." The committee of five deleted the reference to subordination and inserted "political bands which have connected them with another" in its place, and the Continental Congress accepted the implication of a historical equality and liberty under monarchy. Congress similarly altered the beginning of Jefferson's and the committee's conclusion from stating that George III was unfit to be the ruler "of a people who mean to free" to an evidently historically "free people."[17]

It was indeed only very late in the day that the colonists turned against George III. Long after they suspected that he was attempting to impose an absolute tyranny, colonists continued to petition him to desist or to intercede against Parliament. It was only after war had broken out and the king had answered colonists' petitions with repeated injuries, including a proclamation that they were outside his protection, that the Declaration finally held him singularly responsible for events. And it was specifically King George III at whom the Declaration aimed its ire, and not the institution of monarchy. The reason he was unfit to be the ruler of a free people was not because he was "A Prince" but because his "character" was "marked by every act which may define a Tyrant," as shown by his "history of repeated injuries and usurpations, all having in direct object the establishment of an absolute Tyranny," as demonstrated by the grievances and his ignoring of his subjects' petitions. If the Declaration influenced the United States to become a (nonmonarchical) republic, then, it was because of its recounting of recent historical experience, not because of its pronouncements about equality or liberty.[18]

For some historians, an ideological form of republicanism was latent in Americans even before independence, with relatively widespread distribution of colonial wealth preconditioning them for a more egalitarian society and polity in the new nation. That argument is less prevalent than it used to be, with increased acknowledgment of persisting inequalities in the early United States. It may nonetheless be the case that some were converted to ideological republicanism by Thomas Paine. Paine attributed loyalty to monarchy to "local or long standing prejudices" and argued, in direct contrast to Locke but using the same methodology, that monarchy and heredity defied the laws of nature and God. As well as acknowledging the supposedly just distinctions of rich and poor, and claiming that "Male and female are the distinctions of nature" and "good and bad the distinctions of heaven," Paine identified "another and greater distinction for which no truly natural or religious reason can be assigned, and that is, the distinction of men into *kings* and *subjects*." Paine's antimonarchism was also historical. He pointed out that "In the early ages of the world, according to the scripture chronology, there were no kings," and that "Government by kings was first introduced into the world by the Heathens, from whom the children of Israel copied the custom." Yet, Paine added, "As the exalting one man so greatly above the rest cannot be justified on the equal rights of nature, so neither can it be defended on the authority of scripture, for the will of the Almighty, as declared by Gideon and the prophet Samuel, expressly disapproves of government by kings"—although he also noted, "All anti-monarchical parts of Scripture have been very smoothly glossed over in monarchical governments." That included the almost "three thousand years . . . from the Mosaic account of the creation, till the Jews under a national delusion requested a king. Till then," he said, "their form of government (except in extraordinary cases, where the Almighty interposed) was a kind of republic administered by a judge and the elders of the tribes."[19]

Locke too had pointed out that people lived without monarchs for long periods of time in order to discredit Filmer's claims about kingship descending directly from Adam. Yet that did not preclude monarchy as a rightful part of government either for Locke or for the authors of the Declaration of Independence. What mainly distinguished Paine, then, was opposition to the principle of heredity. "To the evil of monarchy," Paine noted, "we have added that of hereditary succession; and as the first is a degradation and lessening of ourselves, so the second, claimed as a matter of right, is an insult and an imposition on posterity. For all men being originally equals," he argued, "no one by birth could have a right to set up his own family in perpetual preference to all others for ever, and though himself might deserve some decent degree of honors of his contemporaries, yet his descendants might be far too unworthy to inherit them." And, he added, "One of the strongest natural proofs of the folly of hereditary right in kings, is, that nature disapproves it, otherwise she would not so frequently turn it into ridicule by giving mankind an ass for a lion." Though opposing Lockean conclusions about the benignity of limited monarchy, Paine used the Lockean argument that all are born as well as created equal to make his case against heredity. As "no man at first could possess any other public honors than were bestowed upon him, so the givers of those honors could have no power to give away the right of posterity." And "though they might say, 'We choose you for our head,' they could not, without manifest injustice to their children, say, 'that your children and your children's children shall reign over ours for ever.' Because such an unwise, unjust, unnatural compact might (perhaps) in the next succession put them under the government of a rogue or a fool."[20]

Yet some prominent authors of the Declaration, and apparently many other Americans, remained monarchists long after 1776. John Adams had argued in early March 1775, before war broke out, that "we are not a part of the British empire. Because the British government is not an empire." It is, rather, "a limitted monarchy" and thus "much more like a republic than an empire . . . a government of laws, and not of men . . . in which the king is first magistrate. This office being hereditary, and being possessed of such ample and splendid prerogatives, is no objection to the government's being a republic," he explained, "as long as it is bound by fixed laws, which the people have a voice in making, and a right to defend. An empire," however, "is a despotism, and an emperor a despot, bound by no law or limitation, but his own will."[21]

And Adams's monarchism endured long after independence, as is evident during a heated exchange of letters with Benjamin Rush in 1789. Rush had ruefully admitted what he saw as a continuing public admiration of monarchy that he feared might encourage abuse of executive power under the new constitution. "Why should we accelerate the progress of our Government towards monarchy?" he asked, especially as "Every part of the conduct of the americans tends to it." Adams agreed: "That every Part of the Conduct and feelings of the Americans tends to that Species of Republick called a limited Monarchy I agree.—They were born and brought up in it.—Their Habits are fixed in it." And "I also, am as much a Republican as I was in 1775." Then, apparently paraphrasing *Common Sense*, which Adams later called "a poor, ignorant, malicious, short-sighted, Crapulous mass," he noted, "I do not 'consider hereditary Monarchy or Aristocracy as Rebellion against Nature.' on the contrary I esteem them both Institutions of admirable Wisdom and exemplary Virtue, in a certain Stage of Society in a great Nation." They were, he said, "The only Institutions that can possibly preserve the Laws and Liberties of the People. and I am clear that America must resort to them as an Asylum against Discord Seditions and Civil War and that at no very distant Period of time. . . . I think it therefore impolitick," he added, "to cherish Prejudices against Institutions which must be kept in View as the Hope of our Posterity." He qualified himself, but only slightly, by adding, "I am by no means for attempting any Such thing at present.— Our Country is not ripe for it, in many respects and it is not yet necessary but our ship must ultimately land on that shore or be cast away." Adams may have overstated his position out of apparent irritation with Rush, but it is remarkable that one of the main authors of the Declaration would make such claims over a decade after independence and so soon after taking office as the first vice president of the American Republic.[22]

If the Declaration of Independence did not make a natural law or historical case against monarchy, the recent experience it described nevertheless augured changes in the operations of executive power in the new states and nation. The "history of the present King of Great Britain" as "a history of repeated injuries and usurpations" not only discouraged the resurrection of monarchy in the new United States, it brought about new checks and balances aimed at limiting the powers of future governors and presidents. As the last chapter showed, the crown exercised extensive powers in the colonies, including those of proroguing and dissolving legislatures and suspending and vetoing legislation: powers that, as the Declaration's grievances alleged, George III repeatedly abused. Neither the Articles of Association nor the Articles of Confederation created separate executive offices or powers, and new states initially either abolished the executive branch of government altogether or else subjected governors to election or appointment by assemblies, and substantially diminished their powers. The states that initially abolished separate executives all later revived them, however; and when the Constitutional Convention created the presidency of the United States in 1787, it resorted to colonial tradition, creating an executive as a separate power with separate powers.

Yet the political leaders of the United States ultimately decided on an entirely different solution to the problem of executive abuse of power that the English and British had adopted after 1688, reflecting their differing experiences and memories of the Glorious Revolution. As noted previously, the British answer was the absorption of most royal prerogative into the legislature in the form of the crown-in-Parliament. For colonists, however, the Glorious Revolution had simply restored colonial property rights and self-government under assemblies and limited monarchy. That did not require or result in any principle of coordination in colonial America. There were no governors-in-the-assemblies in any of the American colonies, and to that extent those colonies retained the constitutional characteristics of the English seventeenth century, with separate executive and legislatures with distinct responsibilities and powers. Indeed, while the colonists eventually blamed the king for abusing what they believed were his prerogatives in his different realms, they also believed that collusion between the king and Parliament was part of the problem. When the new states and the new United States restored executive offices, then, they ensured that they were separate powers—that governors and presidents were elected and appointed distinctly from houses of the legislatures, and that they had separate powers or responsibilities as well. In these respects, the modern differences of the U.S. presidential system and the British parliamentary system are institutionalized legacies of different experiences and memories of the Glorious Revolution. The U.S. Constitution is widely thought to be more modern than the British one, and, in the sense of being explicitly based on the sovereignty of "We the People," that is true—although contemporaries believed that all previous legitimate governments had been implicitly based on that principle. But in the separation of the executive and legislative branches of government that the federal Constitution and all revised state constitutions restored, the American political system continued to operate and still operates on a pre–Glorious Revolution basis.[23]

The retention of a separate and empowered executive, however, did not mean that the United States became "a monarchy without a king," as one historian has argued. The limits on presidential powers, inscribed into a written constitution—most especially advice and consent, the override of the veto, powers of impeachment and removal, and above all quadrennial elections—make the American presidency different from Locke's elective monarchy or any kind of kingship. Indeed, no president of the United States could or can do what George III did—as long as the principles of the Declaration of Independence and the laws of the Constitution are upheld. So, although the United States obviously did become a republic, it is the checks and balances against executive power rather than republicanism per se that are the real legacies of one king's "history of repeated injuries and usurpations" as portrayed in the Declaration.[24]

If the Declaration's principles of government did not require the new nation to be a nonmonarchical republic, neither did they require it to be a democracy, at least as we understand the term today. "Democracy" often then signified an estate—the people as the democracy—as distinct from the aristocracy and monarchy. If the word referred to a political system, it signified the direct rule of the people, evoking either happy images of ancient Greece or New England towns, or the less happy prospect of conflict in larger, more diverse states, and certainly in an extended polity such as a United States would be. In this respect, then, the Declaration's principles were antidemocratic—lawlessness being contrary to the laws of nature and God, which directed that government should secure a people's lives, liberty, property, safety, and happiness. Early state constitutions nevertheless instituted forms of government that would count as democratic by later standards, at least in terms of government structure if not in terms of electoral inclusiveness. The most famous example was Pennsylvania's of 1776, which created a state government comprising an annually elected unicameral legislature whose acts would not take effect unless passed a second time, following an election, thereby creating a kind of lawmaking by plebiscite. Subsequently, however, states, including Pennsylvania, extended the periods between elections, and restored upper houses of assembly and governors with vetoes and other executive powers. And the Philadelphia Convention did the same when it drafted the federal Constitution in 1787.

John Adams certainly favored a more complex and remote form of government. He authored his "Thoughts on Government" in response to a request from North Carolina delegates who, in the spring of 1776, were considering their own state's new constitution, though he subtitled the work more generally as "Applicable to the Present State of the American Colonies." He described "the end of government" as "the happiness of society," just as "the happiness of the individual is the end of man." And "From this principle it will follow, that the form of government, which communicates ease, comfort, security, or in one word happiness to the greatest number of persons, and in the greatest degree, is the best." Citing "Sidney, Harrington, Locke, Milton, Nedham, Neville, Burnet, and Hoadley," he stated that "there is no good government but what is Republican," and he added, "the very definition of a Republic, is 'an Empire of Laws, and not of men.'" Adams agreed that representation was necessary for a republic as "the best of governments," but he also stated that the "particular arrangement of the powers of society, or in other words that form of government, which is best contrived to secure an impartial and exact execution of the laws, is the best of Republics."[25]

For Adams, though, happiness and the rule of law were not possible under simple representation alone. Like any other branch of government, a legislature had to be checked and balanced. Thus "A REPRESENTATION of the people in one assembly being obtained, a question arises whether all the powers of government, legislative, executive, and judicial, shall be left in this body? I think a people cannot be long free, nor ever happy, whose government is in one Assembly." He then gave six reasons why. First, because "A SINGLE Assembly is liable to all the vices, follies and frailties of an individual." The next two reasons cited "the vices of avarice and ambition for perpetual power," and the next described representative assemblies as "unfit to exercise the executive power, for want of . . . secrecy and dispatch" and as "still less qualified for the judicial power; because it is too numerous, too slow, and too little skilled in the laws." Finally, "a single Assembly, possessed of all the powers of government, would make arbitrary laws for their own interest, execute all laws arbitrarily for their own interest, and adjudge all controversies in their own favour."[26]

On these grounds, Adams rejected not only government by a legislature alone but also by a unicameral legislature. He argued that "the legislative power ought to be more complex" than that to obviate the legislature and executive opposing each other to the point of war and usurpation by "the strongest." He therefore advocated a "distinct Assembly . . . as a mediator between the two extreme branches of the legislature, that which represents the people and that which is vested with the executive power." This

"Council" would advise the executive and be elected by the representative house, but "should have a free and independent exercise of its judgment, and consequently a negative voice in the legislature," as had been the case in Massachusetts from 1692 to 1774. The two "integral parts of the legislature" should "by joint ballot choose a Governor, who, after being stripped of most of those badges of domination called prerogatives, should have a free and independent exercise of his judgment, and be made also an integral part of the legislature." Still, potential legislative encroachment on executive prerogative "shews the necessity . . . of giving the executive power a negative upon the legislative." The "Governor should have the command of the militia, and of all your armies," with "pardons" by the Governor and Council, and "JUDGES, Justices and all other officers, civil and military, should be nominated and appointed by the Governor, with the advice and consent of Council." Even so, "the judicial power ought to be distinct from both the legislative and executive, and independent upon both, that so it may be a check upon both, as both should be checks upon that." Judges "should not" therefore "be distracted with jarring interests" or "be dependant upon any man or body of men," and so "should hold estates for life in their offices, or in other words their commissions should be during good behaviour, and their salaries ascertained and established by law."[27]

Otherwise, Adams advocated annual elections for representatives, councilors, and the governor on the "maxim" that "'Where annual elections end, there slavery begins.'" He also promoted rotation in office for all officials except judges. Notwithstanding his belief in the ultimate sovereignty of the people and these partial concessions to democratic practice, Adams's "Thoughts on Government" aligned with structures implemented in the later state constitutions and in the federal Constitution that checked and balanced the powers of the people. There has been a long debate over the relationship between the Declaration and the U.S. Constitution, with some arguing that the Constitution embodied the democratic principles of the Declaration and that the two founding documents were therefore similar to each other, and others arguing that the Constitution betrayed the democratic principles of the Declaration and the two founding documents were therefore distinct. In fact, while the Constitution certainly embodied the Declaration's principle of popular sovereignty, the form of government it created also reflected the Declaration's antidemocratic implications.[28]

Nor did the Declaration's principles necessitate democracy in the modern sense that all adult citizens should have the vote. The "public," after all, was then considered only part of, and the only enfranchised part of, the "demos." Indeed, elements of the Declaration's social contract theory militated against universal suffrage. Today, we regularly conflate the general principle of consent of the governed with the particular right of individuals to vote, and thus consider the franchise a natural right rather than a social one, even though the word *franchise* originally signified something handed down by a higher authority. Although some argued for a natural right to vote in the early modern era, the prevailing beliefs were that only those who were presumed to have a stake in society and who were independent of the will of others should be enfranchised. Both criteria were widely thought to require ownership of property, as well as the supposed virtues of masculinity. And some believed that enfranchising people with little or no property would tempt them to violate the rights of others by voting to redistribute their estates and other possessions. Universal suffrage was therefore thought by many to be inimical to the security of property. Hence many colonies retained the English requirement of ownership of a forty shilling freehold or equivalent personal property to qualify to vote, and all retained some form of property qualification. And many states would retain the same, or at least a taxpaying requirement, long after independence. But the most prevalent anti-enfranchisement argument in the later eighteenth century was based on personal independence as conferred by property ownership, and it was most famously expressed in William Blackstone's *Commentaries on the Laws of England.* In a passage that Alexander Keyssar notes was "repeated endlessly during the revolutionary era," Blackstone stated that the "true reason" for property qualifications for voting "is to exclude such persons, as are in so mean a situation, that they are esteemed to have no will of their own. If these persons had votes, they would be tempted to dispose of them, under some undue influence, or other," giving "a great, an artful, or a wealthy man, a larger share in elections, than is consistent with general liberty." Hence "all popular states have been obliged to establish certain qualifications, whereby, some who are suspected to have no will of their own, are excluded from voting," in favor of "those whose wills may be supposed independent."29

Though remembered as a democrat, Thomas Jefferson agreed with Blackstone. When Jefferson described "Those who labour in the earth" as "the chosen people of God . . . whose breasts he has made his peculiar deposit for substantial and genuine virtue," he was imagining such persons as landowners rather than as the white tenants, indentured servants, laborers, or free or enslaved African Americans who together constituted a majority of the Chesapeake population and who worked far more of its land than the minority of landowning yeoman farmers did. Hence he was able to state that "Corruption of morals in the mass of cultivators is a phenomenon of which no age nor nation has furnished an example. It is the mark set on those, who," looking "to their own soil and industry, as does the husbandman, for their subsistence, depend for it on the casualties and caprice of customers." On the other hand, dependence, which he saw as characteristic of urban industrialism, despite its prevalence in the Chesapeake as well, "begets subservience and venality, suffocates the germ of virtue, and prepares fit tools for the designs of ambition." This was the basis for his plea to "let our workshops remain in Europe," but it was also the rationale for limiting the franchise to freeholders. Jefferson's vision for an extension of the franchise thus depended on the wider distribution of western lands.[30]

John Adams explicitly opposed extending the franchise in a May 1776 letter to John Sullivan, an advocate of abolishing property qualifications. Adams agreed that "It is certain in Theory, that the only moral Foundation of Government is the Consent of the People. But," he asked, "to what an Extent Shall We carry this Principle?" After pointing out the impossibility of every person consenting to every piece of legislation, he argued that those "who are wholly destitute of Property, are also too little acquainted with public Affairs to form a Right Judgment, and too dependent upon other Men to have a Will of their own." Thus, by giving "to every Man, who has no Property, a Vote," he further asked, "will you not make a fine encouraging Provision for Corruption by your fundamental Law? Such is the Frailty of the human Heart, that very few Men, who have no Property, have any Judgment of their own. They talk and vote as they are directed by Some Man of Property, who has attached their Minds to his Interest." Adams's answer to the problem of political representation was therefore similar to Jefferson's: to encourage wider property ownership rather than extend the vote to those without property. "Harrington has Shewn that Power always follows Property," Adams argued, and "We may advance one Step farther and affirm that the Ballance of Power in a Society, accompanies the Ballance of Property in Land." Thus "The only possible Way . . . of preserving the Ballance of Power on the side of equal Liberty and public Virtue, is to make the Acquisition of Land easy to every Member of Society: to make a Division of the Land into Small Quantities, So that the Multitude may be possessed of landed Estates."[31]

Adams also made the Pandora's box argument against extending suffrage, and it was one that undercut any natural rights case for extension as it posited that demands for the vote would be perniciously endless. "The same reasoning which will induce you to admit all men who have no property, to vote, for those Laws, which affect the Person," he informed Sullivan, "will prove that you ought to admit Women and Children: for generally Speaking, Women and Children, have as good Judgment, and as independent Minds as those Men who are wholly destitute of Property: these last being to all Intents and Purposes as much dependent upon others, who will please to feed, cloath, and employ them, as Women are upon their Husbands, or Children on their Parents." And so, he reiterated, it is "dangerous to open So fruitfull a Source of Controversy and Altercation. . . . There will be no End of it. New Claims will arise. Women will demand a Vote," he repeated. And, he added, "Lads from 12 to 21 will think their Rights not enough attended to," and "every Man, who has not a Farthing, will demand an equal Voice with any other in all Acts of State." That kind of equal voice, he argued, "tends to confound and destroy all Distinctions, and prostrate all Ranks, to one common Levell."[32]

Adams had already revealed his anti-egalitarianism in his famous exchange of letters with his wife in March–April 1776. Abigail Adams added a woman's voice to calls for independence and to advocacy for aspects of new governance and law. "I long to hear that you have declared an independency," she told her husband, and "in the new Code of Laws which I suppose it will be necessary for you to make," she added, "I desire that you would Remember the Ladies, and be more generous and favourable to them than your ancestors." She then made a claim for a form of women's equality by adding, "If perticuler care and attention is not paid to the Laidies we are determined to foment a Rebelion, and will not hold ourselves bound by any Laws in which we have no voice, or Representation." Her husband responded by acknowledging the tumult around him. "We have been told that our Struggle has loosened the bands of Government every where," he observed. "That Children and Apprentices were disobedient," he continued, and "that schools and Colledges were grown turbulent—that Indians slighted their Guardians and Negroes grew insolent to their Masters. But your Letter," he added, "was the first intimation that another Tribe more numerous and powerfull than all the rest were grown discontented."[33]

He was confident of retaining patriarchal control of the course of human events, however, and determined to do so. "Depend upon it," he replied,

"We know better than to repeal our Masculine systems. Altho they are in full Force, you know they are little more than Theory. We dare not exert our Power in its full Latitude. We are obliged to go fair, and softly, and in Practice you know We are the subjects. We have only the Name of Masters," he concluded, "and rather than give up this, which would compleatly subject Us to the Despotism of the Peticoat, I hope General Washington, and all our brave Heroes would fight." Even Abigail Adams had not requested the overthrow of the masculine system, however, and did not demand anything as substantive as suffrage. In fact, what she requested was the further institutionalization of patriarchy, or at least paternalism. Expressing a form of gender essentialism, she observed, "That your Sex are Naturally Tyrannical is a Truth so thoroughly established as to admit of no dispute." She thus asked that it be "put it out of the power of the vicious and the Lawless to use us with cruelty and indignity with impunity," urging her husband to "Regard us . . . as Beings placed by providence under your protection and in immitation of the Supreem Being make use of that power only for our happiness."[34]

Nor did it occur to Thomas Jefferson that the Declaration's ideas about equality and liberty should lead to civil equality or liberty for women. Jefferson apparently considered women to be among the "all men" who were created equal, judging by the undiscriminating references to "men" in his comments on a slave trade that violated the lives, liberties, and happiness of as many women as it did men. Yet the Declaration had stated that the king had "dissolved Representative Houses repeatedly, for opposing with manly firmness his invasions on the rights of the people," and Jefferson had written in his draft that "manly spirit bids us to renounce forever" American attachment to the British (though that was removed for reasons previously explored). Jefferson thus articulated the common notion that the capacity for defending liberty was masculine. That in turn helps explain his belief that women did not belong in politics or in the public sphere at all. While president, he wrote, "The appointment of a woman to public office is an innovation for which the public is not prepared, nor am I." He later observed that nature had "marked infants and the weaker sex for the protection, rather than the direction of government." On the women he saw in politics in France, he wrote to George Washington that he was thankful that in Virginia, women's roles did not "extend beyond the domestic line," which he apparently turned a blind eye to at Monticello and elsewhere in Virginia. And, in his observations on Native Americans, he wrote that "women are submitted to unjust drudgery. This I believe is the case with every barbarous people. With such, force is law. The stronger sex therefore imposes on the weaker. It is civilization alone," he therefore argued, "which replaces women in the enjoyment of their natural equality." Jefferson's ideas that women were created equal but were not equal and that their "natural equality" entitled them to civil inequality demonstrate again that when the founders used the word *equal,* it did not mean what we think it means.[35]

The idea of voting as a natural right that followed from the Declaration's natural right of consent to be governed was rarely more than ambiguously advanced, at least by political elites. When the Constitutional Convention debated voting rights, one of the most powerful advocates of extension was Benjamin Franklin. Yet even he couched his arguments in terms of earned and civil rights rather than inherent and natural ones. "It is of great consequence that we shd. not depress the virtue & public spirit of our common people, of which they displayed a great deal during the war, and which contributed principally to the favorable issue of it," Franklin agued. "He related," as James Madison recalled, "the honorable refusal of the American seamen who were carried in great numbers into the British Prisons during the war, to redeem themselves from misery or to seek their fortunes, by entering on board the Ships of the Enemies to their Country." Franklin was also reported by others to have attacked property restrictions for voting by positing, "Today a man owns a jackass worth fifty dollars and he is entitled to vote; but before the next election the jackass dies. The man in the meantime has become more experienced, his knowledge of the principles of government, and his acquaintance with mankind, are more extensive, and he is therefore better qualified to make a proper selection of rulers—but the jackass is dead and the man cannot vote." Franklin then concluded with an implicit—though notably not explicit—natural rights argument: "Now gentlemen, pray inform me, in whom is the right of suffrage? In the man or in the jackass?"[36]

Yet Gouverneur Morris, the framer who drafted the claim that the new government was ordained and established by "We the People of the United States" and thus wrote the idea of the consent of the governed and the sovereignty of the people into the Constitution's preamble, firmly believed that only freeholders should be enfranchised. "The aristocracy will grow out of the House of Representatives," he argued, if votes were given "to people who have no property" and who "will sell them to the rich who will be able to buy them." "The time is not distant when this Country will abound with mechanics & manufacturers who will receive their bread from their employers. Will such men be the secure & faithful Guardians of liberty? Will they be the impregnable barrier agst. aristocracy?" James Madison agreed that "the freeholders of the Country would be the safest depositories of Republican liberty. In future times," he predicted, "a great majority of the people will not only be without landed, but any other sort of, property. These will either combine under the influence of their common situation; in which case, the rights of property & the public liberty, will not be secure in their hands: or which is more probable, they will become the tools of opulence & ambition, in which case there will be equal danger on another side." Madison nevertheless felt that the extent of voting rights was best left to the states to decide, and the Constitutional Convention concurred.[37]

At that point, however, few states had significantly extended voting rights. In 1776, Pennsylvania allowed all taxpaying men to vote for delegates to its constitutional convention, as did Massachusetts in 1779, although only the former retained this limited extension of the franchise. By the time of the first federal elections in 1788, twelve years after independence, not a single state offered universal manhood suffrage—eleven still had property requirements, and only Pennsylvania and New Hampshire (from 1784) allowed all taxpaying men to vote. New Hampshire dropped the taxpaying requirement in 1792, becoming the first of the original thirteen states to adopt universal male suffrage (albeit following Vermont, which joined the Union in 1791). The next to do so were Maryland and South Carolina in 1810, and then New York in the year of the semicentennial. New Jersey and Connecticut followed, in 1844 and 1845, and Virginia and North Carolina as late as 1850 and 1854. Massachusetts retained a taxpaying requirement until 1891, Delaware until 1897, and Georgia, Pennsylvania, and Rhode Island until the Twenty-Fourth Amendment to the Constitution was passed in 1964. The Northwest Ordinance of 1787 included a fifty-acre freehold requirement for voting, although none of new western states afterward retained a property requirement, and only a few required tax paying, many soon adopting suffrage for all white men, but only white men.[38]

New Jersey's 1776 constitution had allowed all propertied inhabitants of the state to vote, but legislation forbade women from voting after 1807. No state allowed women to vote again until Wisconsin in 1877, and women were finally guaranteed a federal right to vote only with passage of the

Nineteenth Amendment in 1920, almost a century and a half after independence and despite the invocations of the Declaration of Independence in the Seneca Falls Declaration of Sentiments of 1848. Furthermore, the same legislation that ended women's suffrage in New Jersey in 1807 did the same to Black men. Eleven of the original thirteen colonies had no racial restrictions on suffrage, but seven of them explicitly banned free Black men from voting after independence. Delaware extended the vote to taxpaying white men and introduced a ban on free Black men from voting in the same year, 1792. Connecticut abolished its property requirement for white men in 1817 and abolished voting rights for free Black men in 1818. New York imposed a $250 freehold property qualification exclusively on Black men from 1821. Kentucky and Tennessee, though both slave states, initially had no race restrictions on voting but then banned free Black men from voting in 1799 and 1834, respectively. Vermont maintained Black male suffrage, but all the other new states restricted voting to white men only. The Fifteenth Amendment of 1871 was supposed to resolve the matter when it stated: "The right of citizens of the United States to vote shall not be denied or abridged by the United States or by any State on account of race, color, or previous condition of servitude," and the Voting Rights Act of 1965 was supposed to close the loopholes of Jim Crow. Yet the struggle for voting rights and other forms of equality continues today.[39]

The Declaration of Independence changed the course of human events in significant ways. Its persuasive argument and rhetoric helped win the War of Independence and thereby found a new nation. It thus helped create the early American chronology we are familiar with today—a British colonial past, an American revolutionary era, and the founding of a republic. Its new and unique civics lessons have perhaps helped the United States survive to this day, although recent events remind us that there is no guarantee of its indefinite survival. The Declaration is, by these high standards, one of the most significant achievements in human history.

Yet many today hold the Declaration to even higher and in fact impossible standards. It did not, as some have claimed, create a people or a nation all by itself but was instead part of a historical process of nation formation that both preceded and postdated it. Nor did it establish the first government in human history to be founded on the consent of the governed and for the securing of unalienable rights to life, liberty, and the pursuit of happiness but, by its own reckoning, it merely advocated instituting the latest of such governments. Nor did it ground a government on the basis of equality for all. Its idea that all are created equal applied to self-sovereignty and access to property in a state of nature. In civil society, the equality and liberty of individual sovereignty would be sacrificed for the collective sovereignty of the people as a whole. That still implied a form of equality in that the people would ultimately retain a sovereign right of a majority to overthrow a government that was manifestly and deliberately tyrannical, but otherwise people would submit to a supreme magistrate, usually a monarch. Although the Declaration helped create a republic, it was only because it recounted the historical experience of one bad king, not because of any ideological antipathy to monarchy. Each member of a civil society was also equal to all the others and to the people as a whole in possessing certain unalienable rights to life, liberty, and the pursuit of happiness that their government was entrusted to secure. But other rights, including the right to vote, would be distributed unequally in accordance with supposed individual competences as defined by property ownership, gender, and, for some, race. Even unalienable rights were only unalienable during the act of consenting to be governed and for as long as citizens obeyed the law. Those who broke the social contract by committing crimes against others might, by due process of law, forfeit life, liberty, and property by execution, imprisonment, and fines, depending on the severity of their offenses.

And it was the very purpose of government to establish legal differentiations among its people and to deprive enemies within of their unalienable rights. For the Declaration's authors did not intend to establish a "natural rights republic" that gave equal reign to all individuals but rather a *natural law republic* in which each person would be subject to inequalities and to limits on their freedoms for the greater good of all—for the sake of a commonwealth. The Declaration indeed was not a manifesto for individual rights but for "the Right of the People" as a whole. And, as the next chapter shows, it was not a manifesto for "all men" or women. For if "the Right of the People" included protection from internal threats such as lawlessness or excessive empowerment of the demos, it also included protection from the "rest of mankind," those who had not subscribed to their social contract. That meant Britons, other foreign enemies, and others closer to home, such as those engaged in "domestic insurrections" and "the inhabitants of our frontiers."

6

The Rest of Mankind

We must, therefore, acquiesce in the necessity, which denounces our Separation, and hold them, as we hold the rest of mankind, Enemies in War, in Peace Friends.

The Declaration of Independence is commonly remembered for its pronouncements of the equality and unalienable rights of "all men." Yet its principal purpose was to help establish the independence of one people from another. And to justify that act, it concerned itself, from its introduction to its conclusions, with the founding of governments and of peoples who thereby distinguished themselves from "the rest of mankind." The document's opening words identify a moment "in the Course of human events" when "it becomes necessary for one people to dissolve the political bands which have connected them with another, and to assume among the powers of the earth, the separate and equal station to which the Laws of Nature and of Nature's God entitle them." It states straight afterward that its purpose is to "declare the causes which impel" that "one people" to that "separation." The preamble then goes back to the beginning of time, when "all men are created equal," but only in order to describe the unalienable rights they aim to secure when "Governments are instituted among Men"—the process by which individuals in a state of nature first form a society or people and then constitute themselves as a particular nation by consenting to be governed. The document then describes "the Right of the

People" to alter or abolish any government that has become destructive of its ends before describing the sufferance of "these Colonies" and the necessity of separation caused by the king attempting to establish an absolute tyranny over "these States." All the grievances are predicated on the notion that the colonists were distinct peoples with their own governments. Some were explicit about that. The seventh grievance complains that the king had restricted the "population of these States," and the thirteenth also indicates that "these Colonies" or indeed "States" were already distinct political communities by accusing the king of combining "with others to subject us to a jurisdiction foreign to our constitution, and unacknowledged by our laws." The conclusion refers to reminders to the British people of how Americans had become distinct peoples initially, before becoming "one people" through "the circumstances of our emigration and settlement here."

The Declaration's general history of humankind and its particular history of the American colonies and American Revolution thus focus on the constituting of distinct peoples. And that past and present segued into a future in which Americans would not only be distinct peoples but an independent nation. The king's dismissal of colonists' petitions and British deafness "to the voice of justice and of consanguinity" finally forced Americans to "acquiesce in the necessity, which denounces our Separation, and hold them, as we hold the rest of mankind, Enemies in War, in Peace Friends." Immediately after that, the Declaration's authors made the most emphatic statement of separateness of all:

> We, therefore, the Representatives of the united States of America, in General Congress, Assembled . . . do, in the Name, and by Authority of the good People of these Colonies, solemnly publish and declare, That these United Colonies are, and of Right ought to be Free and Independent States; that they are Absolved from all Allegiance to the British Crown, and that all political connection between them and the State of Great Britain, is and ought to be totally dissolved.

And in a future as "as Free and Independent States," they would "have full Power to levy War, conclude Peace, contract Alliances, establish Commerce, and to do all other Acts and Things which Independent States may of right do."

For the final Declaration of Independence, the committee of five and the Continental Congress both enhanced and moderated Thomas Jefferson's original accounts of the separateness of peoples and of the American people. The drafting committee altered his introductory "a people" to a more specific "one people," and his "change" to a more specific "separation." Congress retained the alterations and the substitution of "equal & independant station" for "separate and equal station" among the powers of the earth. Jefferson may have used "independant" to distinguish a fuller future break with Britain than a past in which the colonies had already been "separate" in the sense of being self-governing under the British crown. The committee and Congress seemed to feel, however, that such subtle distinctions were unnecessary at this point, and may have decided to match the future fact of a "separate" status with the act of "separation" referred to at the end of the introduction. Neither the committee nor Congress made any significant changes to the preamble's depictions of the origins of nations or of the American colonies except that both the Dunlap broadside of July and the Matlack version of August capitalized the word "States" in both the preamble and the seventh grievance. On the other hand, in the conclusion, the committee altered Jefferson's reference to warnings to the British people "of attempts by their legislature to extend a jurisdiction over these our states" to "an unwarrantable jurisdiction," indicating that the British Parliament had some jurisdiction in the colonies. And Congress moderated the passage further by substituting "over these our states" with "over us," and it deleted Jefferson's and the committee's explanation of "the circumstances of our emigration here" and thus their free state theory of the origins of the colonies—although, as chapter 2 showed, it otherwise hinted at an original independence of the American peoples.

The drafting committee toned down and Congress eliminated much of Jefferson's denunciations of the British people for failing to remove "from their councils the disturbers of our harmony" and of having instead "by their free elections re-established them in power," perhaps deeming it best to avoid alienating the British people more than necessary in the hope they might eventually turn against their rulers and become friends "in Peace" sooner rather than later. The future would nevertheless be one in which Britain and the United States would be separate nations, as the final section of the conclusions reiterated. It was perfectly clear, then, that the former colonies would in the future be "Free and Independent States" with "full Power to levy War, conclude Peace, contract Alliances, establish Commerce, and to do all other Acts and Things which Independent States may of right do."

Establishing independence from Britain entailed war against other peoples, too. One of the final five grievances, concerning the conflict then raging, was that the king was "transporting large Armies of foreign Mercenaries to compleat the works of death, desolation and tyranny, already begun." Jefferson's original conclusion had also complained of the king deploying not only "soldiers of our common blood" but also "Scotch & foreign mercenaries to invade & deluge us in blood." The committee changed "deluge us in blood" to the slightly less emotive "destroy us," and Congress deleted the charge entirely. This may have once again been for diplomatic reasons, but it is also worth adding that Jefferson's representation of Scottish people as "foreign" was somewhat anachronistic. Scottish people may, in Jefferson's terms, have been historically not of "our" English or Welsh "common blood," but since the 1707 Act of Union and abolition of the Scottish parliament, they had been members of a single British nation and equal participants in its empire.

But there were yet other enemies. The final Declaration's final grievance stated that the king "has excited domestic insurrections amongst us, and has endeavoured to bring on the inhabitants of our frontiers, the merciless Indian Savages, whose known rule of warfare, is an undistinguished destruction of all ages, sexes and conditions." It thereby identified three more peoples, besides Britons and Hessian mercenaries, who were at war against American independence and who were not therefore among the Declaration's "one people": Loyalists, enslaved African Americans, and Native Americans (the position of free African Americans varied, as shown in the previous chapter and below). The grievance was set in the present moment of the Revolutionary War, but, as this chapter will show, it had profound implications for the future that were grounded in the past and the present: in the laws of nature and God and in a course of human events that would rationalize the alienation of these peoples' natural rights in the new nation.

The position of Loyalists changed from members to nonmembers of American political communities as a direct consequence of the Declaration of Independence. It is well known that the final grievance referred to enslaved people and Native Americans, but it seems likely that the reference to "domestic insurrections" included Loyalists too. The final grievance was a distillation of three that featured in Jefferson's original, the first of which read that the king "has incited treasonable insurrections in our fellow-subjects, with the allurements of forfeiture & confiscation of our property."

The committee changed "fellow-subjects" to "fellow-citizens" but otherwise left it as it was when it submitted its draft to Congress. In portraying Loyalists as "our fellow" subjects or citizens, Jefferson, and especially the committee, once again emphasized that the colonies had been separate political communities before independence. Furthermore, defining their actions as "treasonable insurrections" signified an assumption that colonists' first loyalty was supposed to be to those colonial communities rather than to a British one, and that colonial polities had a constitutional right to insist on such a primary allegiance. And Loyalists' present breaking of past allegiance would have consequences for the near future, in the form of loss of life in war, confiscation of property, and expulsion.

These violations of their natural rights did not contradict the principles of the Declaration of Independence, however. Loyalists had supposedly alienated their natural and previous civil rights by failing to subscribe to a new social contract and by fighting against the course of human events that the Declaration depicted. They thus represented a mortal danger to the "one people" the emerging governments of the United States were duty-bound to protect and on this ground could be divested of their lives, liberties, estates, and happiness in accordance with the laws of nature and God, in particular the first of those laws—of self-preservation. As Locke had explained, if any member of a political community were to "disclaim the lawful Government of the Country he was born in, he must also quit the Right that belong'd to him by the Laws of it, and the Possessions there descending to him from his Ancestors, if it were a Government made by their consent." In any case, Loyalists were supposedly free to pursue their happiness elsewhere, as countless dissenting peoples in history had done before, including some of the now Loyalists' ancestors when they emigrated to America.[1]

The other enemies identified in the final grievance would see their rights violated far more egregiously still. They also would prove to be more intractable and longer-term problems for the future United States. While Loyalists either left U.S. territory permanently or later returned and reintegrated, enslaved people remained "domestic" enemies and Indigenous people remained "inhabitants of our frontiers," and this chapter therefore focuses on the latter groups. Once again, the grievance identified a moment in the present when enslaved people and Native Americans were particularly dangerous antagonists. But that moment cannot be detached from the past, or indeed from a course of human events that linked the past and present to the future. First, the slave trade had rendered Africans and their enslaved descendants distinct from the "one people" forged by "our" emigration and settlement here, and rendered these distinct peoples a part of the "rest of mankind." They were also "Enemies in War" with the Declaration's "one people," according to contemporary concepts of slavery under the laws of nature and of nations—a war that escalated when the king excited enslaved people into "domestic insurrections amongst us."

Again, the first law of nature and God required the suppression of enslaved people unless the war somehow abated. Some believed a truce could be called through emancipation and the incorporation of formerly enslaved people into the Declaration's "one people." Others, however—not least the principal author of the Declaration of Independence himself—believed that Black people were created equal in the senses of possessing self-sovereignty and property rights in a state of nature but were nevertheless so unequal in other respects that they could not live freely among white people, and that future emancipation would have to be accompanied by expatriation. The failure to eradicate slavery after the American Revolution was therefore not only attributable to economic interests and the ideology of property rights. The impulse to enslave was in fact more deeply embedded in the Declaration's ideology than we are accustomed to thinking, and the imperative to emancipate less so.

Second, the circumstances of "our" emigration and settlement "here" had clearly rendered Native Americans distinct from the "one people" those circumstances forged. Those circumstances included the presumption that North America was in a state of nature and therefore open to European migration and settlement, according to the laws of nature and God. The wars and land purchases that followed were part of what made Europeans into Americans, and were rationalized again by the necessities of self-defense. And if Native Americans west of the Appalachians remained so-called "Savages," inhabitants of a state of nature, then the circumstance of emigration and settlement of the colonies would repeat themselves after 1776—except that the U.S. government would lay claim to and assist in the resettlement of western lands more actively than any British government had ever done.[2]

The final grievance is often abstracted from analyses of the rest of the Declaration, as if its sentiments contradicted a document that otherwise chartered the equality and natural rights of "all men." As this chapter shows, however, the passage in fact harmonized perfectly with the sentiments of a document that, as originally written and read, chartered the safety and happiness of "one people" against anyone among "the rest of mankind" who might in the future course of human events threaten that one people's lives, liberties, property, and happiness.

Thomas Jefferson enslaved around two hundred people at the time he drafted the Declaration of Independence, and at least 607 during the course of his life. He was far from alone. Among the fifty-six signers of the Declaration, forty-one either were or had been enslavers, as were other prominent founders, not least George Washington. Critics then were as willing as many are today to point out the apparent hypocrisy, one example being Samuel Johnson, who famously asked the obvious question: "How is it that we hear the loudest yelps for liberty among the drivers of Negroes?" Johnson's question was rhetorical, but there was an answer of sorts, and it lay in contemporary perceptions of the laws of nature and God combined with the course of human events. We can begin to find that answer by looking at Jefferson's draft Declaration.[3]

The king, Jefferson alleged in the last of his original grievances,

> has waged cruel war against human nature itself, violating it's most sacred rights of life & liberty in the persons of a distant people who never offended him, captivating & carrying them into slavery in another hemisphere, or to incur miserable death in their transportation thither. this piratical warfare, the opprobrium of infidel powers, is the warfare of the CHRISTIAN king of Great Britain. determined to keep open a market where MEN should be bought & sold, he has prostituted his negative for suppressing every legislative attempt to prohibit or to restrain this execrable commerce: and that this assemblage of horrors might want no fact of distinguished die, he is now exciting those very people to rise in arms among us, and to purchase that liberty of which he has deprived them, & murdering the people upon whom he also obtruded them; thus paying off former crimes committed against the liberties of one people, with crimes which he urges them to commit against the lives of another.

It is clear, then, that Jefferson and the other members of the committee of five, who submitted the passage intact to Congress on June 28, considered Africans and their American descendants as among the "all men" who were "created equal" and "endowed by their Creator with . . . unalienable Rights" to "Life, Liberty and the pursuit of Happiness." The passage refers to Africans and their American descendants three times as "people" and once as "MEN," the latter in emphatic capitals in Jefferson's draft—and Jefferson was not a habitual user of uppercase letters—and with a capital M in the version submitted by the drafting committee. The king had thus conducted a "cruel war against human nature itself" that violated "it's most sacred rights of life & liberty in the persons of a distant people." The references to "warfare of the CHRISTIAN king of Great Britain" and "the opprobrium" even "of infidel powers" confirm their view that this "execrable commerce" and "assemblage of horrors" violated the laws of nature and God.[4]

As is well known, however, Jefferson's tirade was edited out of the final Declaration for a number of possible reasons. One may have been its blatantly supply-side bias that blamed the king alone for the slave trade and erased colonial settlers' demand for the cheap labor that underlay the fortunes of many of the founders, including Jefferson's. Jefferson later implicitly admitted the role of American demand in the slave trade when he stated that the passage was struck out because South Carolinians and Georgians wished to continue importing Africans. Another possible reason for the elision, though, was that, if the clause blamed Americans for slavery at all, then it held New England merchants, as slave traders, more responsible than, say, Chesapeake tobacco planters and South Carolina rice planters who had subsequently purchased the people "obtruded" on them and enslaved their children. Whatever the precise reason for it, Jefferson regretted the ultimate exclusion of the passage, no doubt sincerely. As noted previously, he had written in 1774 that the "abolition of domestic slavery is the great object of desire in those colonies, where it was unhappily introduced in their infant state. But previous to the enfranchisement [emancipation] of the slaves we have, it is necessary to exclude all further importations from Africa" and to effect what he believed to be abolition's necessary corollary—expatriation. He thus lamented, as he would in the first and the final grievance of the Declaration, that "our repeated attempts to effect" an end to slave trading "by prohibitions, and by imposing duties which might amount to a prohibition, have been hither to defeated by his majesty's negative."[5]

Yet the passage was not quite the "vehement philippic against negro slavery" that John Adams and many historians since have claimed that it was.

First, if "the circumstances of our emigration and settlement here" established Americans as free peoples and eventually helped them reformulate themselves as "one people," that only served to distinguish European arrivals in America from Africans who arrived enslaved. And for Jefferson, the "distant people" of Africa and their descendants retained their distantness and differentness after arrival in America, and with terrible repercussions. Second, the slave trade itself was not the real grievance but was a context for what remained in the final Declaration: that the king (or Virginia governor Dunmore and others) "has exited domestic insurrections amongst us." The comments on the slave trade thus merely highlighted the king's hypocrisy in later "exciting those very people" whom he had enslaved "to rise in arms among us, and to purchase that liberty of which he has deprived them, & murdering the people upon whom he also obtruded them"—the actual substance of the grievance. Third, the passage was not an attack on the slave trade per se but on the illegal conduct of it as allegedly practiced by George III and his predecessors. The slave trade was a legal business, after all. As John Locke stated, slaves, "being Captives taken in a just War, are by the Right of Nature subjected to the Absolute Dominion and Arbitrary Power of their Masters." Jefferson would later support the abolition of all slave trading to the United States, but when he referred to the trade as "a *cruel* war" against "a distant people who *never offended him*," as "*piratical* warfare," and as a series of "*crimes committed* against the liberties of one people," he was not referring to slave trading in general. Rather, he was making a legal point, alleging that the particular practices of the Royal African Company and other agents empowered by the king were not part of a "just war" as described by Locke and before him by the jurist Hugo Grotius, and therefore were not in accord with the laws of God, nature, and nations. And some of those other nations, notably the Netherlands, France, and Spain, were still trafficking human beings—often legally—and an attack on slave trading in general might have alienated them and harmed the cause of American independence. In any case, the Declaration was a legalistic document, and as such could only expose the king's illicit activities. Any attack on the slave trade would have to target illegal trafficking only.[6]

Furthermore, one of the reasons for the claim that enslaved people had been somehow "obtruded" by the king on unwilling or unwitting colonists may have been the imperative to deny American aiding and abetting the crimes Jefferson described. Even if that plea of innocence were plausible, though, and it clearly was not, the continuing enslavement of the descendants of the original victims of the slave trade still represented, at least prima facie, a crime against the laws of nature and God that stated all are born as well as created equal and free. Locke had written that, under natural law, a man, "not having the Power of his own Life, *cannot*, by Compact, or his own Consent, *enslave himself* to anyone, nor put himself under the Absolute, Arbitrary Power of another, to take away his Life, when he pleases." That was distinct, however, from enslavement as a result of a just war. "*Slaves*, who being Captives taken in a just War, are by the Right of Nature subjected to the Absolute Dominion and Arbitrary Power of their Masters," Locke wrote. However, whatever "Engagements or Promises any one has made for himself, he . . . *cannot*, by any *Compact* whatsoever, bind *his children* or Posterity. For his Son, when a Man, being altogether as free as the Father, any *act of the Father can no more give away the liberty of the Son*."[7]

Jefferson himself acknowledged the principle that all are thus born free. Five years before independence, Jefferson had acted as a lawyer for Samuel Howell, who was suing for his freedom on the grounds that his mother's mother had been an indentured servant and not enslaved, and therefore he should have inherited free status according to the law of *partus sequitur ventrem*. Yet Jefferson argued more broadly: "Under the law of nature, all men are born free, every one comes into the world with a right to his own person, which includes the liberty of moving and using it at his own will. This is what is called personal liberty, and is given him by the author of nature, because necessary for his own sustenance," and "Under that law [of nature], we are all born free." Jefferson appeared therefore to believe that American slavery, as a heritable condition, violated the "most sacred rights of life & liberty" as surely as did the illegal version of the Atlantic slave trade allegedly practiced by George III. The court appears to have disagreed, however, as Jefferson lost the case.[8]

For Jefferson, though, there were two resolutions to the problem of hereditary slavery—two ways to rationalize the enslavement of descendants of victims of the slave trade. One was to regard enslaved people collectively, rather than individually. Hence perhaps the draft passage began by referring to violations against the lives and liberties of "the persons of a distant people" rather than persons as individuals. Hence also the stress on warfare throughout the passage—something that can only happen between people collectively, not between individuals—the "cruel war" and "piratical warfare" the king had waged via the slave trade, but above all the warfare the king had incited them into against the colonists. His "exciting" the enslaved "to rise in arms among us, and to purchase that liberty of which he has deprived them, & murdering the people upon whom he also obtruded them," or his "exciting domestic insurrections amongst us," distinguished African Americans as well as their African forbears as a different people and confirmed that they were a people at war with the Declaration's "one people," or indeed, as the final grievance put it, against "us."[9]

In these respects, Jefferson's original passage was less a philippic against the Atlantic slave trade than it was a defense of American slavery. It was certainly not the kind of "positive good" proslavery that would become prominent in the antebellum era, and Jefferson maintained throughout his life that slavery was antithetical to the laws of nature and God, except in certain circumstances, and had everyday ill effects on both enslavers and enslaved people that could lead to the erosion of republican principles, even the destruction of republics, as well as to domestic insurrections. Yet slavery was still war, and as long as enslaved people collectively represented a threat of violence, then the first law of nature, self-preservation, rationalized the enslavement of one people by another. The final grievance was therefore not a contradiction of the rest of the Declaration but represented, for Jefferson and many of the founders, the contingencies of the course of human events and the complexities of the laws of nature and God. George III had "obtruded" enslaved people on "us" and then excited them into domestic insurrections, and so the colonists had a natural right and even duty to defend themselves. When Jefferson wrote in 1820 to John Holmes of the continuation of slavery that "we have the wolf by the ear, and we can neither hold him, nor safely let him go, justice is in one scale, and self-preservation in the other," he was not contradicting but repeating the conditional proslavery position of the Declaration of Independence.[10]

Jefferson wrote that letter in the middle of the Missouri Crisis, some forty-four years after independence and with the abolition of slavery a seemingly more distant prospect than ever. Yet for Jefferson, the process of emancipation would inevitably be long because he believed it required a gradual expatriation of those born after the beginning of the process, their numbers replaced by white immigrants and their former owners compensated from the sale of western lands. And in Jefferson's argument for the necessity of expatriation lay his second justification for the enslavement of those who were born as well as created free and equal: race. Jefferson raised the possibility of a more immediate emancipation when he asked, rhetorically, in his *Notes on the State of Virginia*, "Why not retain and incorporate the blacks into the state, and thus save the expence of supplying, by importation of white settlers, the vacancies they will leave?" He began his answer historically, but with a past that bore upon the future. "Deep rooted prejudices entertained by the whites; ten thousand recollections, by the blacks, of the injuries they have sustained," he wrote, "will divide us into parties, and produce convulsions which will probably never end but in the extermination of the one or the other race." For Jefferson, then, the course of human events militated against immediate emancipation.[11]

But almost all of Jefferson's answer focused on what he called "the real distinctions which nature has made," for, while Jefferson believed that Black people were created equal in terms of rights of self-sovereignty and property, he did not believe they were equal to whites in other ways. The first inequality he claimed to identify was "that of colour," calling it "the foundation of a greater or less share of beauty in the two races"—a judgment that led him to his infamous remark about the sexual preferences of Black people. But what really made Black people incapable of membership in America's "one people," for Jefferson, was what he saw as their intellectual deficiencies, including an inability to analyze history. Judging "them by their faculties of memory, reason, and imagination," he wrote, "it appears to me, that in memory they are equal to the whites; in reason much inferior." He continued, "never yet could I find that a black had uttered a thought above the level of plain narration." In other words, Jefferson believed that Black people were incapable of one the most fundamental elements of good citizenship—the ability to analyze the course of human events according to the laws of nature and God. According to him, they could never therefore understand the foundations of government and never be incorporated "into the state." For Jefferson, then, they were and would forever be, as Peter Onuf described it, "a separate nation."[12]

While Jefferson believed that emancipation must eventually happen, he nevertheless maintained that Black people must remain enslaved until expatriated. The many incapacities he alleged in his *Notes on the State of Virginia*, not least the laziness and consequent poverty and likely criminality of Black people, would lead to the race war and extermination he feared. Freedom would also lead to race mixing and therefore the supposed degradation of the white race—something he persistently preached against even as he practiced it. Once again, though, it was Jefferson's inability to see Black people as intellectual equals that accounts for his conditional proslavery. While Jefferson thought that Black people were incapable of the kind of reasoning that would result in legitimate revolution, he also believed them incapable of the kind of prudence that would result in due sufferance. He knew that Black people understood the injustice of their enslavement, as he acknowledged in his frequently expressed fears of insurrection, including in his draft Declaration of Independence. For him, however, that danger was heightened by Black people's concept of justice and injustice doing "more honour to the heart than the head," as he said of the letters of Ignatius Sancho. He described Sancho's "imagination" as "wild and extravagant," escaping "incessantly from every restraint of reason and taste," his "trail of thought as incoherent and eccentric" and free from "sober reasoning," and so "we find him always substituting sentiment for demonstration." And Jefferson rated Sancho in "first place among those of his own colour." It seems likely, then, that for Jefferson, Black rebellion would amount to mindless violence rather than reasoned actions in accordance with the laws of nature and God.[13]

Jefferson even appears to have believed that Black people were not only inferior but also a different species of human being. He momentarily equivocated on this matter toward the end of Query XIV of *Notes on the State of Virginia*, expressing reluctance to "degrade a whole race of men from the rank in the scale of beings which their Creator may perhaps have given them" without sufficient evidence, and he thus regretted that Black people had "never yet been viewed by us as subjects of natural history." He therefore advanced "a suspicion only, that the blacks, whether originally a distinct race, or made distinct by time and circumstances, are inferior to the whites in the endowments both of body and mind." Yet Jefferson had in previous pages provided copious argument, and what he believed to be powerful evidence, that Black people were in fact inferior. In any case, that was hardly a controversial view among whites, especially among enslavers. Jefferson's real if slightly disguised question, then, was not whether Black people were inferior, but whether "they were originally a distinct race or made distinct by time and circumstances." Unlike the racism he expressed, though, that question was controversial, as Anglo-American religious and scientific orthodoxy held that all human beings were descended from

Adam and Eve. Jefferson may have thus used the pretext of lack of scientific knowledge, alongside the uncharacteristic absence of clarity of expression in this passage, to avoid answering or even asking the question directly.[14]

Yet his answer to his question of whether Black people were "originally a distinct race, or made distinct by time and circumstances," lies in his other writings. At the beginning of Query XIV, he described color as "fixed in nature," and Jefferson elsewhere expressed his belief that no form of flora or fauna had changed its nature since Creation, that what God had created had never altered, evolved, or even become extinct. If Jefferson believed that Black people were inferior, then he must have believed they were created that way. And, toward the end of his comments on race and slavery, he asserted, "It is not against experience to suppose, that different species of the same genus, or varieties of the same species, may possess different qualifications." In other words, he argued for polygenesis, even while avoiding an explicit commitment to it. And he also must have believed that the laws of nature not only justified the continuation (though not the perpetuation) of slavery not only for reasons of self-protection but also because nature and God had rendered Black people immutably inferior to white people. They were still people and were thus created equal in the Lockean senses of possessing self-sovereignty and equal access to the earth in a state of nature. But, for Jefferson, they were nevertheless created aesthetically, morally, and intellectually unequal, and eternal and unchanging natural law therefore directed that they should be treated unequally under civil government and law if, in the course of human events, they were somehow "obtruded" on their superiors.[15]

There were, of course, many contemporaries who took a very different view from Jefferson, not only on polygenesis but even on slavery itself. Among the committee of five, for example, John Adams never enslaved anyone, although he and Abigail hired enslaved people as household servants in Philadelphia in the 1790s and he never spoke publicly against the practice. Benjamin Franklin had enslaved people, but later turned more publicly against the institution. Nevertheless, as a founder of the Society for the Relief of Free Negroes Unlawfully Held in Bondage, he implicitly conceded that some people *were* lawfully held in bondage. More significant were the Black founders—African Americans who used the context of the American Revolution to fight against enslavement and thereby expand the meanings of liberty. Among their number were the enslaved people who petitioned the Massachusetts Assembly for their liberty in the mid-1770s. Even then their arguments began modestly, with appeals based more on their own particular predicaments rather than on the injustice of enslavement per se. One of the earlier petitions, from 1773, asked for that "ample relief which, as men, we have a natural right to." And yet instead of asking for immediate abolition or even manumission, or full incorporation into the state, it suggested that the authors be allowed to work one day a week to acquire the means to purchase themselves and then move to "some part of the Coast of Africa." And the petition concluded that "since the wise and righteous governor of the universe, has permitted our fellow men to make us slaves, we bow in submission to him, and determine to behave in such a manner as that we may have reason to expect the divine approbation of, and assistance in, our peaceable and lawful attempts to gain our freedom." The unnamed petitioners thus promised "to submit to such regulations and laws, as may be made relative to us, until we leave the province." In other words, while the petitioners saw no racial justification for their continuing enslavement, as Jefferson did, they accepted a supposed practical necessity for its temporary continuation and saw that as consistent with the laws of nature and God. Or at least they accepted the political reality that others saw things that way and so worked within the limits of possibility offered by the then prevailing ideology.[16]

The 1774 petition was more assertive. It was written for "those, who, by divine permission, are held in a state of Slavery, within the bowels of a free and Christian Country"—an ambiguous title that seemed to concede that slavery was allowed under the laws of God and yet also seemed to posit a contradiction with a civil norm of freedom. It also stated that "your Petitioners apprehend we have in common with all other men a naturel right to our freedoms without Being depriv'd of them by our fellow men as we are a freeborn Pepel and have never forfeited this Blessing by aney compact or agreement whatever," and described the slave trade as at least sometimes illegal, with "sum of us stolen from the bosoms of our tender Parents and from a Populous Pleasant and plentiful country" or "unjustly dragged by the cruel hand of power." It also argued that slavery violated civil law, stating that "the laws of the Land . . . doth not justifi but condemes Slavery." And it referenced the idea that all are born free, for "if there had bin aney Law to hold us in Bondage we are Humbely of the Opinion ther never was aney to inslave our children for life when Born in a free Countrey." And its request that "an act of the legislative to be pessed that we may obtain our Natural right our freedoms and our children be set a lebety at the yeare of twenty one" without colonization elsewhere was certainly more than Thomas Jefferson would have allowed and was more than the previous petitioners had asked for.[17]

The 1777 petition, however, was considerably more assertive. Prince Hall and others titled their entreaty "The petition of A Great Number of Blackes detained in a State of Slavery in the Bowels of a free & christian Country," this time unambiguously and as if that were a self-evident contradiction. They even pointed explicitly at their enslavers' hypocrisy, describing themselves as "Brought hear Either to Be sold Like Beast of Burthen & Like them Condemnd to Slavery for Life—Among A People Profesing the mild Religion of Jesus" and "in Violation of Laws of Nature and off Nations And in defiance of all the tender feelings of humanity." Furthermore, taking notice of events that had happened since the previous petition, they complimented the "Lawdable Example of the Good People of these States" in their own fight for liberty, but also expressed frustration at the failure to include the truly enslaved in the struggle, stating that "your petitiononers have Long and Patiently waited the Evnt of petition after petition By them presented to the Legislative Body of this state and cannot but with Grief Reflect that their Success hath ben but too similar they Cannot but express their Astonishment that It has Never Bin Consirdered that Every Principle from which Amarica has Acted in the Cours of their unhappy Deficultes with Great Briton Pleads Stronger than A thousand arguments in favowrs of your petioners." The reference to long and patiently waiting for responses to "petition after petition" echoed the reference in the Declaration of Independence to the king answering the colonists' "repeated Petitions" only with "repeated injury." That, as noted previously, represented proof of the king's intent on absolute tyranny and was thus the final part of the colonists' case for revolution. There was also a powerful warning in the petitioners comparing themselves to American revolutionaries as "Not Insensible of the Secrets of Rational Being Nor without spirit to Resent the unjust endeavours of others to Reduce them to a state of Bondage and Subjection."

The three petitions together thus reveal a profound shift in thinking about the essence of liberty—away from the view that the laws of nature and God sometimes allowed enslavement in civil law, if necessitated by the course of human events, and toward the view that the laws of nature and

God always and unconditionally forbade enslavement. The shift was not from complete acceptance of slavery to complete rejection, though. The first petitioners presumed that even enslaved people had some civil rights, as the act of petitioning itself implied a kind of enfranchisement in, if not full membership of, a political community. The third petitioners asked for "an act of the Legislatur to be past Wherby they may Be Restored to the Enjoyments of that which is the Naturel Right of all men" but only asked in practice that "their Children who wher Born in this Land of Liberty may not be heald as Slaves after they arive at the age of Twenty one years" rather than for immediate abolition. Yet the shift in emphasis is clear, and so is the direction of travel. And the journey would soon reach its end, at least in the state of Massachusetts, where the Supreme Court would accept the new and radical argument that natural equality and liberty should extend to all who wished to be members of a commonwealth.[18]

In 1780, Massachusetts adopted a new constitution that stated in its Article I, "All men are born free and equal, and have certain natural, essential, and unalienable rights; among which may be reckoned the right of enjoying and defending their lives and liberties; that of acquiring, possessing, and protecting property; in fine, that of seeking and obtaining their safety and happiness." Of course, several earlier state constitutions had included bills of rights to the same effect, and the preamble of the Massachusetts constitution contained the usual provisos that a social contract secures the rights only of those who are party to it. Yet Elizabeth Freeman, enslaved and a woman, decided she was sufficiently included in the "social compact, by which the whole people covenants with each citizen," that the Massachusetts constitution's Article I should set her free. She then recruited antislavery lawyer Theodore Sedgwick to go to court to have her enslavement by John Ashley (at whose home the Suffolk Resolves were most likely written) annulled. In 1781, though, the court avoided judgment on the legality of slavery generally by freeing her on the grounds of technical issues with Ashley's title to her.

Two years later, however, antislavery arguments from *Brom and Bett v. Ashley* were cited in the Quock Walker case. The latter began as a series of civil suits, with Walker charging that Nathaniel Jennison had reneged on previous promises that he be freed, and that Jennison had then violently and illegally recaptured him after he absconded. Jennison countersued those who had housed Walker during his absence for depriving him of his property—John and Seth Caldwell, brother of James, who had been Walker's earlier enslaver but who had promised him his freedom. In 1783, though, the Commonwealth of Massachusetts prosecuted Jennison for assault and battery. Chief Justice William Cushing's advice to the jury, however, went beyond the details of the case and addressed "the doctrine of slavery" more generally. It began by describing the institution as a British colonial "usage" and arguing that "a different idea has taken place with the people of America, more favorable to the natural rights of mankind," wherein "all men are born free and equal—and that every subject is entitled to liberty, and to have it guarded by the laws, as well as life and property—and in short is totally repugnant to the idea of being born slaves. This being the case," he continued, "I think the idea of slavery is inconsistent with our own conduct and Constitution." Cushing argued further that there was a "natural, innate desire of Liberty, with which Heaven (without regard to color, complexion, or shape of noses—features) has inspired all the human race." He thus concluded that "there can be no such thing as perpetual servitude of a rational creature, unless his liberty is forfeited by some criminal conduct or given up by personal consent or contract." He thereby accepted the idea of slavery as a punishment for a crime, as the later Thirteenth Amendment would, and even as an individual choice, but he rejected any collective racial justification for slavery.

No less an authority than the chief justice of Massachusetts thus accepted the idea that universal equality and liberty should apply under civil law and government, that every "subject" was entitled to liberty under the laws and Constitution, not just "all men" in a state of nature. This advice to a jury did not make slavery illegal in Massachusetts, but it did make it impossible to maintain as it withdrew the support that enslavers always need from the state. Consequently, slavery ended in Massachusetts much more quickly than it did in states that legislated for gradual emancipation. And this moment in the course of human events followed from that fundamental shift in thinking about the relationship of natural law to civil law initiated and developed by the Massachusetts petitioners of 1773–1777.[19]

That shift seems to have had other and opposite effects elsewhere, however. Just four years after the Quock Walker case concluded, the framers at the Philadelphia Convention did not include the words that all men are created or born equal and entitled to unalienable rights to life, liberty, and the pursuit of happiness when they drafted a new constitution. Now that one state had deemed that universal equality and liberty applied not only in a state of nature but in civil society too, there was a danger that this idea might be applied as civil law across the newly federal Union. Instead, the Constitution encapsulated the Declaration's more traditional and broader natural law precept that allowed the securing of the unalienable rights of one people at the expense of those of others if supposedly necessitated by the course of human events.

Indeed, that Constitution supported slavery. Its preamble, for example, stated: "We the People of the United States, in Order to form a more perfect Union, establish Justice, insure domestic Tranquility, provide for the common defence, promote the general Welfare, and secure the Blessings of Liberty to ourselves and our Posterity, do ordain and establish this Constitution for the United States of America." Insuring "domestic Tranquility" and providing "for the common defence" included preventing or repressing slave insurrections. Hence Article I, Section 8, empowered Congress "To provide for calling forth the Militia to execute the Laws of the Union, suppress Insurrections and repel Invasions," and Article 4, Section 4, promised that the "United States shall guarantee to every State in this Union a Republican Form of Government," which included protecting "each of them against Invasion" and, "on Application of the Legislature, or of the Executive (when the Legislature cannot be convened) against domestic Violence." The Constitution also secured enslavers' property by means of the fugitive slave clause and subsequent legislation, and the three-fifths clause that gave slave states a bigger voice in revenue bills and regulation of interstate commerce, all of which originated in the House of Representatives. And the three-fifths clause increased enslaver representation not only in the people's chamber but also in the Electoral College, helping to elect southern slaveholding presidents for forty of the first forty-eight years of the federal republic.

As David Waldstreicher has shown, all of the above not only enhanced the economic and political power of enslavers but also made slavery a national institution—as especially did the requirement of Article IV, Section 1, that "Full Faith and Credit shall be given in each State to the public Acts, Records, and judicial Proceedings of every other State." Northern states might abolish slavery within their own borders, but they remained under the authority of federal laws and powers that protected it, as confirmed by the Fugitive Slave Acts of 1793 and 1850, passed under the authority of the Constitution's fugitive slave clause. Abolitionists might increasingly use new interpretations of the Declaration of Independence as a civil charter for natural rights, as shown in this book's postscript, but they faced opposition from originalists, who saw it as a charter for natural law that sometimes overrode natural rights.[20]

Furthermore, the Constitution might only temporarily protect enslavers' economic interests by preventing but then allowing the federal abolition of the slave trade, but it protected them more permanently with another matter of interpretation. The slave trade clause stated, "The Migration or Importation of such Persons as any of the States now existing shall think proper to admit, shall not be prohibited by the Congress" before 1808. Had "Migration" been interpreted as referring to internal movement, Congress would have had the power to prohibit the interstate as well as the international slave trade. James Madison and others, however, interpreted migration and importation as one and the same, and as applying only to transatlantic and not to domestic slave trading. That interpretation allowed slavery to spread rapidly through slave sales across the Southwest even while forbidden in the Northwest. In the meantime, the enslaved population of the United States rose from just over half a million in 1776 to four million by 1865. As Adam Rothman has pointed out, the Declaration of Independence did not set the United States on a course to abolition. In fact, an original interpretation of the Declaration combined with the protections of a proslavery constitution allowed enslavement to thrive for nearly nine decades after independence.[21]

The section of the final grievance regarding enslaved people and domestic insurrections during the then present war against Britain was thus grounded in the past and had implications for the future—in a long course of human events as defined by the laws of nature and God. It was the same for the next section of that same grievance, this time regarding Native Americans.

The language on Native Americans in the Declaration's final grievance read, "He has . . . endeavoured to bring on the inhabitants of our frontiers, the merciless Indian Savages, whose known rule of warfare, is an undistinguished destruction of all ages, sexes and conditions." This passage, with its brutally racist language and allegations, is often seen as out of line with the rest of a text that supposedly emphasized the equality and natural rights of all men. Yet its meanings are in fact embedded in the document's concepts of the laws of nature and God, its general history of humankind, especially its ideas about the state of nature, and its particular history of colonial British America, beginning with "the circumstances of our emigration and settlement here" and culminating in the War of Independence. Indeed, the most fundamental of those circumstances, the one that allowed for all the others, was that "here" was a state of nature at the time the first migrants arrived, a purported wilderness inhabited only by "Savages." As so-called "Savages," Native Americans were deemed not to own the land they occupied as personal property and to own only little of it as communal territory. Those lands were therefore deemed open and available to those who would exercise dominium and imperium over them. This theory of property and the colonizing practices that followed from it were ancient. The ideology rested in part on the biblical injunction, in Genesis 1:28, that people should have dominion over the earth and every living thing, encouraging the notion of a God-given right to expropriate lands from those who did not exercise the colonizers' idea of dominion or imperium. The notions of *res nullius* had negated Indigenous peoples' claims to their land since the expansion of the Roman Empire, either by *terra nullius* (nonoccupancy) or by *vacuum domicilium* (occupancy without legitimate use and title). As numerous historians have shown, these ideas were later adapted as a "doctrine of discovery" to justify the European colonization of America and the expropriation of Indigenous peoples' lands after 1492. And it justified the removal and killing of Indigenous people if they failed to cooperate.[22]

Lockean historiography aligned with this settler-colonial ideology. As John Locke famously wrote, "In the beginning all the World was *America*": that is, America was mostly part of "the common stock of mankind" and open to European settlement and use. As Locke claimed, "There are still *great Tracts of Ground* to be found, which . . . *lie waste*, and are more than the People, who dwell on it, do, or can make use of, and so still lie in common." "There cannot be a clearer demonstration of any thing," he continued, "than several Nations of the *Americans* . . . are rich in Land, and poor in all the Comforts of Life; whom Nature having furnished as liberally as any other people, with the materials of Plenty, *i.e.* a fruitful Soil, apt to produce in abundance, what might serve for food, rayment, and delight; yet for want of improving it by labour, have not one hundredth part of the Conveniencies we enjoy: And a King of a large and fruitful Territory there feeds, lodges, and is clad worse than a day Labourer in *England*." Because Native Americans had no individual possession of land and no money, they had little need of society and almost none of government. The "*Kings* of the *Indians* in *America*," Locke thus wrote, "are little more than *Generals of their Armies;* and though they command absolutely in War, yet at home and in time of Peace they exercise very little Dominion, and have but a very moderate Sovereignty."[23]

According to the settler-imperial literature explored in chapter 2, English and British settlers occasionally recognized Native Americans' territorial rights and thus purchased lands from them, though for the most part they did not, and therefore fought wars for those lands whenever Native Americans stood their ground. Hence the sacrifices of "blood and treasure" frequently mentioned in that literature and that Thomas Jefferson mentioned in his draft elaboration of the Declaration's "circumstances of our emigration and settlement here." Those circumstances also account for other aspects of the final grievance. First, it was through the history of European-Indian wars that settlers learned to think of Native Americans as "merciless . . . Savages, whose known rule of warfare, is an undistinguished destruction of all ages, sexes and conditions." And it was also those "circumstances of our emigration and settlement here" that made Native Americans "the inhabitants of our Frontiers"—frontiers that had moved westward to the Appalachian Mountains during the colonial era and would continue on to the Mississippi River and the Pacific Ocean after independence. The Declaration of Independence thus indicated once again, this time in relation to Indigenous Americans, that past and present practices would continue in the future.

As Craig Yirush has shown, Lockean settler-colonial ideology was a part of Anglo-American political economy from early on, and this earlier literature gave meaning to the Declaration's historic "emigration and settlement here" and the document's mention of current war with "merciless Indian Savages," and gave impetus to the future movement of "our frontiers." The 1684 Virginia House of Burgesses' petition to the king against Lords of Trade oversight of their legislation protested that settlers had "Aduentured" their "Liues, fortunes and all that are deare to us" in "Inhabiting a Barbarous and Malancholy part of the world" and facing "the Incursions . . . and depredations of a skulking, Cruell, inhumane . . . Enemie." Edward Rawson's 1691 *The Revolution in New-England Justified* recounted Reverend John

Higginson's testimony that the earliest settlers "had for more than sixty years had the possession and use of" Massachusetts lands "by a twofold right warranted by the word of God. 1. By a right of just occupation from the grand charter in *Genesis*" and "2. By a right of purchase from the Indians, who were native inhabitants, and had possession of the land before the English came hither," and therefore "that from the beginning of these plantations our fathers entered upon the land, partly as a wilderness and *Vacuum Domicilium*, and partly by the consent of the Indians."[24]

As that testimony indicates, settlers sometimes conquered lands by violence and at other times purchased them—hence the "blood and treasure" argument for the colonists' own property rights against English claims. Rawson himself argued that the king's claim to native peoples' lands by conquest "was clearly against *Jus Gentium & Jus Naturale*, which instructs every man . . . that shall violently, and without just cause take from the infidels their lands . . . does them manifest injury." By contrast, he claimed that "first Planters in *New-England*" were not "willing to *wrong the Indians in their property*" and "purchased from the natives their right to the soil." Jeremiah Dummer's *Defence of the New-England Charters* stressed the dangers emigrants and settlers faced after they had "arriv'd at an Inhospitable Shore and a waste Wilderness" and "found themselves inevitably engag'd in a War with the Natives. So that by Fatigue and Famine, by the Extremity of the Seasons, and by a War with the Savages, the first Planters soon found their Graves, leaving the young Settlements to be perfected by their Survivors." Also, Elizabeth I had not conquered or purchased any American lands, and so settlers had either "purchas'd it with their money" or else claimed "*derelict Lands*," of which there were plenty, as Indians "liv'd chiefly on Fish and Fowl, and Hunting."[25]

Connecticut clergyman John Bulkley probably gave the most detailed British American account of American rights arising from wars against Native Americans and purchases from them in his 1725 argument against crown attempts to protect Mohegan rights to land from settler encroachment. Bulkley cited "that Great Man Mr. *Lock*" to make a case that "Two Things" established property rights—"Either the *Law of Nature*, or *Positive Laws* or Constitutions . . . Regulating or Determining the matter of *Property*," arguing that Native Americans could claim "here and there a *few spots of*" land by the former but none by the latter. He even quoted Locke: "*Thus* says he, *this Law of Reason makes the* Deer *the* Indians *who has Kill'd it, tis allow'd to be his Goods, who has bestow'd his Labour upon it,*" but a "*Right of Property in Land particularly* . . . can't be of great Extent during mens continuance *in this State* [of Nature] at least so long as they continue their Simple, Mean, Inartful way of Living, are mainly fed and cloth'd with *Roots, Fish, Fowl, Deer, Skins,* &c." Native Americans made "very little use . . . of the Earth further than to walk upon it," however, so American land mostly "lay *in Common* and was Equally the Right of *every Man.*" Bulkley also quoted "*Gen.* 1.28" to argue "that *Cultivating and Subduing the Earth, and having Dominion* are joyned together," and therefore inhabitants of a state of nature could not possess land beyond whatever they applied individual labor to. Again, though, he relied mostly on Locke to argue that extended territories could only be rightly claimed by "*Those* says that Worthy Person—before mentioned, *who are United into one Body, and have a Common, Establish'd Law and Judicature to Appeal to, with Authority to Decide Controversies arising between them, and Punish Offenders, are in Civil Society one with another.*" Of Native Americans, Bulkley asked, "Who that is not a Stranger to them will say the aforementioned Essentials of a state of Civil Policy are to be found among them? that they have any Established, Settled, common Law" or, quoting Locke again, "a known, Indifferent Judge with Authority to determine differences according to this Established Received Law?"[26]

Bulkey admitted the "undoubted Truth, that the *Aborigines of this Country,* some or all of them had Right to *Lands* in it," and "so is it equally certain that of what Extent soever it was it arose from one of these Two Things, *viz.* Either the *Law of Nature,* or *Positive Laws* or Constitutions of their own (Tacit or Express) Regulating or Determining the matter of *Property,* one or other of these must give them what they had." But, answering arguments that Mohegans had "entred into Communities, and by Compact, and at least Tacit Constitutions of their own, settled the matter of Property," Bulkley claimed that even "the making of one Person a King, and another a Subject simply in it self, will not make a Right of Property" if he was no more than king of a state of nature. As the English were thus "*the first* (of Civiliz'd Nations)" to make a "*Discovery of the Country, they had* . . . *an Undouted Right to Enter upon and Impropriate all such parts of it as lay Wast or Unimproved by the Natives and this without any consideration or allowance made to*" them. Settlers had for "*Prudential Considerations*" paid "*Gratuities* under the Notion of their being a Price for Lands; yet all such Lands being like the Ocean it self, *Publici vel Communis juris,* they could be under no Obligation from the Head of Justice."[27]

Conflict with Native Americans was a distant memory for most eastern seaboard colonists by the Revolutionary era. Yet, while their writings about the place of Native Americans in the process of settlement carried less urgency than those of some of their forebears, the issue retained its place in early revolutionary histories of the founding of the colonies. James Otis wrote in 1764 that "Our fore-fathers" had secured American lands by "hard labour on their little plantations" and by having "defended themselves against the frequent incursions of the most inhuman Salvages, perhaps on the face of the whole earth." Richard Bland in 1766 referred to "*North America*" before 1607 as an "uncultivated and almost uninhabited Country," thereby evoking the idea that it was not only largely vacuum domicilium but almost terra nullius. James Wilson was similarly dismissive, referring to pre-European America as "a wilderness, inhabited only by savage men and savage beasts." Johns Adams's 1774–1775 *Novanglus Letters* argued that America "was not a conquered, but a discovered country." It thus "came not to the king by descent, but was explored by the settlers. It came not by marriage to the king, but was purchased by the settlers of the savages. It was not granted of the king by his grace, but was dearly, very dearly earned by the planters, in the labor, blood, and treasure which they expended to subdue it by cultivation."[28]

The Boston Massacre orators popularized the idea that Massachusetts was once in a state of nature and that their forebears had fought for it or bought it from its Indigenous occupants. In 1771 James Lovell claimed that "Our fathers" arrived in a "then-savage desart" and "for a long course of years . . . defended their liberty, their religion and their lives against the greatest inland danger from the savage natives." The following year Joseph Warren stated that "the first settlers of this country" came "to this new world, which they fairly purchased of the Indian natives, the only rightful proprietors" and "cultivated the then barren soil, by their incessant labour, and defended their dear bought possessions with the fortitude of the Christian, and the bravery of the hero." In his more vivid and detailed history in 1775, Warren claimed that "This country" had "been discovered by an English subject" and that settlers had "found the land swarming with savages who threatned death with every kind of torture." Afterward, they "entered into a treaty with the natives, and bought from them the lands," although those "savage natives saw with wonder the delightful change, and quickly formed a scheme to obtain that by fraud or force, which nature meant as the reward of industry alone," after which "the illustrious emigrants soon convinced the rude invaders that they were as ready to take the field for battle as for labor; and the insidious foe was driven from their borders as often as he ventured to disturb them." It was thus thrгough "infinite expense of toil and blood" that this "continent had been cultivated and defended."[29]

Public documents expressed similar statements. The Stamp Act Congress's Petition to the King in 1765 noted that settlers established colonies through "Perseverance in the midst of innumerable Dangers and Difficulties, together with a Profusion of their Blood and Treasure" in "the inhospitable Desarts of *America*." Individual colonial resolves repeated these words or made similar claims. Nine years later, the Fairfax Resolves asserted that Virginia was not "a conquered Country; and if it was, that the present Inhabitants are the Descendants not of the Conquered, but of the Conquerors." A few months later, the Suffolk Resolves stated that the "savage and uncultivated desert" of Massachusetts "was purchased by the toil and treasure, or acquired by the valor and blood, of . . . our venerable progenitors."[30]

The Continental Congress's Declaration of the Causes and Necessity of Taking Up Arms of 1775 also explicitly mixed settler imperialism and settler colonialism, attributing the origins of colonists' rights to "*Our Forefathers,*" who, "*At the Expence of their Blood, at the Hazard of their Fortunes, . . . effected Settlements in the distant and inhospitable Wilds of America,* then filled with numerous and warlike Nations of Barbarians." However, while earlier literature had mentioned Native Americans, sometimes at length, even if only to instrumentalize them in arguments against British authority, another element of settler colonial ideology was becoming increasingly evident in later literature: the disappearance of Native Americans from European American histories of the colonies. It was John Dickinson who had suggested the inclusion of the term "then filled with numerous and warlike Nations of Barbarians" in the 1775 Declaration—a term that did not appear in Thomas Jefferson's drafts. Nor did Jefferson mention Native Americans explicitly in his *Summary View of the Rights of British America*. Jefferson noted there that "America was conquered, and her settlements made, and firmly established, at the expence of individuals, and not of the British public. Their own blood was spilt in acquiring lands for their settlement, their own fortunes expended in making that settlement effectual; for themselves they fought, for themselves they conquered, and for themselves alone they have right to hold."[31]

Jefferson's erasure of Native Americans may have been deliberate, given the literary gymnastics he performed in writing the passage. The passive voice of the first sentence and first two phrases of the second one does some of the work of not mentioning Native Americans. By contrast, the active voice of the conclusion of the second sentence ascribes agency to the settlers who "fought" and "conquered," thus identifying those settlers, rather than the British crown, as having "the right to hold." What Jefferson strenuously avoided mentioning is whom the settlers fought, whom they conquered, and who otherwise might have had "the right to hold."

Jefferson's silence about Native Americans suggests that he regarded "the wilds of America" before English settlement not only as vacuum domicilium, unused, but even as terra nullius, unoccupied. He hinted at a potential mention of Indigenous Americans when he referred to how Saxons "had possessed themselves of the island of Britain, then less charged with inhabitants." It is all the more striking, therefore, that he represented the much more recent contest over title to American property and territory as one exclusively between American settlers and British authorities, with no mention of America being "charged with inhabitants." Furthermore, the title page of *A Summary View* described the work as authored "BY A NATIVE, AND MEMBER OF THE HOUSE OF BURGESSES"—the only use of the word "native" in the pamphlet, except for a reference to Saxons leaving their "native wilds and woods in the north of Europe." *A Summary View* not only thereby erased Indigenous peoples' claims to American land and territory but appropriated their title as "native" inhabitants as well.[32]

Jefferson's and the Declaration's erasure of Native American history (in its circumstances of emigration and settlement if not in its account of the present war against Britain) thus exemplifies what Michel-Rolph Trouillot in 1995 called the silencing of the past in the making of history. "Silences enter the process of historical production," Trouillot wrote, "at four crucial moments: the moment of fact creation (the making of *sources*); the moment of fact assembly (the making of *archives*); the moment of fact retrieval (the making of *narratives*); and the moment of retrospective significance (the making of *history* in the final instance)." The Declaration of Independence, ending the colonies' ties with Britain, is an example of the making of history in the final instance, written in a moment of retrospective significance, one in which Native Americans were deemed insignificant and were therefore erased from the history in this particular record. One might understand the Declaration's silence on Native Americans in the context of the severing of the imperial relationship. It was, after all, deploying the history of emigration and settlement in an argument against parliamentary authority rather than Native Americans' claims. We cannot dismiss its silence on Indigenous Americans that easily, however, for the Declaration's making of history in the final instance rested on a previous "moment of fact retrieval"—Jefferson's *Summary View*—an example of the making of a narrative in which Native Americans were silenced at greater length. And that in turn rested on an older archive of material that had assembled at least some Native American history, if only that which seemed relevant to arguments against Britain. What we see in the Declaration, then, especially in its references to "the circumstances of our emigration here," is the "Vanishing Indian" in the later stages of disappearing before our very eyes.[33]

Jefferson did, of course, mention Native Americans on other occasions, in moments when they still had retrospective or current significance to him. One instance was in the Declaration's reference to "merciless Indian Savages" who had allied with the king. Even then, though, he practiced other forms of literary erasure, in this case in the immediately preceding description of Native Americans as "the inhabitants of our frontiers." Jefferson committed a similar erasure in his "survey, in time, of the progress of man from the infancy of creation to the present day," in which a "philosophic observer" journeying from the west would first see "the savages of the Rocky mountains . . . the earliest stage of association living under no law but that of nature, subsisting and covering themselves with the flesh and skins of wild beasts," before finding "those on our frontiers in the pastoral state, raising domestic animals to supply the defects of hunting." Then, further east, they were replaced by "our own semi-barbarous citizens, the pioneers of the advance of civilization, and so on in his progress he would meet the gradual shades of improving man until he would reach his, as yet, most improved state in our seaboard towns."[34]

Jefferson's "survey in time" also suggested that the conquering of Native American peoples and lands in the past would continue in the future. The scene for that was partly set in the Declaration's statement that the king had "endeavoured to bring on the . . . merciless Indian Savages," which invoked natural law and the sacred duty to defend life and liberty by wars of conquest if necessary. That Native Americans' supposed "known rule of warfare is an undistinguished destruction of all ages, sexes and conditions" both reflected the past—the known—but could rationalize any atrocity in the near or distant future. And the same phrase, combined with others in the Declaration, also foreshadowed a longer-term future of westward expansion. The use of the term "frontiers" (as opposed to borders) did the same work as "inhabitants" and "Savages." If those people were in a state of nature, then so was their land, and so there no demarcated territorial borders, only limits of purportedly civilized settlement. The fact that the Declaration called them "our" frontiers further implied the possibility of future European-American possession, even a form of preemption. And the seventh grievance was even more indicative on this matter. Its complaints about the king preventing "the population of these States" by "raising the conditions of new Appropriations of Lands" referred to the Proclamation Line of 1763 as well as to increasing quitrents in Virginia and elsewhere. And that, of course, pointed to a postindependence determination to take possession of the lands beyond the Appalachian Mountains and for European Americans to settle them in even greater numbers than they had already.

The United States did indeed take formal possession of those lands under the 1783 Treaty of Paris, whereby the British abandoned their obligations to their erstwhile Indigenous allies. The Confederation Congress subsequently declared in its Land Ordinances of 1784 and 1785 that new states would be formed in the region and the land sold to settlers, and the Ordinances of 1787 and subsequently of the federal Congress gave greater detail and substance to these plans. By 1819 the entire region had been filled with new states except for the northern extremities that would constitute Michigan and Wisconsin, which joined the Union in 1837 and 1848, respectively. By then the United States extended beyond the Mississippi, following the Louisiana Purchase of 1803 and statehood for Missouri in 1821. The United States also stretched across the Gulf of Mexico region from lands acquired in the Adams-Onis Treaty of 1819 (also known as the Florida Purchase Treaty) and was on the verge of becoming a continental nation with the acquisition of vast tracts of the Southwest and Pacific Coast acquired during the Mexican-American War of 1846–1848. A series of treaties with Britain and Russia had also established the border between the United States and Canada.[35]

All of this, of course, was accompanied by numerous negotiations, purchases, removals, and wars against Native Americans that replicated the expenditures of "blood and treasure" recorded in colonial and revolutionary political literature and that informed the Declaration of Independence—but with one crucial difference. The Treaty of Paris and the various ordinances and actions that followed meant that later western settlement occurred under the territorial jurisdiction and with the assistance of the U.S. government, in contrast to the alleged absence of substantive British claims and assistance that colonial and revolutionary settler-imperial literature frequently referred to. Future western migrants would indeed be "migrants" within federal territory or immigrants into western territories, rather than emigrants to foreign or unclaimed lands. With the exception of southern proslavery secessionists, western settlers would therefore not be able to assert the kind of autonomy and ultimately independence from the United States that their predecessors had claimed in the face of usurpations by Great Britain. Ironically, therefore, the United States would be more of an imperial nation than Britain had hitherto been.[36]

Another possible difference between the circumstances of settlement in the past and future that Thomas Jefferson envisioned was by amalgamation of peoples. As president, for example, he counseled the Delaware people to "give up war and hunting" and "adopt the culture of the earth and raise domestic animals." And then "Unite yourselves with us" and "join our Great Councils and form one people with us, and we shall all be Americans; you will mix with us by marriage, your blood will run in our veins." This advice, repeated to other Native American peoples, certainly proposed another form of erasure: the cultural extinction of Native Americans. As Jefferson put it, if Native Americans did not accept agriculture and other elements of European American civilization, they would "disappear from the earth."[37]

If the "one people" of the Declaration of Independence did not encompass "all men," then neither did the *E Pluribus Unum* of the new nation's Great Seal. Indeed, the development of images on the seal confirms that, for the founders, "out of many, one" did not apply to all. On the fourth of July, 1776—the same day the Continental Congress approved an official version of the Declaration of Independence—it appointed three of that Declaration's drafters, "Dr. Franklin, J. Adams, and Mr Jefferson," to "a committee, to prepare a device for a Seal of the United States of America." The three then independently drew up designs they believed would project the identity of the

American people, each recalling different aspects of a past that, in their view, symbolically represented the new United States. Thomas Jefferson's sketches of Saxon chiefs Hengist and Horsa reflected his concept of Americans as descendants and inheritors of the economic, social, and political liberties of ancient Britons and their German forebears, as expressed in his *Summary View of the Rights of British America*. John Adams's efforts reflected more a sense of political and cultural inheritance than a supposed ancestral lineage, and his design incorporated southern and not just northern Europe by recalling Greek mythology, with Hercules choosing virtue over vice. Benjamin Franklin depicted Moses and the Israelites abandoning Pharaoh as they emerged from the Red Sea, thus extending even beyond the northern Mediterranean littoral and across the sea to Africa and Asia, if only to appropriate non-European traditions for a Europeanized Judeo-Christian heritage and an American political liberation.

Finding no way of reconciling their different representations of American inheritance, however, the three turned to Pierre-Eugène du Simitière, a Genevan emigré, naturalist, and man of letters living in Philadelphia at the time. On August 10, Simitière submitted his design, and, after making some alterations, the committee proposed to the Continental Congress a seal design with "the Eye of Providence" on top, a ribbon flag bearing the legend "E PLURIBUS UNUM" at the bottom, a "Goddess of Liberty" on one side, and a buckskinned rifleman on the other. In the middle would be a shield with escutcheons at the center containing the initials of each of the states, surrounded by six symbols representing "the countries from which these States have been peopled." Thus: "The 1st Or, a Rose enammelled gules and argent for England; the 2nd Argent, a Thistle Proper for Scotland: the 3rd Vert a harp Or for Ireland: the 4th Azure a Flower de luce Or for France: the 5th Or the Imperial Eagle Sable for Germany; and the 6th Or the Belgic Lion Gules for Holland." The seal thereby confirmed the notion implicitly advanced by the Declaration's circumstances of emigration and settlement that "these States" had "been peopled" by northern Europeans, and not by the Indigenous inhabitants of North America or by those captured from among the peoples of western Africa, and that the new United States belonged to European Americans and not to "all men" or "the rest of mankind."

The American identity stamped into this first Great Seal was therefore distinctly ethnocultural and racial—the more so when the committee replaced Simitière's original buckskinned rifleman and tomahawk with the "Goddess Justice," thus replacing an American icon, albeit with the Indigenous trappings of European imaginations, for a classical European one. Over the next few years Congress further fiddled with the iconography, later adding a Roman soldier, an armored knight, and a Native American depicted as a "naked savage," another European American image of a Native American, until they finally agreed on the eagle design concocted by Secretary Charles Thomson and heraldry enthusiast William Barton on June 20, 1782. These final imaginings and images were also imperialistic. The eagle, with thirteen stars and stripes across its breast, was described as "symbol of empire" by *The Colombian Magazine*, which printed and popularized it along with Thomson's "Remarks and Explanation." With a bundle of arrows clasped in one claw, the eagle was as much a representation of conquest as the buckskinned rifleman with the tomahawk. The Great Seal thereby expressed a notion of American national identity based not on the Declaration's self-evident truths of the equality and unalienable rights of "all men" but on its exclusivist idea of "one people" forged by "the circumstances of our emigration and settlement here"—not on new-fangled ideas but on old-fashioned blood and treasure.[38]

POSTSCRIPT

We Hold These Truths to Be Self-Evident

The authors of the Declaration of Independence never intended that the self-evident truths of equality and unalienable rights be indiscriminately applied under the government and law of the United States. Absolute equality and liberty existed in a state of nature, and, even then, they implied nothing more than individual sovereignty and common access to the earth and its resources for subsistence and survival. Natural equality and liberty would translate, by natural law, into civil government and law through the consent of the governed, the purpose of government in securing certain unalienable rights, and a popular sovereignty that gave the people collectively (though not all the people individually) a right to representation in their government and a right to revolution, if the latter became necessary. But the social contract nevertheless required that perfect natural equality and liberty be abandoned in civil government and society. All sacrificed something in the sense that individual self-sovereignty was absorbed into a collective sovereignty of the people, and all submitted themselves to the rule of a legislative and the civil laws it produced. Some sacrificed more natural equality and liberty than others, for although the authors of the Declaration meant that all people were created equal as self-sovereign individuals and with equal endowments of rights to life, liberty, and the pursuit of happiness, they did not mean that all were born with equal natural or civil capacities or competencies. Some were men, some were not. Some were white, some were not. Some were economically independent, some were not. Some were intelligent, educated, industrious, sober, and generally virtuous, and some were not. Most of the founders believed that these inequalities of capacity and competence should translate into civil governance and law just as firmly as they believed other elements of equality should translate into civil governance and law. They also believed that the purpose of civil government and law was to protect its subjects or citizens from enemies within and without—criminals, traitors, enslaved people, and "merciless Indian Savages," and even to deprive those others of their lives, liberties, and pursuits of happiness if necessary in "the Course of human events." In short, the authors of the Declaration of Independence envisioned a *natural law republic* that would secure the safety and happiness of its own citizens, not a natural rights republic that would institute equality and liberty for all.

Yet the idea of the United States as a natural rights republic eventually came to prevail, though its emergence was slow and hesitant. In 1776, the year of independence, the former Massachusetts Minuteman and Continental Army private Lemuel Haynes began authoring an essay titled *Liberty Further Extended: Or Free thoughts on the illegality of Slave-keeping*. Haynes never completed the work, and it was not published in his lifetime, but the African American future preacher had been thinking deeply about natural law and its relationship to liberty and slavery. "Liberty is a Jewel," he wrote, "which was handed Down to man from the cabinet of heaven, and is Coaeval with his Existance. And as it proceed from the Supreme Legislature of the univers, so it is he which hath a sole right to take away; therefore, he that would take away a mans Liberty assumes a prerogative that Belongs to another, and acts out of his own domain." Haynes admitted, as per Grotius, Locke, and others, that "sometimes men by their flagitious practise forfeit their Liberty into the hands of men, By Becomeing unfit for society." But, challenging the orthodoxy that a people at war may be enslaved indiscriminately by another, he asked, "have the affricans Ever as a Nation, forfited their Liberty in this manner? What Ever individuals have done; yet, I Believe, no such Chaleng can be made upon them, as a Body." Haynes thereby deployed a new doctrine, that of individual rights, to argue against the orthodoxy that persons might justly be enslaved through membership in a community of people. He thus rejected entirely the idea that the laws of nature and God might allow for enslavement, and he did so a year before the 1777 Massachusetts petitioners hinted at the same and seven years before the chief justice of Massachusetts endorsed this idea as the basis of that state's constitution.[1]

How could Haynes make such claims against the contemporary orthodoxies of the laws of nature and God and the course of human events? The clue to the answer lies in his epigraph. Immediately under the title and before the essay begins, he inserted the following: "We hold these truths to be self-Evident, that all men are created Equal, that they are Endowed By their Creator with Ceartain unalienable rights, that among these are Life, Liberty, and the pursuit of happyness." Haynes thus skipped right over the Declaration's first paragraph, with its context about the course of human events and the laws of nature and God that was so important to the original authors of the document. And the selected extract was also cut off from everything that followed it and that it had framed: the Declaration's general history of humankind and its particular history of colonial and revolutionary British America, all of which had given the document so much of its original meaning. As Hannah Spahn has put it, Haynes thus transformed the Declaration's self-evident truths into "ahistorical universals." And as such, they could form the basis of a more philosophical argument against enslavement, an argument untethered from the course of human events. It was thus Haynes who first presented the Declaration of Independence as a break with the past.[2]

Lemuel Haynes was probably also the first to quote the Declaration directly to argue comprehensively against slavery as a violation of the laws of nature and God that could never be excused in the course of human events. But he would not be the last. Haynes's manuscript would not be published until the late twentieth century, and the Declaration of Independence itself was somewhat forgotten in the years between the end of the War of Independence and the end of the War of 1812. Certain ideas about equality and liberty remained well known, however, deployed as they were in the Massachusetts petitioners' reaching toward an interpretation of natural law that outlawed slavery, in Elizabeth Freeman's more complete articulation of this idea, and in Chief Justice William Cushing's deployment of them to end enslavement in Massachusetts. Then, in the decade preceding the 1826 semicentennial, the Declaration of Independence itself returned to prominence as Americans began to celebrate the anniversary of their revolution. By this time, however, the events that had underwritten the Declaration's historical content had largely been forgotten. And the laws of nature and God were thereby less a basis for analyzing the course of human events—that is, history—and more a basis for abstract theorizing in favor of natural rights.

The Declaration of Independence could thus be more widely reinterpreted, shorn of its history and historical consciousness, and in this way become an "American scripture."[3]

One year after the semicentennial, William Hamilton, son of Alexander, gave "An Address to the New York African Society for Mutual Relief" celebrating the final July 4 abolition of slavery in the state—"a victory obtained," he said, "by the principles of liberty, such as are broadly and indelibly laid down by the glorious sons of 76." Yet he described Thomas Jefferson as "an ambidexter philosopher, who can reason contrarywise," who "first tells you 'that all men are created equal, and that they are endowed with unalienable rights of life, liberty, and the pursuit of happiness,'" and "next proves that one class of men are not equal to another." Jefferson did, of course argue both these things, but Hamilton ignored the Lockean argument that all men are *created* equally free in a state of nature and argued instead the radically different view that all men *are* equal and their equality should apply in civil society.[4]

Two years later, David Walker's *Appeal to the Colored Citizens of the World* took a lesson from Timothy Matlack's orthography and ran with it in a Haynesian truncation of the Declaration:

> See your Declaration Americans!!! Do you understand your own language? Hear your language, proclaimed to the world, July 4th, 1776—☞ "We hold these truths to be self evident—that ALL MEN ARE CREATED EQUAL!! That they are endowed by their Creator with certain unalienable rights; that among these are life, liberty, and the pursuit of happiness!!" Compare your own language above, extracted from your Declaration of Independence, with your cruelties and murders inflicted by your cruel and unmerciful fathers and yourselves on your fathers and on us—men who have never given your fathers or you the slightest provocation!!!!!![5]

Walker's friend and ally, William Lloyd Garrison, would write in the first issue of *The Liberator* two years afterward: "Assenting to the 'self-evident truth' maintained in the American Declaration of Independence, 'that all men are created equal, and endowed by their Creator with certain inalienable rights—among which are life, liberty and the pursuit of happiness,' I shall strenuously contend for the immediate enfranchisement of our slave population." Frederick Douglass would later declaim to his audience: "You declare, before the world . . . that you *hold these truths to be self evident, that all men are created equal; and are endowed by their Creator with certain inalienable rights; and that, among these are, life, liberty, and the pursuit of happiness;* and yet, you hold securely, in a bondage which, according to your own Thomas Jefferson, *is worse than ages of that which your fathers rose in rebellion to oppose,* a *seventh part* of the inhabitants of your country." And John Adams would no doubt have found himself surprised to find "that another Tribe more numerous and powerfull than all the rest were grown discontented" enough by 1848 to issue a Declaration of Sentiments stating, "We hold these truths to be self-evident: that all men and women are created equal" and deserve civil equality. If the Declaration of Independence is to be celebrated today, then, it is really thanks to the self-evident truths of Lemuel Haynes and the men and women who have followed him since, rather than to the document's original authors.[6]

But we should celebrate with caution, because the Declaration's truths were not and never have been universally "self-evident," and so the American revolutionary settlement remains contested to this day. Most people now accept the creedal interpretation of the Declaration; that is, they accept that the idea that all people are created equal and endowed with unalienable rights is or should be the basis of American society and government. But too many accept this idea in word only. The Declaration's past, as originally understood, therefore continues to shape the American present; its "Laws of Nature and of Nature's God" and "Course of human events," and most especially its "circumstances of our emigration and settlement here," still exert their influence some 250 years after the founding of the nation, to the detriment of many American citizens today.

NOTES

INTRODUCTION

1. The various versions of the Declaration referred to in this book—Thomas Jefferson's first draft, the committee draft submitted to the Continental Congress on June 28, 1776, the Dunlap broadside, the versions in the journal of the Continental Congress, and the parchment edition of August 2—can be found at the U.S. National Archives online: America's Founding Documents | National Archives. I will be using Timothy Matlack's August 2 edition, the final version produced by Congress, as definitive.
2. Maier, *American Scripture*. Maier rejects the idea of the Declaration as a charter for the future, seeing it as set in its present, but she does not connect it to the past in any sustained way. For her exploration of the Declaration's emergence as "scripture," see 175–208, and Maier, "The Strange History of 'All Men Are Created Equal.'" Philip Detweiler also points out that this interpretation of the Declaration emerged in the approach to the fiftieth anniversary of independence in "The Changing Reputation of the Declaration of Independence." See also Onuf and McDonald, *Revolutionary Prophecies*, "Introduction," 4; Tsesis, *For Liberty and Equality*; Brown, *Self-Evident Truths*; Lepore, *These Truths*; Sarson, *Barack Obama*; Hattem, *The Memory of '76*.
3. Becker, *The Declaration of Independence*, 6; Anderson, *Imagined Communities*, 193, although there is a case for Herbert Friedenwald's 1904 *The Declaration of Independence* as the first major academic study of the document. On ideological liberalism, see Becker, *The Declaration of Independence*; Diggins, *Lost Soul of American Politics*; Kramnick, *Republicanism and Bourgeois Radicalism*; Appleby, *Liberalism and Republicanism*; Gerber, *To Secure These Rights*. On individualism, see Eicholz, *Harmonizing Sentiments*, and some works on Locke cited below. On natural law and rights, see Wright,

American Interpretations of Natural Law; Zuckert, *The Natural Rights Republic*; Carey, "Natural Rights, Equality, and the Declaration of Independence," 51–59. On republicanism, see Bailyn, *Ideological Origins*; Pocock, *Machiavellian Moment*; Wood, *The Creation of the American Republic*. On Scottish moral philosophy, see Wills, *Inventing America*, never to be read without Ronald Hamowy's "Jefferson and the Scottish Enlightenment." On activist government, see Pincus, *The Heart of the Declaration*. On aristocracy, see Eidelberg, *On the Silence of the Declaration of Independence*. On equality, see Allen, *Our Declaration*. On religion, see Jayne, *Jefferson's Declaration of Independence*; Anderson, *The Declaration of Independence and God*. On constitutionalism and law, see Black, "The Constitution of Empire"; Greene, *Peripheries and Center* and *The Constitutional Origins of the American Revolution*; Reid, *Constitutional History of the American Revolution* (5 vols.) and *Constitutional History of the American Revolution: Abridged Edition*; Bilder, *The Transatlantic Constitution*; Crow, *Thomas Jefferson*. On social imperatives, see Holton, *Forced Founders* and *Liberty Is Sweet*; Parkinson, *Common Cause* and *Thirteen Clocks*. On international imperatives, see Armitage, "The Declaration of Independence and International Law" and *The Declaration of Independence*; Gould, *Among the Powers of the Earth*. Even historians of colonial and revolutionary history have found little history in the Declaration: Colbourn, *Lamp of Experience*; Spahn, *Thomas Jefferson, Time, and History*; Hattem, *Past and Prologue*. Historians of the early republic tend to see American history as a whole, as opposed to local histories, as a product of nation formation and thus nonexistent at the time of the founding: Shaffer, *The Politics of History* and *To Be an American*; Waldstreicher, *In the Midst of Perpetual Fetes*; Furstenberg, *In the Name of the Father*; Shalev, *Rome Reborn on Western Shores*.

4. I use the term "historical consciousness" rather than the more commonly used and often useful term "historical memory" for two reasons. First, "consciousness" captures the systematic nature of the Declaration's authors' theory and methods of historical analysis—their idea that the laws of nature and of God were both a theory of history and a method for analyzing history—while the more general term "historical memory" implies a broader and often vague corpus of knowledge or beliefs about the past. Second, "historical consciousness" better captures the Declaration's account of "the Course of human events" as a whole—past, present, and future, and how the three related to each other—an important element of this book's interpretation of the Declaration. On historical consciousness and memory, see Burke, "History as Social Memory"; Halbwachs, *On*

Collective Memory; Confino, "Collective Memory and Cultural History" and "Memory and the History of Mentalities"; and Bruner, *Strategies of Remembrance.*

5. Historians differ in describing the structure of the Declaration, but I refer to the first paragraph (beginning "When in the Course of human events") as the introduction and the second paragraph (beginning with the self-evident truths) as the preamble, followed by the grievances (each beginning "He has" or in one case "He is") and the conclusions (beginning "In every stage of these Oppressions"). I separate the introduction from the preamble in order to stress the importance of the former. George Carey associates equality with entitlement to unalienable rights, but that applies to civil rather than natural equality: "Natural Rights, Equality, and the Declaration of Independence," 59–67. Bruce Hunt also associates Lockean equality with entitlement to unalienable rights and also with equal capacity to understand natural law, which Locke emphatically denied: "Locke on Equality."

6. On the influence of Locke, see Friedenwald, *The Declaration of Independence,* esp. chapter 9; Becker, *The Declaration of Independence,* esp. chapter 2; Dworetz, *Unvarnished Doctrine;* Huyler, *Locke in America;* Arneil, *John Locke and America;* Ward, *The Politics of Liberty in England and Revolutionary America;* Brown, *The Consent of the Governed;* Thompson, "John Locke and the American Mind"; Amar, *The Words That Made Us;* Gerber, *To Secure These Rights,* 20–56. On Burlamaqui, see White, *The Philosophy of the American Revolution.* On Trenchard and Gordon ("Cato"), see Bailyn, *Ideological Origins.* On Machiavelli, see Pocock, *Machiavellian Moment.* On Hutcheson, see Wills, *Inventing America.* Some acknowledge Locke as important but stress the idea of the Declaration as an amalgam of ideas from many sources: Wright, *American Interpretations of Natural Law,* 1–62; May, *The Enlightenment in America;* Reck, "The Enlightenment in American Law I," 549–66; Zuckert, *Launching Liberalism;* Arcenas, *America's Philosopher,* 49–55.

7. Thomas Jefferson to Henry Lee, 8 May 1825, *Papers of Thomas Jefferson,* National Archives, https://founders.archives.gov/documents/Jefferson/98-01-02-5212. Sarson, "Harmonizing the 'Sentiments of the Day.'" On the evolution and nature of the text, see Hazelton, *The Declaration of Independence;* Boyd, *The Declaration of Independence;* Lucas, "Justifying America" and "The Stylistic Artistry of the Declaration of Independence"; Ritz, "From the Here of Jefferson's Handwritten Rough Draft"; Fliegelman, *Declaring Independence,* 28–35, 164–89; Allen, *Our Declaration,* 275–82.

See also Chartier, *Inscription and Erasure*, 28–45, on how printers visually reinforced the arguments of texts. Jefferson always used an apostrophe in the possessive "its."

8. For recent reiterations of the view that natural law or rights arguments emerged late in the revolutionary era, see Hattem, *Past and Prologue*, 8–9, 127–38, and Greene, *The Constitutional Origins of the American Revolution*, 149–86. The most extreme position on this issue is John Philip Reid's dismissal of the Declaration and its natural rights theory as entirely detached from all other American jurisprudence: "The Irrelevance of the Declaration." Yirush, *Settlers, Liberty, and Empire*, 215–62, on the other hand, identifies a long history of natural rights theory, although I differ in emphasizing the importance of natural law (which sometimes supposedly overrode natural rights in highly consequential ways).

9. On changes generally, see esp. Becker, *The Declaration of Independence*, 194–223; Lucas, "Justifying America" and "The Stylistic Artistry of the Declaration of Independence"; Fliegelman, *Declaring Independence*; Jefferson, *The Autobiography of Thomas Jefferson*, 35–42. The Continental Congress made no record of its deliberations of July 2–4 over the draft declaration, and this book continues the debate over why certain changes were made, but also tries to contextualize those changes in long-running historical and political debates in colonial and revolutionary protest literature.

10. Allen, *Our Declaration*, esp. 43, 45–104. I more closely follow Maier's idea that the Declaration's "original creation was . . . a collective act that drew on the words and thoughts of many people, dead and alive, who struggled with the same or closely related problems" (*American Scripture*, xx, 97–153). I also like her likening of the Declaration's authoring to a "symphony" or "choir" (xviii). Maier, Becker, and others have also referred to Jefferson as a "draftsman" working with older designs to craft something useful, which is fair enough, although I think authoring carries that meaning too. Maier also used ninety local declarations of independence extensively and appended a selection of them in *American Scripture*, esp. 47–96 and 217–34. They can be found in full in Force, *American Archives*, vols. 5, 6, and 7, https://digital.lib.niu.edu/amarch.

11. On natural law and rights in earlier writings, see Yirush, *Settlers, Liberty, and Empire*; Zuckert, *The Natural Rights Republic* and *Launching Liberalism*. On public knowledge, see Hattem, *Past and Prologue*, 33–39; Brown, *Knowledge Is Power* and *The Strength of a People*; Thompson, *Rum Punch and Revolution*; Irvin, *Clothed in Robes of Sovereignty*; Adelman,

Revolutionary Networks; Carey, "Natural Rights, Equality, and the Declaration of Independence."

12. Maier noted that equality was a condition of the state of nature, but placed the Declaration in the context of its present rather than connecting it to a past: *American Scripture,* 135–36, 192. Roosevelt also noted in *The Nation That Never Was* that equality was a condition of the state of nature, but claims, as many do, that Locke and the founders saw the state of nature as theoretical rather than historical.

1. THE LAWS OF NATURE AND OF NATURE'S GOD

1. Maier noted the "epic" nature of the opening sentence, although she depicted it as rhetorical rather than historical: *American Scripture,* 132–33.
2. Thomas Jefferson to Henry Lee, 8 May 1825, in *Papers of Thomas Jefferson,* National Archives, https://founders.archives.gov/documents/Jefferson/98-01-02-5212.
3. Becker, *The Declaration of Independence,* 175n1; Lucas, "Justifying America" and "The Stylistic Artistry of the Declaration of Independence"; Maier, *American Scripture,* 236n1, 134–35; Allen, *Our Declaration,* 76 (see also 72–79 and 246–48 for Matlack's other contributions). Chartier, *Inscription and Erasure,* 28–45, also shows how early modern printers visually reinforced the arguments of texts.
4. Thomas Jefferson to John Trumbull, 15 February 1789, in *Papers of Thomas Jefferson,* National Archives, https://founders.archives.gov/documents/Jefferson/01-14-02-0321; Thomas Jefferson to Benjamin Rush, 16 January 1811, ibid., https://founders.archives.gov/documents/Jefferson/03-03-02-0231.
5. Miller, *Jefferson and Nature,* 11, 19–28, 35–38, 194; O'Shaughnessy, *The Illimitable Freedom of the Human Mind,* 17–21; Cogliano, *Thomas Jefferson,* 1–4. See also Jayne, *Jefferson's Declaration of Independence,* 87–89; Cohen, *Science and the Founding Fathers,* 61–134; Crow, *Thomas Jefferson,* 265–71.
6. Jayne, *Jefferson's Declaration of Independence,* 81–86, 98–108. Crow, *Thomas Jefferson,* 250–64.
7. Allen, *Our Declaration,* 110–11; Spahn, *Jefferson, Time, and History*: for the point about rivers, see 103–4, for the quotations from "Scholium" in Newton's *Mathematical Principles,* see 21–24, and for Hume's *Enquiry Concerning Human Understanding* and Bolingbroke's *Letters on the Study and Use of History,* see 106. Spahn dates the completion of this shift in Jefferson's historical thinking to the 1780s and 1790s (143), while I see it as fundamental to the Declaration. On earlier concepts of time and history,

see Lovejoy, *The Great Chain of Being*; Wilcox, *Measures of Times Past*, 1–82, 187–251. See also Valsania, *The Limits of Optimism*, esp. 9–31; Jayne, *Jefferson's Declaration of Independence*, 19–40. Crow explores Jefferson's historical thought, but in the context of its utility in law and with recognition of but skepticism about the connection of natural law and history: *Thomas Jefferson*, 32, 37–38, 86–87, 112–15, 126, 133–36, 139–42, 233–35.

8. Thomas Jefferson to James Madison, 30 August 1823, *Papers of Thomas Jefferson*, National Archives, https://founders.archives.gov/documents/Jefferson/03-20-02-0123.

9. Cicero, *De Legibus*, II, 4, 10, cited in Wright, *American Interpretations of Natural Law*, 2. The case for the Declaration as a synthesis of many thinkers is powerfully made by Wright, 1–62, esp. 56–58; May, *The Enlightenment in America*; Reck, "The Enlightenment in American Law I," 549–66; Zuckert, *The Natural Rights Republic* and *Launching Liberalism*; and Arcenas, *America's Philosopher*. Locke himself regarded Pufendorf's 1672 *De Jure naturali & gentium* (*On The Law of Nature and of Nations*) as "the best book" on the origins of society and government. "Some Thoughts Concerning Reading and Study for a Gentleman," cited in Arcenas, *America's Philosopher*, 13. Blackstone opposed Locke on many matters but said that the "law of nature being coeval with mankind, and dictated by God himself, is of course superior in obligation to any other. It is binding all over the globe, in all countries and at all times: no human laws are of any validity, if contrary to this; and such of them as are valid derive all their force and all their authority, mediately or immediately, from this original." *Commentaries*, I, 40, cited in Wright, *American Interpretations of Natural Law*, 5. For those who stress the preeminence of Locke, see Becker, *The Declaration of Independence*, 24–79, and more recently Jayne, *Jefferson's Declaration of Independence*, 41–51, 55–56, and Amar, *The Words That Made Us*, although most who emphasize Locke focus on his natural rights theory rather than on natural law and history. An exception, at least for natural law, is Eicholz, *Harmonizing Sentiments*, 80–88.

10. Locke, *Two Treatises*, 271, 357–58, 395–96.

11. Locke, *An Essay Concerning Human Understanding*, 317. Jefferson recommended the *Essay* for Robert Skipwith's library five years before independence, under the heading of "Locke's conduct of the mind in search of truth": Thomas Jefferson to Robert Skipwith, with a List of Books for a Private Library, 3 August 1771, *Papers of Thomas Jefferson*, National Archives, https://founders.archives.gov/documents/Jefferson/01-01-02-0056. This moral philosophy and the historical trajectory that follows

from it confirm that portraits of Locke as an extreme individualist and liberal or libertarian are caricatures: Strauss, *Natural Right and History*; McPherson, *The Political Theory of Possessive Individualism*; Dunn, *The Political Thought of John Locke*. For critiques of the caricaturing, see Dworetz, *Unvarnished Doctrine*, 97–134; Huyler, *Locke in America*, 29–41; Arneil, *John Locke and America*, 2–16; Arcenas, *America's Philosopher*, 8–57; Gerber, *To Secure These Rights*, 23–40.

12. Locke, *Two Treatises*, 276, 365, 277, 326. See also Dumbauld, *The Declaration of Independence* and "Independence under International Law"; Onuf, "A Declaration of Independence for Diplomatic Historians"; Armitage, "The Declaration of Independence and International Law" and *The Declaration of Independence*, 25–102; Sadosky, *Revolutionary Negotiations*; Gould, *Among the Powers of the Earth*, 1–13, 111–44.

13. Ibid., 277–78, 270. Zuckert quoted Jefferson as indicating that morality is innate rather learned by reason and observation when he wrote to Peter Carr in 1787 that "[Man] was endowed with a sense of right and wrong" that "is as much a part of his nature as the sense of hearing, or feeling; it is the true foundation of morality": "Thomas Jefferson and Natural Morality," 64. See also Wills, *Inventing America*, 165–319; Jayne, *Jefferson's Declaration of Independence*, 62–86, 116–17; Eicholz, *Harmonizing Sentiments*, 96–102.

14. Locke, *Two Treatises*, 135, 265, 157.
15. Ibid., 147, 255, 252–53.
16. Ibid., 156, 161–62, 285–86.
17. Ibid., 204–5, 286, 286–87, 288.
18. Ibid., 207.
19. Ibid., 350, 283.
20. Ibid., 345, 333, 334, 334–35.
21. Ibid., 334, 344, 345, 335.
22. Ibid., 340, 341.
23. Ibid., 335, 336.
24. Ibid., 339, 335, 337, 301.
25. Ibid., 412, 412–13, 413.
26. Ibid., 414, 417–18, 415, 412–13.
27. Colonial and revolutionary sermons as well as political writings familiarized many with Locke's ideas, as is stressed in Wright, *American Interpretations of Natural Law*, 9–34; Rossiter, *The Political Thought of the American Revolution*; Morgan, "The Puritan Ethic and the American Revolution"; Arcenas, *America's Philosopher*, 8–30. Lutz calculated that Locke was the

most cited author in America in the 1760s and 1770s: *The Origins of American Constitutionalism*, 143. See also Amar, *The Words That Made Us*, and Marshall, *John Locke, Resistance, Religion, and Responsibility*.
28. Yirush, *Settlers, Liberty, and Empire*, 34–35. Dulany (the Elder), *The Right of the Inhabitants of Maryland*, 84, 87, 88. As Yirush notes, Dulany's citation of Locke referred to "Locke of Civil Government, Chap.2, Sec. 4": 156n68. See also Arcenas, *America's Philosopher*, 8–30, although she argues that Locke's influence was greatest in the areas of education and epistemology.
29. Otis, *A Vindication of the Conduct of the House of Representatives*, 17–20, 51, 52.
30. Otis, *The Rights of the British Colonies*, 8, 9, 10, 35, 38.
31. Ibid., 23, 22, 23–24.
32. Dulany (the Younger), *Considerations on the Propriety of Imposing Taxes*, 4, 30; Hicks, *The Nature and Extent of Parliamentary Power Considered*, and the introductory section titled "Advertisement to the Printer," 3, 18, 16.
33. Wilson, *Considerations on the Nature and Extent of the Legislative Authority*, 2–3.
34. Warren, *An Oration, Delivered March 5th, 1772*, 5, 6, 7.
35. Paine, *Common Sense*, 3–4.
36. Ibid., 3–4, 4, 4–5, 5; Spahn, *Jefferson, Time, and History*, 103–4; Allen, *Our Declaration*, 110–11.
37. Yirush, *Settlers, Liberty, and Empire*, 1, 2. The explanation of the instructions is in Greene and Yirush, *Exploring the Bounds of Liberty*, 3:1723–24; the quotations are from "Massachusetts House of Representatives: Instructions to Jasper Manduit (June 15, 1762)," ibid., 3:1725–26, 1729, 1730.
38. "The Declarations of the Stamp Act Congress, October 19, 1765," in Morgan, *Prologue to Revolution*, 62–63; "Calvin's Case," in Sheppard, *Selected Writings and Speeches of Sir Edward Coke*, 1:224.
39. "The South Carolina Resolves, November 29, 1765," "The New Jersey Resolves, November 30, 1765," "The Pennsylvania Resolves, September 21, 1765," "The Massachusetts Resolves, October 29, 1765," in Morgan, *Prologue to Revolution*, 58, 59–60, 51, 56. "The Connecticut Resolutions on the Stamp Act: December 10, 1765," *Massachusetts Gazette*, December 19, 1765: Avalon Project—Connecticut Resolutions on the Stamp Act: December 10, 1765 (yale.edu); "The Resolutions as Printed in *The Journal of the House of Burgesses*, 1765" and "The Virginia Petitions to the King and Parliament, December 18, 1764," in Morgan, *Prologue to Revolution*, 47–48, 14, 15.

40. Massachusetts House of Assembly to the King, January 20, 1768, in Wright, *American Interpretations of Natural Law*, 43–44; Greene, *Constitutional Origins of the American Revolution*, 129; Huyler, *Locke in America*, 222; Yirush, *Settlers, Liberty, and Empire*, 240.
41. Constitution of New Hampshire, 1776; Constitution of South Carolina, 1776; Constitution of South Carolina, March 26, 1776; Constitution of New Jersey—1776.
42. "The Virginia Bill of Rights, June 12, 1776," and "The Constitution of Virginia, 29 June, 1776," National Archives, *The Virginia Declaration of Rights | National Archives; VII. The Constitution as Adopted by the Convention, [29 June 1776]*, https://founders.archives.gov/documents/Jefferson/01-01-02 -0161-0008.
43. Continental Congress, Articles of Association, October 20, 1774; Continental Congress, Declaration and Resolves, October 14, 1774.
44. "A Declaration ... setting forth the Causes and Necessity of their taking up Arms, 6 July, 1775," *Papers of Thomas Jefferson*, National Archives, https://founders.archives.gov/documents/Jefferson/01-01-02-0113-0005; Calvert, *Penman of the Founding*, 247–48.

2. OUR EMIGRATION AND SETTLEMENT HERE

1. Becker argues that the Declaration's assertions about the origins and development were distorted by the political needs of 1776: *The Declaration of Independence*, 80–134. Wills alleges that fellow delegates at the Continental Congress found Jefferson's account of the origins of colonies and empire "embarrassing": *Inventing America*, 311. Maier argues that Jefferson inserted his views on emigration and settlement "so inconspicuously that not every reader might catch its assertion that the colonists had settled America entirely at their own cost": *American Scripture*, 139–41, 147–48 (quotation at 141). Unlike Becker, I see the Declaration's history as informing revolutionary politics. Unlike Wills, I see Jefferson's version as radical and unsettling but increasingly attractive as an argument for independence. Unlike Maier, I see the idea of colonists settling at their own expense as a commonplace; the controversy was over whether settlers had expatriated and formed new "states" in America—and its inclusion in Jefferson's draft was so conspicuous that it had to be removed from the final version.
2. Jack P. Greene has used the term "settled constitutionalism" in a yet unpublished essay titled "The Empirical Roots of Settler Constitutionalism in Colonial British America: James Knight and the Jamaica Exemplar,"

cited courtesy of the author. I see "settler constitutionalism" as the outcome of a historical "settler imperialism." See also Greene, *Peripheries and Center* and *The Constitutional Origins of the American Revolution* (where Greene argues, in contrast to me, that natural law fully entered colonial arguments only in 1774); see also Greene, "The Glorious Revolution and the British Empire, 1688–1783," and "The Limits of the American Revolution." Craig Yirush uses the terms "settler vision of the empire" and "settler political theory" to describe the idea that settlers' efforts and expenses earned them rights to property and self-government. All these terms are apt, but I prefer "settler imperialism" as it is more descriptive of the theory's ideas and also has the advantage of implying its close relationship with settler colonialism (explored more in chapter 6). Yirush, *Settlers, Liberty, and Empire*, 4, 266, 270. See also Greene, *Pursuits of Happiness*, for settler motivations for colonization, and Messer, *Stories of Independence*, for patriot histories of colonial autonomy and Loyalist histories of attachments to Britain.
3. Thomas Jefferson to Henry Lee, 8 May 1825, *Papers of Thomas Jefferson*, National Archives, https://founders.archives.gov/documents/Jefferson/98-01-02-5212.
4. Sarson, "Harmonizing the 'Sentiments of the Day.'"
5. Yirush, *Settlers, Liberty, and Empire*, 216.
6. John Adams to Timothy Pickering, 6 August 1822, *Adams Papers*, National Archives, https://founders.archives.gov/documents/Adams/99-02-02-7674. Becker, *The Declaration of Independence*, 194–223; Maier, *American Scripture*, 97–153; Fliegelman, *Declaring Independence*, 4–35; Lucas, "The Stylistic Artistry of the Declaration of Independence"; Allen, *Our Declaration*, 47–104.
7. Jefferson, *Summary View*, 5.
8. Ibid., 5–6. Onuf, *Jefferson's Empire*, 61–62; Brewer, *By Birth or Consent*, 17–149; Steele, *Thomas Jefferson and American Nationhood*, 21–28; Crow, *Thomas Jefferson*, 13–14, 47–48, 75–77, 96–103.
9. Jefferson, *Summary View*, 6.
10. Ibid., 6, 20, 7.
11. Ibid., 19.
12. Ibid., 19–20. Jefferson quoted the principle that "all lands in England were held either mediately or immediately of the crown" from Edward Coke, *Commentary on Littleton's Tenures* (1628), and copied extensive sections from histories and legal tracts in his commonplace book, including from Salkfield, Kames, Dalrymple, Hale, and others, as well as Coke: Konig and Zuckert, *Jefferson's Legal Commonplace Book*, 112–40; 226–97.

13. Jefferson, *Summary View*, 20.
14. "Refutation of the Argument that the Colonies were Established at the Expense of the British Nation, [after 19 January 1776]." Unpublished manuscript, *Papers of Thomas Jefferson*, National Archives, https://founders.archives.gov/documents/Jefferson/01-01-02-0147.
15. Locke, *Two Treatises*, 393–94, 346, 389–90, 392.
16. Ibid., 387.
17. Ibid., 345.
18. Yirush, *Settlers, Liberty, and Empire*, 59, 60.
19. Rawson, *The Revolution in New-England Justified*, 46, 19, 20, 12, 13, 17–18, 20 25; Yirush, *Settlers, Liberty, and Empire*, 72–73. Also Hall et al., *The Glorious Revolution in America*; Lovejoy, *The Glorious Revolution in America* (stressing liberty); Webb, *Lord Churchill's Coup* (stressing oppression); Stanwood, *The Empire Reformed* (somewhere in between); and Sosin, *English America and the Revolution of 1688* (stressing local variations).
20. Dummer, *A Defence of the New-England Charters*, 2, 5, 6, 5, 8, 8–9; Yirush, *Settlers, Liberty, and Empire*, 83–112.
21. Dulany (the Elder), *The Right of the Inhabitants of Maryland*, 85; Dulany (the Younger), *Considerations on the Propriety of Imposing Taxes in the British Colonies*, 29, 30; Kammen, "The Meaning of Colonization," 341; Colbourn, *The Lamp of Experience*, 163–65; Yirush, *Settlers, Liberty, and Empire*, 142–57.
22. Otis, *The Rights of the British Colonies*, 11, 25, 34, 57.
23. Bland, *An Inquiry into the Rights of the British Colonies*, 7, 10, 14. Private citizens expressed settler-imperial opinions, some even explicitly approving Bland's argument for a confederal empire. A "meeting of a considerable number of inhabitants of the town and county of Norfolk, and others, SONS OF LIBERTY, at the Court House of the said county, in the colony of Virginia, on Monday the 31st of March, 1766" adopted six resolves against the Stamp Act. The fifth determined "That a committee be appointed to present the thanks of the Sons of Liberty to Colonel Richard Bland, for his treatise entitled 'An Inquiry into the Rights of the British Colonies.'" "Norfolk, Virginia, March 31, 1766," in Morgan, *Prologue to Revolution*, 116. Gutzman, "Jefferson's Draft Declaration of Independence"; Steele, *Thomas Jefferson and American Nationhood*, 17–18, 25–28; Crow, *Thomas Jefferson*, 5, 48, 68–69.
24. Bland, *An Inquiry into the Rights of the British Colonies*, 7, 21, 13–14.
25. Ibid., 20, 15, 20–21, 15–16, 16, 16–17, 17.
26. Ibid., 17–18.
27. Ibid., 19–20.

28. Dickinson, *Letters from a Farmer in Pennsylvania*, 13, 49. According to William Wirt, Jefferson later wrote to Patrick Henry that Bland was "the most learned and logical man of those who took a prominent lead in public affairs; profound in constitutional lore," and that his *Inquiry into the Rights of the British Colonies* was "the first pamphlet on the nature of the connexion with Great Britain, which had any pretension to accuracy of view on that subject," containing "more sound matter" than "the celebrated Farmer's Letters, which were really but an *ignis fatuus*, misleading us from true principle." Wirt, *Sketches of the Life and Character of Patrick Henry*, 46.
29. Dickinson, *Letters from a Farmer in Pennsylvania*, 50, 51, and *Essay on the Constitutional Power of Great-Britain*, 68–69, 111, 94, 95; Calvert, *Penman of the Founding*, 233–34.
30. Hicks, *The Nature and Extent of Parliamentary Power Considered*, 22, 23–24.
31. Wilson, *Considerations on the Nature and Extent of the Legislative Authority*, 19, 20, 22, 26.
32. Ibid., 26, 34, 16.
33. Ibid., 30–31.
34. "VIII. To the Inhabitants of the Colony of Massachusetts-Bay, 13 March 1775," *Adams Papers, Letters of Novanglus*, National Archives, https://founders.archives.gov/documents/Adams/06-02-02-0072-0009.
35. Ibid. "King Massachusetts" was presumably Ousamequin, "Massasoit" or sachem of the Wampanoag Confederacy at the time English settlers arrived at Plymouth and Massachusetts.
36. Ibid.; "XII. To the Inhabitants of the Colony of Massachusetts-Bay, 17 April 1775," Founders Online, National Archives, https://founders.archives.gov/documents/Adams/06-02-02-0072-0014.
37. "VII. To the Inhabitants of the Colony of Massachusetts-Bay, 6 March 1775," *Adams Papers, Letters of Novanglus*, National Archives, https://founders.archives.gov/documents/Adams/06-02-02-0072-0008.
38. Ibid.; "XI. To the Inhabitants of the Colony of Massachusetts-Bay, 10 April 1775," Founders Online, National Archives, https://founders.archives.gov/documents/Adams/06-02-02-0072-0013.
39. Lovell, *An Oration Delivered April 2d, 1771*, 7, 13, 14, 12.
40. Warren, *An Oration, Delivered March 5th, 1772*, 7; Warren, *An Oration, Delivered March Sixth, 1775*, 6, 6–7. See also Lee, *Essay in Vindication*; Hopkins, *Rights of the Colonies*; Downer, *Discourse Delivered in Providence*; Allen, *American Alarm*; Webster, *Misery and Duty*.
41. "Convention of Suffolk County," in Lincoln, *The Journals of Each Provincial Congress of Massachusetts*, 601.

42. "Fairfax County Resolves, 18 July 1774," *Papers of George Washington*, National Archives, https://founders.archives.gov/documents/Washington/02-10-02-0080.
43. "The New York Petition to the House of Commons, October 18, 1764," in Morgan, *Prologue to Revolution*, 9, 10; "The Virginia Petitions to the King and Parliament, December 18, 1764: The Remonstrance to the House of Commons," ibid., 16.
44. "The Stamp Act Congress, October 7–24, 1765: The Petition to the King," ibid., 64.
45. "The Connecticut Resolves, October 25, 1765," ibid., 54–55; "The Massachusetts Resolves, October 29, 1765," ibid., 56, 56–57, 57; "The New York Resolves, December 18, 1764," ibid., 61.
46. All drafts and the final version of the Declaration can be found at National Archives, *Declaration of the Causes and Necessity for Taking Up Arms [26 June–6 July 1775]*, https://founders.archives.gov/ancestor/TSJN-01-01-02-0113. Maier argues that Dickinson's draft was the strongest, even though Jefferson later described his own draft as "too strong for Mr. Dickinson": *American Scripture*, 19–20. Seen in the light of the debate over the origins of colonies and empire, however, Jefferson's version was certainly more historically and politically radical. Calvert, *Penman of the Founding*, 247–48.
47. "The Twelve United Colonies, by their Delegates in Congress, to the Inhabitants of Great Britain," July 8, 1775, *Journals of the American Congress*, 1:108.
48. Jefferson, *Summary View*, 6.
49. Thomas Jefferson to John Manners, 12 June 1817, *Papers of Thomas Jefferson*, National Archives, https://founders.archives.gov/documents/Jefferson/03-11-02-0360. The letter suggests that Jefferson moved away from Lockean epistemology and toward a more Scottish "moral sense" philosophy. See Wills, *Inventing America*, 165–319; Jayne, *Jefferson's Declaration of Independence*, 62–86, 116–17; Eicholz, *Harmonizing Sentiments*, 96–102; Zuckert, "Thomas Jefferson and Natural Morality."
50. "The Revisal of the Laws 1776–1786," in Boyd et al., *Papers of Thomas Jefferson*, 2:476–79. See also Maier, *American Scripture*, 134; Jayne, *Jefferson's Declaration of Independence*, 51–56, 128–38; Eicholz, *Harmonizing Sentiments*, 93; Steele, *Thomas Jefferson and American Nationhood*, 25–26. For the pursuit of happiness as a broader social and economic phenomenon and as an element of American identity, see Greene, *Pursuits of Happiness* and *Intellectual Construction of America*. For a broader approach to

the meaning of "happiness" at the time, see Mumford Jones, *The Pursuit of Happiness*; Lewis, *The Pursuit of Happiness*; Conklin, *The Pursuit of Happiness in the Founding Era*; Rosen, *The Pursuit of Happiness*. Schlesinger's 1964 "The Lost Meaning of 'The Pursuit of Happiness'" addressed the political meaning of happiness and the pursuit thereof, but did not connect it to migration.

51. Calvert, *Penman of the Founding*, 255–373.

3. UNFIT TO BE THE RULER OF A FREE PEOPLE

1. Historians usually count the nine clauses detailing the king's collaboration with Parliament separately, making for twenty-seven grievances, or twenty-eight, if one counts the collaboration itself, or twenty-nine, if one includes the complaint about the king ignoring colonial petitions, which, for reasons explained below, I see as the beginning of the conclusions. Each of these grievances was important, as shown in the next chapter. But, given the emphasis the authors placed on the king, I think it is nevertheless more appropriate to count this one as a single grievance under the heading concerning the king's combination with Parliament, making eighteen grievances altogether (or sets of grievances, as some grievances, beginning with "He has," covered more than one issue). It is also the case that some of the nine clauses of the thirteenth grievance were included in previous grievances, so counting twenty-seven, twenty-eight, or twenty-nine means counting some accusations twice, and not including the collaboration itself means not counting one of the most important grievances in the Declaration, as argued below.
2. Fisher, "The Twenty-Eight Charges against the King," 260–62, 284–85; Becker, *The Declaration of Independence*, 80–134; 194–223; Lucas, "Justifying America."
3. The most powerful case for the king's blamelessness is Dickinson's in "Britain's Imperial Sovereignty."
4. Hutchinson, *Strictures upon the Declaration of the Congress at Philadelphia*; Lind, *An Answer to the Declaration*, 9.
5. For the Declaratory Act, see Morgan, *Prologue to Revolution*, 155–56. The royal colonies up to 1776 included Virginia, Massachusetts, New Hampshire, New York, New Jersey, Delaware, North and South Carolina, and Georgia. The private colonies were the charter colonies of Connecticut and Rhode Island and the proprietaries of Maryland and Pennsylvania.
6. Colley, *Britons*, 56. See also Pocock, *The Ancient Constitution and the Feudal Law*; Reid, *The Ancient Constitution and the Origins of Anglo-American*

Liberty; Harris, *Revolution*; Vallance, *The Glorious Revolution of 1688*; Pincus, *1688*; Gould, *The Persistence of Empire*; Maier, *American Scripture*, 22–23.

7. Knox, "Hints Respecting the Settlement of our American Provinces," 118 (according to Barrow, Knox's pamphlet "was apparently used by government ministers in the preparation of the Sugar Act": "A Project for Imperial Reform"); Morgan and Morgan, *The Stamp Act Crisis*, 54.
8. Burke, "Letter to the Sheriffs of Bristol," in Greene, *Peripheries and Center*, 57; "Speech on Declaratory Resolution, 3 February 1766," in Langford, *Writings and Speeches of Edmund Burke*, 2:48–49. "Debate in the House of Commons: William Pitt versus George Grenville (January 14, 1766)," in Greene, *Colonies to Nation, 1763–1789*, 71–72.
9. Reid, *Constitutional History of the American Revolution: The Authority to Tax*, 226.
10. Anon., *An Argument in Defence of the Exclusive Right*, 104, 127–28, 95, 128; Sarson. "A total contradiction to every principle laid down at the time of the revolution."
11. Gould, *Crucible of Peace*.
12. Thomas Jefferson to Henry Lee, 8 May 1825, *Papers of Thomas Jefferson*, National Archives, https://founders.archives.gov/documents/Jefferson/98-01-02-5212; Jefferson, *Summary View*, title page.
13. Jefferson, *Summary View*, 21–22, 23, 15.
14. Ibid., 15, 22, 16. Dickinson, "Britain's Imperial Sovereignty"; McConville, *The King's Three Faces*; Nelson, *The Royalist Revolution*. For works on the Glorious Revolution in America, see Lovejoy, *The Glorious Revolution in America*; Webb, *Lord Churchill's Coup*; Stanwood, *The Empire Reformed*; and Sosin, *English America and the Revolution of 1688*, although I am focusing here on memory of the Glorious Revolution more than on what actually happened at the time. Sosin is correct to assert that American iterations of the Glorious Revolution varied widely from place to place, but American revolutionary memory tended to homogenize the experiences of 1689 within America while distinguishing that from what resulted in Britain. See Sarson, "A total contradiction," and Maier, *American Scripture*, 51–59, 71–72, 109.
15. Jefferson, *Summary View*, 7–8.
16. Ibid., 8–9.
17. Ibid., 9, 10.
18. Ibid., 10–11.
19. Ibid., 11.

20. Bland, *An Inquiry into the Rights of the British Colonies*, 21. Yirush, *Settlers, Liberty, and Empire*, 158–79, focuses on Bland's earlier works: *A Letter to the Clergy of Virginia* (Williamsburg, 1760) and *The Colonel Dismounted* (Williamsburg, 1764).
21. Bland, *An Inquiry into the Rights of the British Colonies*, 22–23, 24, 23.
22. Ibid., 26.
23. Ibid., 24–25. Steele, *Thomas Jefferson and American Nationhood*, 27–28.
24. Dickinson, *Letters from a Farmer in Pennsylvania*, 13, 49, 23, 24.
25. Ibid., 9, 10.
26. Ibid., 6.
27. Hicks, *The Nature and Extent of Parliamentary Power Considered*, 12, 15.
28. Ibid., 29–30.
29. Ibid., 25, 15.
30. Wilson, *Considerations on the Nature and Extent of the Legislative Authority*, 1, 15, 21–22.
31. Ibid., 27–28, 31, 33.
32. "VIII. To the Inhabitants of the Colony of Massachusetts-Bay, 13 March 1775," *Adams Papers, Letters of Novanglus*, National Archives, https://founders.archives.gov/documents/Adams/06-02-02-0072-0009; "VII. To the Inhabitants of the Colony of Massachusetts-Bay, 6 March 1775," National Archives, *Adams Papers, Letters of Novanglus*, https://founders.archives.gov/documents/Adams/06-02-02-0072-0008.
33. "IV. To the Inhabitants of the Colony of Massachusetts-Bay, 13 February 1775," Founders Online, National Archives, https://founders.archives.gov/documents/Adams/06-02-02-0072-0005; "III. To the Inhabitants of the Colony of Massachusetts-Bay, 6 February 1775," *Adams Papers, Letters of Novanglus*, National Archives, https://founders.archives.gov/documents/Adams/06-02-02-0072-0004; "VII. To the Inhabitants of the Colony of Massachusetts-Bay, 6 March 1775," *Adams Papers, Letters of Novanglus*, National Archives, https://founders.archives.gov/documents/Adams/06-02-02-0072-0008.
34. "IV. To the Inhabitants of the Colony of Massachusetts-Bay, 13 February 1775," *Adams Papers, Letters of Novanglus*, National Archives, https://founders.archives.gov/documents/Adams/06-02-02-0072-0005.
35. "III. To the Inhabitants of the Colony of Massachusetts-Bay, 6 February 1775," *Adams Papers, Letters of Novanglus*, National Archives, https://founders.archives.gov/documents/Adams/06-02-02-0072-0004.
36. "VIII. To the Inhabitants of the Colony of Massachusetts-Bay, 13 March 1775," *Adams Papers, Letters of Novanglus*, National Archives, https://founders.archives.gov/documents/Adams/06-02-02-0072-0009; "VII.

To the Inhabitants of the Colony of Massachusetts-Bay, 6 March 1775," *Adams Papers, Letters of Novanglus,* National Archives, https://founders.archives.gov/documents/Adams/06-02-02-0072-0008.

37. "VII. To the Inhabitants of the Colony of Massachusetts-Bay, 6 March 1775," *Adams Papers, Letters of Novanglus,* National Archives, https://founders.archives.gov/documents/Adams/06-02-02-0072-0008.
38. "III. To the Inhabitants of the Colony of Massachusetts-Bay, 6 February 1775," *Adams Papers, Letters of Novanglus,* National Archives, https://founders.archives.gov/documents/Adams/06-02-02-0072-0004. On the idea of conspiracy in revolutionary politics, see Bailyn, *Ideological Origins* and *Origins of American Politics.* For more on constitutionalism and political culture of the American colonies, see Greene, *Quest for Power* and other works.
39. Otis, *The Rights of the British Colonies,* 31, 15.
40. Warren, *An Oration, Delivered March 5th, 1772,* 8; *An Oration, Delivered March Sixth, 1775,* 8, 10, 11.
41. "The Declarations of the Stamp Act Congress, October 19, 1765," in Morgan, *Prologue to Revolution,* 62–63; Calvert, *Penman of the Founding,* 167–69.
42. Ibid., 63, and "The Petition to the King," in Morgan, *Prologue to Revolution,* 64.
43. *Journal of the Continental Congress,* vol. 1, 1774, 47–49, 132.
44. February 5, 1775, in Smyth, *Writings of Benjamin Franklin,* 6:304. "The Declaration as Adopted by Congress, [6 July 1775]," *Papers of Thomas Jefferson,* National Archives, https://founders.archives.gov/documents/Jefferson/01-01-02-0113-0005.
45. "Second Petition from Congress to the King, 8 July 1775," *Papers of Thomas Jefferson,* National Archives, https://founders.archives.gov/documents/Jefferson/01-01-02-0114. Maier, *American Scripture,* 24–28.

4. A HISTORY OF REPEATED INJURIES AND USURPATIONS

1. Exceptions include Friedenwald, *The Declaration of Independence,* chapters 10 and 11; Herbert, *The Declaration of Independence;* and Fisher, "The Twenty-Eight Charges." Although some of these analyses have been superseded by later research, all three give more detailed accounts than any since, though they relate the charges largely to the king's and Parliament's actions rather than to natural law, natural rights, or the rules of revolution described in this chapter. Parkinson also interprets the grievances as central to the purposes of the Declaration: *The Common Cause,* 249–63, and *Thirteen Clocks,* 153–57, and he is currently working on a detailed study of them.

2. Hutchinson, *Strictures upon the Declaration of the Congress at Philadelphia*, 3; Maier, *American Scripture*, 111. See also Mumford Jones, "The Declaration of Independence," 59–61.
3. Force, *American Archives*, vols. 5, 6, and 7. For a selection, see Maier, *American Scripture*, 217–34. See also Eicholz, *Harmonizing Sentiments*, 42–45; Hattem, *Past and Prologue*, 33–39; Brown, *Knowledge Is Power* and *The Strength of a People*; Thompson, *Rum Punch and Revolution*; Irvin, *Clothed in Robes of Sovereignty*; Adelman, *Revolutionary Networks*; and Carey, "Natural Rights, Equality, and the Declaration of Independence." English Parliament, English Bill of Rights, 1689.
4. Trevor Burnard notes that few historians today address the causes of the American Revolution, focusing instead on ideology and social conflict within the colonies: *Writing Early America*, 7–9, 11, 119–20, 199.
5. Jefferson, *Summary View*, 16. For other commentaries on the grievances, see Fisher, "The Twenty-Eight Charges against the King"; Rakove, *The Annotated U.S. Constitution and Declaration of Independence*, 80–95; Parkinson, *Common Cause*, 251–54, and *Thirteen Clocks*, 153–58.
6. Jefferson, *Summary View*, 16.
7. Dickinson, *Letters from a Farmer*, 7–12; Hicks, *The Nature and Extent of Parliamentary Power Considered*, 9; Jefferson, *Summary View*, 17.
8. English Parliament, English Bill of Rights, 1689, https://www.parliament.uk/about/living-heritage/evolutionofparliament/parliamentaryauthority/revolution/collections1/collections-glorious-revolution/billofrights/. Schwoerer, *The Declaration of Rights, 1689*; Harris, *Revolution*, 329–48; Vallance, *The Glorious Revolution of 1688*, 176–79.
9. Jefferson, *Summary View*, 17.
10. Ibid., 18.
11. Ibid., 18–19.
12. Carpenter, "Naturalization in England and the American Colonies," 293–94; Kettner, *The Development of American Citizenship*, 103–04.
13. Rakove, *The Annotated U.S. Constitution and Declaration of Independence*, 86–87; Allen, *Our Declaration*, 218–21.
14. Jefferson, *Summary View*, 20–21.
15. Ibid., 21.
16. Locke, *Two Treatises*, 355–56.
17. Bland, *An Inquiry into the Rights of the British Colonies*, 23–26; Jefferson, *Summary View*, 8–11; "VIII. To the Inhabitants of the Colony of Massachusetts-Bay, 13 March 1775," Adams Papers, Letters of Novanglus, National Archives, https://founders.archives.gov/documents/Adams/06-02-02-0072-0009; "IV. To the Inhabitants of the Colony of Massachusetts-Bay, 13 February

1775," *Adams Papers, Letters of Novanglus*, National Archives, https://founders.archives.gov/documents/Adams/06-02-02-0072-0005; "VII. To the Inhabitants of the Colony of Massachusetts-Bay, 6 March 1775," *Adams Papers, Letters of Novanglus*, National Archives, https://founders.archives.gov/documents/Adams/06-02-02-0072-0008; Dickinson, *Letters from a Farmer*, 7, 49, 12–13.

18. Vallance, *A Radical History of Britain*. The treatment of taxation in revolutionary history is extensive. The most detailed is by Reid in *Constitutional History of the American Revolution: The Authority to Tax*, although Reid focused on civil law and rejected the idea that natural law and natural rights had much to do with anything. English Parliament, English Bill of Rights, 1689, https://www.parliament.uk/about/living-heritage/evolutionofparliament/parliamentaryauthority/revolution/collections1/collections-glorious-revolution/billofrights/.
19. Locke, *Two Treatises*, 206, 294, 287–88, 296.
20. "The Declaration as Adopted by Congress, [6 July 1775]," *Papers of Thomas Jefferson*, National Archives, https://founders.archives.gov/documents/Jefferson/01-01-02-0113-0005. Locke, *Two Treatises*, 355.
21. John Adams to Horatio Gates, 23 March 1776, *Papers of Thomas Jefferson*, National Archives, https://founders.archives.gov/documents/Adams/06-04-02-0023.
22. Harris, *Revolution*, 276–90; Vallance, *The Glorious Revolution of 1688*, 136–61.
23. As Parkinson has shown, there were multiple threats of slave insurrection and Indian wars across the colonies. And revolutionary leaders ruthlessly exploited the white fear and outrage that resulted as propaganda for independence: *Common Cause*, 98–263, and *Thirteen Clocks*, 82–163.
24. Locke, *Two Treatises*, 405, 418, 415, 412, 418. Maier, *American Scripture*, 24–26.
25. The "long 1774" from the Tea Party of December 1773 to the outbreak of war in April 1774 was, as Mary Beth Norton has argued in *1774: The Long Year of Revolution*, crucial to the revolution, but according to the criteria elaborated in the Declaration of Independence, revolution could only be justified by the proofs of the king's intention on tyranny, which came later.
26. Locke, *Two Treatises*, 426–27. The story of Jephthah, a judge who ruled the Israelites for six years and led them to victory against the Ammonities, is found in *Judges*, 11 and 12.
27. Maier, *American Scripture*, 87–89; Allen, *Our Declaration*, 115–16, 129. Patrick Belanger observes the importance of the word "necessity" but sees it as a rhetorical device rather than grounded on Lockean natural law and the duty of self-defense inherent in the right to life: "Rhetoric and

Collective Necessity." I am especially grateful to former students Guillaume Braquet, Léa Berne, and Domitille Dubois-Athenor for their insights on this subject.

28. "VI. To the Inhabitants of the Colony of Massachusetts-Bay, 27 February 1775," Founders Online, National Archives, https://founders.archives.gov/documents/Adams/06-02-02-0072-0007.

29. Thomas Jefferson to John B. Colvin, 20 September 1810, *Papers of Thomas Jefferson*, National Archives, https://founders.archives.gov/documents/Jefferson/03-03-02-0060; Thomas Jefferson to James Madison, 30 January 1787, *Papers of Thomas Jefferson*, National Archives, https://founders.archives.gov/documents/Jefferson/01-11-02-0095; Thomas Jefferson to William Stephens Smith, 13 November 1787, *Papers of Thomas Jefferson*, National Archives, https://founders.archives.gov/documents/Jefferson/01-12-02-0348. Jayne, *Jefferson's Declaration of Independence*, 117–18.

30. The quotation was attributed by Sparks in his 1840 *Works of Benjamin Franklin*, but Van Doren cast doubt in *Benjamin Franklin's Autobiographical Writings*, 418–19.

31. On orthography and editorial revising generally, see Chartier, *Inscription and Erasure*, 28–45; on the hyphens, em-dashes, and other stylistic elements in the Declaration, see Becker, *The Declaration of Independence*, 175n1, 194–223; Maier, *American Scripture*, 236n1; Allen, *Our Declaration*, 76, and 72–79 and 246–48 for Matlack's other contributions.

32. Jefferson, *The Autobiography of Thomas Jefferson 1743–1790*, ed. Ford, 33. Howell, "The Declaration of Independence and Eighteenth-Century Logic"; Maier, *American Scripture*, 148. For the latest on Jefferson as a thinker led by the heart rather than the head, see Spahn, *Black Reason, White Feeling*, 1–80. On British public opinion, see O'Gorman, "The Parliamentary Opposition"; Bradley, "The British Public and the American Revolution."

33. Allen, *Our Declaration*, 97.

34. Hazelton, *The Declaration of Independence*; Becker, *The Declaration of Independence*, 194–223; Maier, *American Scripture*, 97–153; Lucas, "Justifying America" and "The Stylistic Artistry of the Declaration of Independence"; Fliegelman, *Declaring Independence*, 4–35, 164–89; Ritz, "From the Here of Jefferson's Handwritten Rough Draft"; Allen, *Our Declaration*, 47–104, 275–82; Sarson, "Harmonizing the 'Sentiments of the Day.'"

35. On the toppling of the statue, see McConville, *The King's Three Faces*, 309–11; Patrick Griffin, *America's Revolution*, 137–38, and *The Age of Atlantic Revolution*, 1–3. To George Washington from John Hancock, 6 July 1776, *Papers of George Washington*, National Archives, https://founders.archives.gov

/documents/Washington/03-05-02-0153; "General Orders, 9 July 1776," *Papers of George Washington*, National Archives, https://founders.archives.gov/documents/Washington/03-05-02-0176. Maier, *American Scripture*, 123–32, 155–60; Fliegelman, *Declaring Independence*, 4–35; Parkinson, *Common Cause*, 255–56, and *Thirteen Clocks*, 158; Sneff, "When the Declaration of Independence Was News."

36. Austin, *How to Do Things with Words*. In arguing that the Declaration "performed" independence into existence, some scholars have erased the contributions and sacrifices of countless ordinary people and reascribed to the founders the kind of omniscient power previously ascribed to them in the most old-fashioned examples of intellectual history. See Derrida, "Declarations of Independence"; Hominh, "Re-reading the Declaration of Independence as Perlocutionary Performative." Carlton Larson argues that the Declaration created the nation in a legal sense, but does not take contemporary international law into account: "The Declaration of Independence," 721–62.

5. THE RIGHT OF THE PEOPLE

1. Locke, *Two Treatises*, 304.
2. An "antiquity of the American people" that Benedict Anderson claimed was absent from the Declaration: *Imagined Communities*, 193.
3. For those who see Locke as a liberal individualist, see Strauss, *Natural Right and History*; McPherson, *The Political Theory of Possessive Individualism*; Dunn, *Political Thought of John Locke*. For critics, see Dworetz, *Unvarnished Doctrine*, 3–38, 97–134; Huyler, *Locke in America*, 1–28, 120–48; Arneil, *John Locke and America*, 2–16; Arcenas, *America's Philosopher*, 8–57; Gerber, *To Secure These Rights*, 23–40.
4. Virgil, *The Eclogues of Virgil*, 274.
5. Warren, *An Oration, Delivered March 5th, 1772*, 6–7. Shalev, *Rome Reborn on Western Shores*; Shalev, "Thomas Jefferson's Classical Silence, 1774–1776," and Rahe, "Cicero and the Classical Republican Legacy in America," both essays in Onuf and Cole, *Thomas Jefferson, the Classical World, and Early America*, although classical allusions seem a little more present in revolutionary writing and oratory than some of the authors suggest. Jefferson, though he preferred a supposed Anglo-Saxon heritage, cited Cicero in the epigraph of his *Summary View* and Cicero and Aristotle as among those who influenced the Declaration. Thomas Jefferson to Henry Lee, 8 May 1825, *Papers of Thomas Jefferson*, National Archives, https://founders.archives.gov/documents/Jefferson/98-01-02-5212.

6. Trenchard and Gordon were more Lockean that Bailyn suggested in *Ideological Origins*, although Bailyn was less dismissive of Locke than some of his critics and followers have suggested. Trenchard and Gordon, *Cato's Letters*.
7. Spahn, *Thomas Jefferson, Time, and History*; Hattem, *Past and Prologue*. For the quotations from "Scholium" in Newton's *Mathematical Principles*, see Spahn, 21–24, and for Hume's *Enquiry Concerning Human Understanding* and Bolingbroke's *Letters on the Study and Use of History*, see 106. See also Walton, "Hume and Jefferson on the Uses of History," and Wilson, "Jefferson vs. Hume," 49–70; Jayne, *Jefferson's Declaration of Independence*, 19–40; Crow, *Thomas Jefferson*, 127–29, 235, 237, 265–71. More generally, see Lovejoy, *The Great Chain of Being*; Wilcox, *Measures of Times Past*, 1–82, 187–251; Lienesch, *New Order of the Ages*.
8. "III. Thoughts on Government, April 1776," Adams Papers, Letters of Novanglus, National Archives, https://founders.archives.gov/documents/Adams/06-04-02-0026-0004; "79. A Bill for the More General Diffusion of Knowledge, 18 June 1779," Founders Online, National Archives, https://founders.archives.gov/documents/Jefferson/01-02-02-0132-0004-0079.
9. Letter to George Ticknor, 25 November 1817, cited in Spahn, *Black Reason, White Feeling*, 50. Spahn also notes that Bacon may not have said "knowledge is power" in exactly those words, citing Krohn, *Bacon*, 81–89. See also Steele, *Thomas Jefferson and American Nationhood*, 138–39.
10. "Continental Association, 20 October 1774," Founders Online, National Archives, https://founders.archives.gov/documents/Jefferson/01-01-02-0094.
11. Dickinson, *Letters from a Farmer in Pennsylvania*, 13.
12. Jefferson, *Summary View*, 5. Onuf, *Jefferson's Empire*, 65–70, 93–98, 109; Onuf, *Jefferson and the Virginians*; Steele, *Thomas Jefferson and American Nationhood*, 6, 187–290.
13. James Madison to Thomas Jefferson, 8 February 1825, Papers of James Madison, National Archives, https://founders.archives.gov/documents/Madison/04-03-02-0470. Jefferson to the Board of Visitors of the University of Virginia, March 4, 1825, cited in Onuf, *Jefferson's Empire*, 59.
14. Rakove, *Beginnings of National Politics*; Edling, *A Revolution in Favor of Government* and *Perfecting the Union*, 16–104; Blackhawk, *The Rediscovery of America*, 176–247; Roney, "An Expansion of the Same Society." I owe a particular debt to Jack Greene here, who advised me to consider the circumstances of emigration and settlement as a source of states' rights

ideology while I was overinterpreting them as the origins of union. See also Greene, *Peripheries and Center,* 151–211.
15. Locke, *Two Treatises,* 357. Morgan, *Inventing the People;* Onuf, *Jefferson's Empire,* 13; Kloppenberg, *Toward Democracy,* 314–453. Carlton Larson makes the unusual case that the Declaration was a legal instrument that had a direct impact on the law and government of the United States: "The Declaration of Independence," 703–21, 762–82.
16. Locke, *Two Treatises,* 338, 337–38.
17. McConville, *The King's Three Faces,* 1–261.
18. Ibid., 261–311; Nelson, *Royalist Revolution,* 108–45.
19. Bailyn, *Ideological Origins;* Wood, *Creation of the American Republic* and *Radicalism of the American Revolution.* Paine, *Common Sense,* 6, 8, 9.
20. Ibid., 11, 11–12, 12.
21. "VII. To the Inhabitants of the Colony of Massachusetts-Bay, 6 March 1775," *Adams Papers, Letters of Novanglus,* National Archives, https://founders.archives.gov/documents/Adams/06-02-02-0072-0008.
22. To John Adams from Benjamin Rush, 4 June 1789, *Adams Papers,* National Archives, https://founders.archives.gov/documents/Adams/06-20-02-0003. From John Adams to Benjamin Rush, 9 June 1789, *Adams Papers,* National Archives, https://founders.archives.gov/documents/Adams/06-20-02-0008. My thanks to Benoit Leridon for bringing this exchange to my attention. John Adams to Thomas Jefferson, 22 June 1819, *Papers of Thomas Jefferson,* National Archives, https://founders.archives.gov/documents/Jefferson/03-14-02-0409-0001.
23. Greene, *Quest for Power,* 3–47; *Peripheries and Center,* 5–76.
24. Nelson, *Royalist Revolution,* 184–232.
25. "III. Thoughts on Government, April 1776," *Adams Papers, Letters of Novanglus,* National Archives, https://founders.archives.gov/documents/Adams/06-04-02-0026-0004. "VII. To the Inhabitants of the Colony of Massachusetts-Bay, 6 March 1775," *Adams Papers, Letters of Novanglus,* National Archives, https://founders.archives.gov/documents/Adams/06-02-02-0072-0008.
26. "III. Thoughts on Government, April 1776," *Adams Papers, Letters of Novanglus,* National Archives, https://founders.archives.gov/documents/Adams/06-04-02-0026-0004.
27. Ibid.
28. Ibid.
29. Greene, "All Men Are Created Equal"; Keyssar, *The Right to Vote,* 8–9; Pole, *Political Representation in England and the Origins of the American*

Republic; Crow, *Thomas Jefferson,* 108–9, 130–31, 236–38. See, for example, Hamilton, *The Farmer Refuted,* in Syrett, *The Papers of Alexander Hamilton,* 1:81–165.

30. Jefferson, *Notes on the State of Virginia,* 290–91; Sarson, *The Tobacco-Plantation South;* Steele, *Thomas Jefferson and American Nationhood,* 93–95, 100, 186, 296–302.
31. John Adams to James Sullivan, 26 May 1776, *Adams Papers,* National Archives, https://founders.archives.gov/documents/Adams/06-04-02-0091.
32. Ibid.
33. Abigail Adams to John Adams, 31 March 1776, *Adams Papers,* National Archives, https://founders.archives.gov/documents/Adams/04-01-02-0241.
34. John Adams to Abigail Adams, 14 April 1776, *Adams Papers,* National Archives, https://founders.archives.gov/documents/Adams/04-01-02-0248. Holton, *Abigail Adams,* 99–105.
35. To George Washington from Thomas Jefferson, 4 December 1788, *Adams Papers,* National Archives, https://founders.archives.gov/documents/Washington/05-01-02-0118; "From Thomas Jefferson to Albert Gallatin, 13 January 1807," National Archives, https://founders.archives.gov/documents/Jefferson/99-01-02-4862; To Thomas Jefferson from John Hampden Pleasants, 12 April 1824, *Papers of Thomas Jefferson,* National Archives, https://founders.archives.gov/documents/Jefferson/98-01-02-4190. Steele, *Thomas Jefferson and American Nationhood,* 53–90; Crow, *Thomas Jefferson,* 167–69. For more on Jefferson and inequality generally, see Gordon-Reed and Onuf, "Most Blessed of the Patriarchs."
36. Keyssar, *The Right to Vote,* 3.
37. Ibid., 19–20.
38. Ibid., 3–21, 306–14. Roney, "An Expansion of the Same Society."
39. Ibid., 22–54, 315–20. Jayne, *Jefferson's Declaration of Independence,* 123–26; Nash, *The Forgotten Fifth,* 123–68; Kerber, "From the Declaration of Independence to the Declaration of Sentiments." On the founders' commitments to various forms of inequality, see Eidelberg, *On the Silence of the Declaration of Independence,* 69–105, and Greene, "All Men Are Created Equal."

6. THE REST OF MANKIND

1. Locke, *Two Treatises,* 394. Lucas, "Justifying America," 109, and Maier, *American Scripture,* 147, agree that the final grievance included Loyalists. For the opposite argument, see Kaplan, "Domestic Insurrections," and Parkinson, *Common Cause,* 254, and *Thirteen Clocks,* 156. On Loyalists, see esp. Norton, *The British Americans;* Jasanoff, *Liberty's Exiles;* Compeau,

Dishonored Americans, the latter an intriguing study of loyalists suffering dishonor and social death.
2. Others have observed that the Declaration's "one people" was exclusivist, both conceptually and in practice, but without attention to the document's context of history and historical consciousness. See esp. Onuf, *Jefferson's Empire,* and Steele, *Thomas Jefferson and American Nationhood,* esp. 11–12, 37–52; Parkinson, *Common Cause,* 254–59, and *Thirteen Clocks,* 157–63.
3. Johnson, *Taxation no Tyranny,* 89.
4. Becker, *The Declaration of Independence,* 212–17; Miller, *The Wolf by the Ears,* 1–12.
5. Jefferson, *The Autobiography of Thomas Jefferson 1743–1790,* ed. Ford, 32; *Summary View,* 16.
6. John Adams to Timothy Pickering, 6 August 1822, *Adams Papers,* National Archives, https://founders.archives.gov/documents/Adams/99-02-02-7674; Locke, *Two Treatises,* 322; Grotius, *On the Law of War and Peace,* ed. Neff; Wills, *Inventing America,* 71–73; Jayne, *Jefferson's Declaration of Independence,* 123–24; Brewer, "Slavery, Sovereignty, and 'Inheritable Blood.'"
7. Locke, *Two Treatises,* 284, 322, 346.
8. "Argument in the Case of Howell vs. Netherland," in Ford, *Works of Jefferson,* 1:470–81, at 474. Crow, *Thomas Jefferson,* 73.
9. Onuf, *Jefferson's Empire,* 94, 148, 151.
10. Thomas Jefferson to John Holmes, 22 April 1820, *Jefferson Papers,* National Archives, https://founders.archives.gov/documents/Jefferson/03-15-02-0518. I am using the term "conditional proslavery" partly in answer to William Freehling's use of "conditional termination" to describe the founders' form of antislavery. "Conditional termination" amounts to conditional continuation, and conditional antislavery is conditional proslavery if the conditions are not met. Freehling, *The Road to Disunion,* 119–210.
11. Jefferson, *Notes on the State of Virginia,* 264.
12. Ibid., 264, 266. Onuf, *Jefferson's Empire,* 140–74, quotation at 148.
13. Jefferson, *Notes on the State of Virginia,* 267. Onuf, *Jefferson's Empire,* 174–88; Steele, *Thomas Jefferson and American Nationhood,* 167–68, 169, 176–86, 298–302; Crow, *Thomas Jefferson,* 132, 136–37, 150–62, 221–22, 155–57. Gordon-Reed, *Thomas Jefferson and Sally Hemings* and *The Hemingses of Monticello.*
14. Jefferson, *Notes on the State of Virginia,* 270. Onuf, *Jefferson's Empire,* 170–74.
15. Jordan's *White over Black* remains the most trenchant statement that the Declaration's ideas of equality and liberty provided an imperative for

the founders to abolish slavery, despite his appreciation of the depth of early American racism. See esp. 269–304, 308–11, 429–35. Jack Greene drew attention to the founders' deep commitment to inequality, but he too accepts the supposition that the Declaration's idea of equality was applicable to civil society rather than only in a state of nature: see esp. "All Men Are Created Equal." These views still dominate a historiography that continues to posit a contradiction between the Declaration's precepts about natural rights and the existence of slavery, rather than a resolution between them based on natural law and the course of human events. See also Diggins, "Slavery, Race, and Equality," and Rogin, "The Two Declarations of Independence." Some historians continued to gloss over Jefferson's involvement with slavery, stressing his statements against the institution. See Malone, *Jefferson and His Time*, esp, vols. 4, 5, and 6; Koch, *Philosophy of Thomas Jefferson*; Boorstin; *The Lost World of Thomas Jefferson*.

16. Holton, *Abigail Adams*, 181–82; *Petition for freedom to Massachusetts Governor Thomas Hutchinson, His Majesty's Council, and the House of Representatives, June 1773*.
17. *Petition for freedom to Massachusetts Governor Thomas Gage, His Majesty's Council, and the House of Representatives, 25 May 1774*.
18. "Petition for freedom (manuscript copy) to the Massachusetts Council and the House of Representatives, [13] January 1777." Davis, "Emancipation Rhetoric"; Cameron, *To Plead Our Own Cause*; Sesay, "The Revolutionary Black Roots of Slavery's Abolition in Massachusetts"; Stanton, "The Freedom Petitions."
19. Breen, "Making History"; Frey, *Water from the Rock*, 45–80, 284–325; Egerton, *Death or Liberty*, 93–121, 169–93; Newman, *The Transformation of American Abolitionism*; Sinha, *The Slave's Cause*, 69–70; Polgar, *Standard Bearers of Equality*.
20. Waldstreicher, *Slavery's Constitution*.
21. Ibid., 3–10, 57–105; Rothman, *Slave Country*, 1–35.
22. See esp. Fitzmaurice, *Sovereignty, Property, and Empire*; Pagden, *The Burdens of Empire*; Macmillan, *Sovereignty and Possession in the English New World*; Armitage, *Ideological Origins of the British Empire*; Greer, *Property and Dispossession*.
23. Locke, *Two Treatises*, 301, 206, 294, 299, 296–97, 339–40. Arneil, *John Locke and America*, 24–44.
24. "Petition of the Virginia House of Burgesses to the King, May 16, 1684," cited in Yirush, *Settlers, Liberty, and Empire*, 60; Rawson, *The Revolution in New-England Justified*, 18–19. I am defining settler colonialism here as an ideology rather than as historical fact. As numerous historians have

shown, Native Americans defied and defined the process of European settlement much more effectively than settler-colonialism as an annihilating historical narrative allows for. On settler colonialism as history, see Wolfe, "Settler Colonialism and the Elimination of the Native," *Settler Colonialism*, and *Traces of History*; Veracini, *Settler Colonialism*. For a variety of views on the concept's applicability to early America, see Ostler and Shoemaker, "Forum: Settler Colonialism and Early American History."

25. Rawson, *The Revolution in New-England Justified*, 44; Dummer, *A Defence of the New-England Charters*, 5, 9, 12; Yirush, *Settlers, Liberty, and Empire*, 72, 4. Prior has dated the origins of American settler colonialism back to Jamestown: "Settlers among Empires."

26. Bulkley, *Poetical Meditations*, xii, xvii–xviii, xxix. xxv, xxvii–xxviii. xxxvii, liii. xxvi. Bulkley cited Locke as follows: "Treatise of Government, p. 247. and afterward p. 280": xxx.

27. Bulkley, *Poetical Meditations*, xviii, lii; liii–liv, liv. Yirush, *Settlers, Liberty, and Empire*, 113–41.

28. Otis, *The Rights of the British Colonies*, 34, 57; Bland, *An Inquiry into the Rights of the British Colonies*, 13–14; Wilson, *Considerations on the Nature and Extent of the Legislative Authority*, 16; "XII. To the Inhabitants of the Colony of Massachusetts-Bay, 17 April 1775," *Adams Papers, Letters of Novanglus*, National Archives, https://founders.archives.gov/documents/Adams/06-02-02-0072-0014. Kammen, "The Meaning of Colonization," 342–43, 349; Yirush, *Settlers, Liberty, and Empire*, 158–79, 256–59.

29. Lovell, *An Oration Delivered April 2d, 1771*, 7, 14; Warren, *An Oration, Delivered March Sixth, 1775*, 6, 6–7, 8, 7, 8, 9, 10.

30. "The Stamp Act Congress, October 7–24, 1765: The Petition to the King," in Morgan, *Prologue to Revolution*, 64; and for individual colonial resolves, see Morgan 50–61. "Fairfax County Resolves, 18 July 1774," *Papers of George Washington*, National Archives, https://founders.archives.gov/documents/Washington/02-10-02-0080; "Convention of Suffolk County," in Lincoln, *The Journals of Each Provincial Congress of Massachusetts*, 601.

31. National Archives, https://founders.archives.gov/ancestor/TSJN-01-01-02-0113; Jefferson, *Summary View*, 6.

32. Jefferson, *Summary View*, 7, 6, 2, 6.

33. Trouillot, *Silencing the Past*, 26. See also O'Brien, *Firsting and Lasting*.

34. From Thomas Jefferson to William Ludlow, 6 September 1824, *Papers of Thomas Jefferson*, National Archives, https://founders.archives.gov/documents/Jefferson/98-01-02-4523. Onuf, *Jefferson's Empire*, 18–52.

35. Onuf, *Jefferson's Empire*, 37.

36. Onuf, *Statehood and Union* and *Jefferson's Empire*, 33–46, 53–65, 143–44; Duffey, "The Northwest Ordinance"; Calloway, *The Scratch of a Pen*; Furstenberg, "The Significance of the Trans-Appalachian Frontier in Atlantic History"; Ford, *Settler Sovereignty*; Saler, *Settlers' Empire*; Ostler, *Surviving Genocide*; Steele, *Thomas Jefferson and American Nationhood*, 173–76; Crow, *Thomas Jefferson*, 216–32; Greer, "Settler Colonialism and Empire in Early America"; Blackhawk, *The Rediscovery of America*, 4–5, 176–247; Roney, "An Expansion of the Same Society"; Hixson, *American Settler Colonialism*; Ostler, "'Just and Lawful War' as Genocidal War in the (United States) Northwest Ordinance and Northwest Territory, 1787–1832."

37. To Captain Hendrick, the Delawares, Mohicans, and Munries, December 21, 1808, To the Chiefs of the Ottawas, Chippewas, Powtowatamies, Wynadots, and Senecas of Sandusky, April 22, 1808, in Onuf, *Jefferson's Empire*, 48, 48–48. See also Miller, *Jefferson and Nature*, 65; Wallace, *Jefferson and the Indians*; Miller, *Native America*; Crow, *Thomas Jefferson*, 5, 53–54, 58, 162–78, 181–88.

38. Greene, "Pluribus or Unum?" Fliegelman, *Declaring Independence*, 160–63; Irvin, *Clothed in Robes of Sovereignty*, 1–3, 129–30; Steele, *Thomas Jefferson and American Nationhood*, 33–35; Crow, *Thomas Jefferson*, 115–16, 238–50.

POSTSCRIPT

1. Haynes, "Liberty Further Extended," 94, 96.
2. Spahn, *Black Reason, White Feeling*, 93–97, quotation at 95.
3. Detweiler, "The Changing Reputation of the Declaration of Independence"; Maier, *American Scripture*, 154–208.
4. Spahn, *Black Reason, White Feeling*, 101–02.
5. Walker cited in Spahn, *Black Reason, White Feeling*, 106.
6. Garrison, "To the Public." Douglass, "The Meaning of the Fourth of July for the Negro," in Foner, *Frederick Douglass*, 197; John Adams to Abigail Adams, 14 April 1776, *Adams Papers*, National Archives, https://founders.archives.gov/documents/Adams/04-01-02-0248; *Seneca Falls Declaration (1848)*, Constitution Center. Maier in *American Scripture* and "The Strange History of 'All Men Are Created Equal'"; Hattem, *The Memory of '76*.

WORKS CITED

PRIMARY SOURCES AND COLLECTIONS

Adams, John. *The Adams Papers.* National Archives, Founders Online: The Adams Papers. https://founders.archives.gov/about/Adams.

Adams, John. *The Letters of Novanglus.* Boston, 1775. National Archives. I. To the Inhabitants of the Colony of Massachusetts-Bay, 23 January 1775. https://founders.archives.gov/?q=Author%3A%22Novanglus%22&s=1111311111&r=1.

Adams, John. "Thoughts on Government." Boston, 1776. National Archives, Founders Online: Thoughts on Government: ante 27 March–April 1776. https://founders.archives.gov/ancestor/ADMS-06-04-02-0026.

Allen, John. *The American Alarm, or, The Bostonian plea, for the rights, and liberties, of the people.* Boston, 1773.

Anon. *An Argument in Defence of the Exclusive Right Claimed by the Colonies to Tax Themselves.* London, 1774.

Bland, Richard. *The Colonel Dismounted: Or the Rector Vindicated.* Williamsburg, 1764.

Bland, Richard. *An Inquiry into the Rights of the British Colonies, Intended as an Answer to The Regulations lately made concerning the Colonies, and the Taxes imposed upon them considered.* Williamsburg, 1766.

Bland, Richard. *A Letter to the Clergy of Virginia in which the Conduct of General-Assembly is Vindicated.* Williamsburg, 1760.

Bulkley, John. *Poetical Meditations, Being the Improvement of some Vacant Hours, By Roger Wolcott, Esq, With a Preface By the Reverend Mr. Bulkley of Colchester.* New London, CT, 1725.

Burke, Edmund. *The Writings and Speeches of Edmund Burke, Volume II: Party, Parliament, and the American Crisis 1766–1774,* ed. Paul Langford. Oxford University Press, 1981.

Coke, Edward. *The Selected Writings and Speeches of Sir Edward Coke*, ed. Steve Sheppard. 3 vols. Liberty Fund, 2003.

Constitution of New Hampshire, 1776. The Avalon Project: Constitution of New Hampshire—1776 (yale.edu). https://avalon.law.yale.edu/18th_century/nh09.asp#1.

Constitution of New Jersey, 1776. The Avalon Project: Constitution of New Jersey, 1776 (yale.edu). https://avalon.law.yale.edu/18th_century/nj15.asp.

Constitution of South Carolina, 1776. The Avalon Project: Constitution of South Carolina—March 26, 1776 (yale.edu). https://avalon.law.yale.edu/18th_century/sc01.asp.

Constitution of Virginia, 1776. "The Virginia Bill of Rights, June 12, 1776," and "The Constitution of Virginia, 29 June, 1776," National Archives, The Virginia Declaration of Rights; *VII. The Constitution as Adopted by the Convention, [29 June 1776]*. https://founders.archives.gov/documents/Jefferson/01-01-02-0161-0008.

Continental Congress. Articles of Association, October 20, 1774. National Archives: *1774 Articles of Association* (ArchivesFoundation.org). https://archivesfoundation.org/documents/1774-articles-association/.

Continental Congress. "A Declaration of the Causes and Necessity of Taking Up Arms" (all versions), National Archives, *Declaration of the Causes and Necessity for Taking Up Arms [26 June–6 July 1775]*, https://founders.archives.gov/ancestor/TSJN-01-01-02-0113.

Continental Congress. The Declaration of Independence (all versions). National Archives. https://www.archives.gov/founding-docs.

Continental Congress. Declaration and Resolves, October 14, 1774. *Avalon Project—Declaration and Resolves of the First Continental Congress* (yale.edu). https://avalon.law.yale.edu/18th_century/resolves.asp.

Continental Congress. *Journals of the Continental Congress, 1774–1789*, ed. Worthington C. Ford et al. 4 vols. Library of Congress, 1904.

Continental Congress. "Second Petition from Congress to the King, 8 July 1775," National Archives, https://founders.archives.gov/documents/Jefferson/01-01-02-0114.

Continental Congress. "The Twelve United Colonies, by their Delegates in Congress, to the Inhabitants of Great Britain," July 8, 1775. *Journals of the American Congress: From 1774 to 1789. In Four Volumes*. Vol. I, 108. Washington, DC, Way and Gideon, 1823.

Dickinson, John. *Letters from a Farmer in Pennsylvania. To the Inhabitants of the British Colonies*. Philadelphia, 1768.

Dickinson, John. *Essay on the Constitutional Power of Great-Britain over the Colonies in America*. Philadelphia, 1775.
Dickinson, John. J. H. Powell, ed. "Speech of John Dickinson Opposing the Declaration of Independence, 1 July, 1776." *Pennsylvania Magazine of History and Biography* 65, no. 3 (October 1941): 458–81.
Downer, Silas. *A Discourse Delivered in Providence*. Providence, 1768.
Douglass, Frederick. "The Meaning of the Fourth of July for the Negro" [commonly known as "What to the Slave is the Fourth of July"]. In *Frederick Douglass: Selected Speeches and Writings*, edited by Philip S. Foner, abridged and adapted by Yuval Taylor. Lawrence Hill, 1999.
Dulany, Daniel (the Elder). *The Right of the Inhabitants of Maryland to the Benefit of the English Laws*. Annapolis, 1728. Reprinted in St. George L. Sioussat, "The English Statutes in Maryland." *Johns Hopkins University Studies in Historical and Political Science* 21, nos. 11–12 (1903): 79–104.
Dulany, Daniel (the Younger). *Considerations on the Propriety of Imposing Taxes in the British Colonies*. Annapolis, 1765.
Dummer, Jeremiah. *A Defence of the New-England Charters*. Boston, 1721.
English Parliament. English Bill of Rights, 1689. The Avalon Project: English Bill of Rights—1689 (yale edu). https://avalon.law.yale.edu/17th_century/england.asp.
Foner, Philip S., ed. *We, the Other People: Alternative Declarations of Independence by Labor Groups, Farmers, Woman's Rights Advocates, Socialists, and Blacks, 1829–1975*. University Press of Illinois, 1976.
Force, Peter, ed. *American Archives: Documents of the American Revolutionary Period, 1774–1776*. Northern Illinois University Digital Library (niu.edu). https://digital.lib.niu.edu/amarch.
Franklin, Benjamin. *The Papers of Benjamin Franklin*. National Archives, Founders Online: The Papers of Benjamin Franklin. https://founders.archives.gov/about/Franklin.
Franklin, Benjamin. *The Writings of Benjamin Franklin*, ed. Albert Henry Smyth. Macmillan, 1905.
Garrison, William. "To the Public." *The Liberator*, January 1, 1831. Boston Public Library, *The Liberator* (Boston, Mass.: 1831–1865)—Digital Commonwealth. https://www.digitalcommonwealth.org/collections/commonwealth:9w032b61n.
Greene, Jack P., ed. *Colonies to Nation, 1763–1789: A Documentary History of the American Revolution*. Norton, 1975.
Greene, Jack P., and Craig B. Yirush, eds. *Exploring the Bounds of Liberty: Political Writings of Colonial British America from the Glorious Revolution to the American Revolution*. 3 vols. Liberty Fund, 2018.

Grotius, Hugo. *On the Law of War and Peace,* ed. Stephen C. Neff. Cambridge University Press, 2013.

Hall, Michael G., Lawrence H. Leder, and Michael G. Kammen, eds. *The Glorious Revolution in America: Documents on the Colonial Crisis of 1689.* University of North Carolina Press, 1964.

Hamilton, Alexander. *The Farmer Refuted, or A more impartial and comprehensive View of the Dispute between Great-Britain and the Colonies.* New York, 1775. In *The Papers of Alexander Hamilton,* vol. 1, ed. Harold C. Syrett, 81–165. Columbia University Press, 1961.

Haynes, Lemuel. "Liberty Further Extended" (unpublished, 1776). In Ruth Bogin, "'Liberty Further Extended': A 1776 Antislavery Manuscript by Lemuel Haynes." *William and Mary Quarterly* 40, no. 1 (January 1983): 85–105.

Hicks, William. *The Nature and Extent of Parliamentary Power Considered.* Philadelphia, 1768.

Hopkins, Stephen. *The Rights of the Colonies Examined.* Providence, 1765.

Hutchinson, Thomas, *Strictures upon the Declaration of the Congress at Philadelphia in a Letter to a Noble Lord, &c.* London, 1776.

Jefferson, Thomas. *The Autobiography of Thomas Jefferson 1743–1790,* ed. Paul Leicester Ford, with a new introduction by Michael Zuckerman. University of Pennsylvania Press, 2005.

Jefferson, Thomas. *The Commonplace Book of Thomas Jefferson: A Repository of His Ideas on Government,* ed. Gilbert Chinard. Johns Hopkins University Press, 1926.

Jefferson, Thomas. *Jefferson's Legal Commonplace Book,* ed. David Thomas Konig and Michael P. Zuckert. Princeton University Press, 2022.

Jefferson, Thomas. *Jefferson's Literary Commonplace Book,* ed. Douglas L. Wilson. Princeton University Press, 1989.

Jefferson, Thomas. *Notes on the State of Virginia.* In *Jefferson: Writings,* ed. Merrill D. Peterson, 123–325. Library of America, 1984.

Jefferson, Thomas. *The Papers of Thomas Jefferson.* National Archives, Founders Online: The Papers of Thomas Jefferson. https://founders.archives.gov/about/Jefferson.

Jefferson, Thomas. *The Works of Thomas Jefferson,* ed. Paul Leicester Ford. 12 vols. G. P. Putnam's Sons, 1904–1905.

Jefferson, Thomas. *A Summary View of the Rights of British America. Set forth in some Resolutions Intended for the Inspection of the Present Delegates of the People of Virginia, Now in Convention.* Williamsburg, 1774.

Johnson, Samuel. *Taxation no Tyranny.* London, 1775.

Journals of the American Congress: From 1774 to 1789. In Four Volumes. Way and Gideon, 1823.

Knox, William. "Hints Respecting the Settlement of our American Provinces." In Thomas C. Barrow, "A Project for Imperial Reform: 'Hints Respecting the Settlement of our American Provinces,' 1763." *William and Mary Quarterly*, 3d Ser., 24, no. 1 (January 1967): 108–26.
Lee, Arthur. *An Essay in Vindication of the Continental Colonies of America*. London, 1764.
Lincoln, William, ed. *The Journals of Each Provincial Congress of Massachusetts*. Dutton and Wentworth, 1838.
Lind, John. *An Answer to the Declaration of the American Congress*. London, 1776.
Locke, John. *An Essay Concerning Human Understanding*, ed. Roger Woolhouse. London, 1997, rev. ed., 2004.
Locke, John. *Two Treatises of Government*, ed. Peter Laslett. Cambridge University Press, 1960, 2004.
Lovell, James. *An Oration Delivered April 2d, 1771*. Boston, 1771.
Madison, James. *The Papers of James Madison*. National Archives, Founders Online: The Papers of James Madison. https://founders.archives.gov/about/Madison.
Morgan, Edmund S., ed. *Prologue to Revolution: Sources and Documents on the Stamp Act Crisis, 1764–1766*. Norton, 1959, 1973.
Otis, James. *A Vindication of the Conduct of the House of Representatives of the Province of the Massachusetts-Bay*. Boston, 1762.
Otis, James. *The Rights of the British Colonies Asserted and Proved*. Boston, 1764.
Paine, Thomas. *Common Sense*, 1776. In *Paine: Political Writings*, ed. Bruce Kuklick, 1–45. Cambridge University Press, 2000, 2012.
Petition for freedom to Massachusetts Governor Thomas Hutchinson, His Majesty's Council, and the House of Representatives, June 1773. Massachusetts Historical Society, Collections Online.
Petition for freedom to Massachusetts Governor Thomas Gage, His Majesty's Council, and the House of Representatives, 25 May 1774. Massachusetts Historical Society, Collections Online.
"Petition for freedom (manuscript copy) to the Massachusetts Council and the House of Representatives, [13] January 1777." Massachusetts Historical Society, Collections Online.
Rawson, Edward. *The Revolution in New-England Justified, and the People there Vindicated from the Aspersions Cast upon them by Mr. John Palmer*. Boston, 1691, 1773.
Rakove, Jack N. *The Annotated U.S. Constitution and Declaration of Independence*. Harvard University Press, 2009.
Sarson, Steven, and Jack P. Greene, eds. *The American Colonies and the British Empire, 1607–1783*. 8 vols. Pickering and Chatto, 2010–11; Routledge, 2020.

Sparks, Jared. *The Works of Benjamin Franklin*. Charles Tappan, 1844.
Stanton, Elizabeth Cady, et al. Declaration of Sentiments, 1848. *Seneca Falls Declaration (1848)*. Constitution Center. https://constitutioncenter.org/the-constitution/historic-document-library/detail/seneca-falls-declaration-1848.
Trenchard John, and Thomas Gordon, *Cato's Letters: Or, Essays on Liberty, Civil and Religious, and Other Important Subjects*. London, 1720. Edited by Ronald Hamowy, 4 vols. in 2, Liberty Fund, 1995.
Van Doren, Carl. *Benjamin Franklin's Autobiographical Writings*. Viking, 1945.
Virgil. *The Eclogues of Virgil*, trans. J. W. MacKail. Modern Library, 1934.
Warren, Joseph. *An Oration, Delivered March 5th, 1772*. Boston, 1772.
Warren, Joseph. *An Oration, Delivered March Sixth, 1775*. Boston, 1775.
Washington, George. *The Papers of George Washington*. University of Virginia, WashingtonPapers.org.
Webster, Samuel. *The Misery and Duty of an Oppress'd and Enslav'd People*. Boston, 1774.
Wilson, James. *Considerations on the Nature and Extent of the Legislative Authority of the British Parliament*. Philadelphia, 1774.
Wirt, William. *Sketches of the Life and Character of Patrick Henry*. Philadelphia, 1817.

SECONDARY SOURCES

Adelman, Joseph M. *Revolutionary Networks: The Business and Politics of Printing the News, 1763–1789*. Johns Hopkins University Press, 2019.
Allen, Danielle. *Our Declaration: A Reading of the Declaration of Independence in Defense of Equality*. Liveright, 2014.
Amar, Akhil Reed. *The Words That Made Us: America's Constitutional Conversation, 1760–1840*. Basic Books, 2021.
Anderson, Benedict. *Imagined Communities: Reflections on the Origin and Spread of Nationalism*. Verso, 1983, rev. ed., 2006.
Anderson, Owen. *The Declaration of Independence and God: Self-Evident Truths in American Law*. Cambridge University Press, 2015.
Appleby, Joyce. *Liberalism and Republicanism in the Historical Imagination*. Harvard University Press, 1992.
Arcenas, Claire Rydell. *America's Philosopher: John Locke in American Intellectual Life*. University of Chicago Press, 2022.
Armitage, David. *The Declaration of Independence: A Global History*. Harvard University Press, 2008.
Armitage, David. "The Declaration of Independence and International Law." *William and Mary Quarterly* 59, no. 1 (January 2002): 39–64.

Armitage, David. *The Ideological Origins of the British Empire*. Cambridge University Press, 2000.
Arneil, Barbara. *John Locke and America: The Defence of English Colonialism*. Clarendon Press of Oxford University Press, 1996.
Ashcraft, Richard. *Revolutionary Politics and Locke's Two Treatises of Government*. Princeton University Press, 1986.
Austin, J. L. *How to Do Things with Words*. 2nd ed., ed. J. O. Urmson and M. Sbisà. Harvard University Press, 1975.
Bailyn, Bernard. *The Ideological Origins of the American Revolution*. Harvard University Press, 1967, 1992.
Bailyn, Bernard. *The Origins of American Politics*. Random House, 1967.
Barrow, Thomas C. "A Project for Imperial Reform: 'Hints Respecting the Settlement of our American Provinces,' 1763." *William and Mary Quarterly*, 3d Ser., 24, no. 1 (January 1967): 108–26.
Becker, Carl. *The Declaration of Independence: A Study in the History of Political Ideas*. Harcourt, Brace, 1922; Dodo Press, 2008.
Belanger, Patrick. "Rhetoric and Collective Necessity: The Declaration of Independence." *Journal of the Canadian Society for the Study of Rhetoric* 6 (2016): 84–98.
Bilder, Mary Sarah. *The Transatlantic Constitution: Colonial Legal Culture and the Empire*. Harvard University Press, 2004.
Black, Barbara. "The Constitution of Empire: The Case for the Colonists." *University of Pennsylvania Law Review* 124, no. 5 (May 1976): 1157–211.
Blackhawk, Ned. *The Rediscovery of America: Native Peoples and the Unmaking of U.S. History*. Yale University Press, 2023.
Boorstin, Daniel. *The Lost World of Thomas Jefferson*. Peter Smith, 1976.
Boyd, Julian P. *The Declaration of Independence: The Evolution of a Text*. Washington, DC: Library of Congress, 1943; repr., ed. Gerald W. Gawait, Library of Congress, 2000.
Bradley, James E. "The British Public and the American Revolution: Ideology, Interest and Opinion." In *Britain and the American Colonies*, ed. H. T. Dickinson, 124–54. Routledge, 1998.
Breen, T. H. "Making History: The Force of Public Opinion and the Last Years of Slavery in Massachusetts." In *Through a Glass Darkly: Reflections on Personal Identity in Early America*, ed. Ronald Hoffman, Mechal Sobel, and Fredrika J. Teute, 67–95. University of North Carolina Press, 1997.
Brewer, Holly. *By Birth or Consent: Children, Law, and the Anglo-American Revolution in Authority*. University of North Carolina Press, 2005.
Brewer, Holly. "Slavery, Sovereignty, and 'Inheritable Blood': Reconsidering John Locke and the Origins of American Slavery." *American Historical Review* 122, no. 4 (October 2017): 1038–78.

Brown, Gillian. *The Consent of the Governed: The Lockean Legacy in Early American Culture.* Harvard University Press, 2001.

Brown, Richard D. *Knowledge Is Power: The Diffusion of Information in Early America, 1700–1865.* Oxford University Press, 1991.

Brown, Richard D. *Self-Evident Truths: Contesting Equal Rights from the Revolution to the Civil War.* Yale University Press, 2017.

Brown, Richard D. *The Strength of a People: The Idea of an Informed Citizenry in America, 1650–1870.* University of North Carolina Press, 2000.

Bruner, M. Lane. *Strategies of Remembrance: The Rhetorical Dimensions of National Identity Construction.* University of South Carolina Press, 2002.

Burke, Peter. "History as Social Memory." In *Memory: History, Culture and the Mind,* 97–114. Blackwell, 1989.

Burnard, Trevor. *Writing Early America: From Empire to Revolution.* University of Virginia Press, 2023.

Calloway, Colin G. *The Scratch of a Pen: 1763 and the Transformation of North America.* Oxford University Press, 2006.

Calvert, Jane E. *Penman of the Founding: A Biography of John Dickinson.* Oxford University Press, 2024.

Cameron, Christopher. *To Plead Our Own Cause: African Americans in Massachusetts and the Making of the Antislavery Movement.* Kent State University Press, 2014.

Carey, George W. "Natural Rights, Equality, and the Declaration of Independence." *Ave Maria Law Review* 3, no. 1 (Spring 2005): 45–68.

Carpenter, A. H. "Naturalization in England and the American Colonies." *American Historical Review* 9, no. 2 (January 1904): 288–303.

Chartier, Roger. *Inscription and Erasure: Literature and Written Culture from the Eleventh to the Eighteenth Century.* University of Pennsylvania Press, 2007.

Cogliano, Francis D. *Thomas Jefferson: Reputation and Legacy.* University of Virginia Press, 2006.

Cohen, I. Bernard. *Science and the Founding Fathers: Science in the Political Thought of Thomas Jefferson, Benjamin Franklin, John Adams, and James Madison.* Norton, 1995.

Colbourn, H. Trevor. *The Lamp of Experience: Whig History and the Intellectual Origins of the American Revolution.* University of North Carolina Press, 1965; Liberty Fund, 1998.

Colley, Linda. *Britons: Forging the Nation, 1707–1837.* Yale University Press, 1992.

Compeau, Timothy. *Dishonored Americans: The Political Death of Loyalists in Revolutionary America.* University of Virginia Press, 2023.

Confino, Alon. "Collective Memory and Cultural History: Problems of Method." *American Historical Review* 102, no. 5 (December 1997): 1386–403.

Confino, Alon. "Memory and the History of Mentalities." In *Cultural Memory Studies: An International and Interdisciplinary Handbook*, 77–84. De Gruyter, 2008.

Conklin, Carli N. *The Pursuit of Happiness in the Founding Era: An Intellectual History*. University of Missouri Press, 2019.

Crow, Matthew. *Thomas Jefferson, Legal History, and the Art of Recollection*. Cambridge University Press, 2017.

Davis, Thomas J. "Emancipation Rhetoric, Natural Rights, and Revolutionary New England: A Note on Four Black Petitions in Massachusetts, 1773–1777." *New England Quarterly* 62, no. 2 (June 1989): 248–63.

Derrida, Jacques. "Declarations of Independence." In *Negotiations: Interventions and Interviews, 1971–2001*, 46–54. Stanford University Press, 2002.

Detweiler, Philip. "The Changing Reputation of the Declaration of Independence: The First Fifty Years." *William and Mary Quarterly* 19, no. 4 (October 1962): 557–74.

Dickinson, H. T. "Britain's Imperial Sovereignty: The Ideological Case against the American Colonies." In *Britain and the American Colonies*, ed. H. T. Dickinson, 64–96. Routledge, 1998.

Diggins, John Patrick. "Slavery, Race, and Equality: Jefferson and the Pathos of the Enlightenment." *American Quarterly* 28, no. 2 (Summer 1976): 208–28.

Diggins, John Patrick. *The Lost Soul of American Politics: Virtue, Self-Interest, and the Foundations of Liberalism*. University of Chicago Press, 1984.

Duffey, Denis P. "The Northwest Ordinance as a Constitutional Document." *Columbia Law Review* 95, no. 4 (May 1995): 929–68.

Dumbauld, Edward. *The Declaration of Independence and What It Means Today*. University of Oklahoma Press, 1950.

Dumbauld, Edward. "Independence under International Law." *American Journal of International Law* 70 (1976): 425–31.

Dunn, John. *The Political Thought of John Locke: An Historical Account of the Argument of the "Two Treatises of Government."* Cambridge University Press, 1988.

Dworetz, Steven M. *The Unvarnished Doctrine: Locke, Liberalism and the American Revolution*. Duke University Press, 1990.

Edling, Max. *A Revolution in Favor of Government: Origins of the U.S. Constitution and the Making of an American State*. Oxford University Press, 2003.

Edling, Max. *Perfecting the Union: National and State Authority in the U.S. Constitution*. Oxford University Press, 2021.

Egerton, Douglas. *Death or Liberty: African Americans in Revolutionary America.* Oxford University Press, 2009.

Eicholz, Hans. *Harmonizing Sentiments: The Declaration of Independence and the Jeffersonian Idea of Self-Government.* Peter Lang, 2001.

Eidelberg Paul. *On the Silence of the Declaration of Independence.* University of Massachusetts Press, 1976.

Fisher, Sydney George. "The Twenty-Eight Charges Against the King in the Declaration of Independence." *Pennsylvania Magazine of History and Biography* 31, no. 3 (1907): 257–303.

Fitzmaurice, Andrew. *Sovereignty, Property, and Empire, 1500–2000.* Cambridge University Press, 2014.

Fliegelman, Jay. *Declaring Independence: Jefferson, Natural Language, and the Culture of Performance.* Stanford University Press, 1993.

Ford, Lisa. *Settler Sovereignty: Jurisdiction and Indigenous People in America and Australia, 1788–1836.* Harvard University Press, 2010.

Freehling, William W. *The Road to Disunion, Vol. 1: Secessionists at Bay, 1776–1854.* Oxford University Press, 1990.

Frey, Sylvia R. *Water from the Rock: Black Resistance in a Revolutionary Age.* Princeton University Press, 1991.

Friedenwald, Herbert. *The Declaration of Independence: An Interpretation and an Analysis.* Macmillan, 1904.

Furstenberg, François. *In the Name of the Father: Washington's Legacy, Slavery, and the Making of a Nation.* Penguin, 2006.

Furstenberg, François. "The Significance of the Trans-Appalachian Frontier in Atlantic History." *American Historical Review* 113, no. 3 (June 2008): 647–77.

Gerber, Scott Douglas. *To Secure These Rights: The Declaration of Independence and Constitutional Interpretation.* New York University Press, 1995.

Gordon-Reed, Annette. *The Hemingses of Monticello: An American Family.* Norton, 2008.

Gordon-Reed, Annette. *Thomas Jefferson and Sally Hemings: An American Controversy.* University of Virginia Press, 1997.

Gordon-Reed, Annette, and Peter S. Onuf. *"Most Blessed of the Patriarchs": Thomas Jefferson and the Empire of the Imagination.* Liveright, 2017.

Gould, Eliga H. *Among the Powers of the Earth: The American Revolution and the Making of a New World Empire.* Harvard University Press, 2012.

Gould, Eliga H. *Crucible of Peace: The Turbulent History of the United States' Founding Treaty.* Oxford University Press, 2025.

Gould, Eliga H. *The Persistence of Empire: British Political Culture in the Age of the American Revolution.* University of North Carolina Press, 2000.

Greene, Jack P. "All Men Are Created Equal: Some Reflections on the Character of the American Revolution." In *Imperatives, Behaviors, and Identities: Essays in Early American Cultural History*, 236–67. University of Virginia Press, 1992.

Greene, Jack P. *The Constitutional Origins of the American Revolution*. Cambridge University Press, 2011.

Greene, Jack P. "The Glorious Revolution and the British Empire, 1688–1783." In *Negotiated Authorities: Essays in Colonial Political and Constitutional History*, 78–92. University of Virginia Press, 1994.

Greene, Jack P. *Intellectual Construction of America: Exceptionalism and Identity from 1492 to 1800*. University of North Carolina Press, 1997.

Greene, Jack P. "The Limits of the American Revolution." In *Understanding the American Revolution: Issues and Actors*, 359–70. University of Virginia Press, 1995.

Greene, Jack P. *Peripheries and Center: Constitutional Development in the Extended Polities of the British Empire and the United States, 1607–1788*. Norton, 1986.

Greene, Jack P. "Pluribus or Unum? White Ethnicity in the Formation of Colonial American Culture." In *Creating the British Atlantic: Essays on Transplantation, Adaptation, and Continuity*, 381–400. University of Virginia Press, 2013.

Greene, Jack P. "The Pursuit of Happiness, the Private Realm, and the Movement for a Stronger National Government." In *Imperatives, Behaviors, and Identities: Essays in Early American Cultural History*, 310–16. University of Virginia Press, 1992.

Greene, Jack P. *Pursuits of Happiness: The Social Development of the Early Modern British Colonies and the Formation of American Culture*. University of North Carolina Press, 1988.

Greene, Jack P. *The Quest for Power: The Lower Houses of Assembly in the Southern Royal Colonies, 1689–1776*. University of North Carolina Press, 1963.

Greene, Jack P. "State Identities and National Identity in the Era of the American Revolution." In *Creating the British Atlantic: Essays on Transplantation, Adaptation, and Continuity*, 340–59. University of Virginia Press, 2013.

Greer, Allan. *Property and Dispossession: Natives, Empires and Land in Early Modern North America*. Cambridge University Press, 2018.

Greer, Allan. "Settler Colonialism and Empire in Early America." *William and Mary Quarterly* 76, no. 3 (July 2019): 383–90.

Griffin, Patrick. *The Age of Atlantic Revolution: The Fall and Rise of a Connected World*. Yale University Press, 2023.

Griffin, Patrick. *America's Revolution*. Oxford University Press, 2012.

Gutzman, K. R. Constantine. "Jefferson's Draft Declaration of Independence, Richard Bland, and the Revolutionary Legacy: Giving Credit Where Credit Is Due." *Journal of the Historical Society* 1, nos. 2–3 (Winter 2000–Spring 2001): 137–54.

Halbwachs, Maurice. *On Collective Memory*. University of Chicago Press, 1992.

Hamowy, Ronald. "Jefferson and the Scottish Enlightenment: A Critique of Garry Wills's *Inventing America: Jefferson's Declaration of Independence.*" *William and Mary Quarterly* 36, no. 4 (October 1979): 503–23.

Harris, Tim. *Revolution: The Great Crisis of the British Monarchy, 1685–1720*. Allen Lane, 2006.

Hattem, Michael. *The Memory of '76: The Revolution in American History*. Yale University Press, 2024.

Hattem, Michael. *Past and Prologue: Politics and Memory in the American Revolution*. Yale University Press, 2020.

Hazelton, John H., *The Declaration of Independence: Its History*. Dodd, Mead, 1906.

Hixson, Walter L. *American Settler Colonialism: A History*. Palgrave Macmillan, 2013.

Holton, Woody. *Abigail Adams*. Free Press, 2009.

Holton, Woody. *Forced Founders: Indians, Debtors, Slaves, and the Making of the American Revolution in Virginia*. University of North Carolina Press, 1999.

Holton, Woody. *Liberty Is Sweet: The Hidden History of the American Revolution*. Simon and Schuster, 2021.

Hominh, Yarran. "Re-reading the Declaration of Independence as Perlocutionary Performative." *Res Publica: A Journal of Moral, Legal, and Political Philosophy* 22, no. 4 (November 2016): 423–44.

Howell, Wilbur Samuel. "The Declaration of Independence and Eighteenth-Century Logic." *William and Mary Quarterly* 18, no. 4 (October 1961): 463–84.

Hunt, Bruce A. Jr. "Locke on Equality." *Political Research Quarterly* 69, no. 3 (September 2016): 546–56.

Huyler, Jerome. *Locke in America: The Moral Philosophy of the Founding Era*. University Press of Kansas, 1995.

Irvin, Benjamin H. *Clothed in Robes of Sovereignty: The Continental Congress and the People Out of Doors*. Oxford University Press, 2011.

Jasanoff, Maya. *Liberty's Exiles: American Loyalists in the Revolutionary World*. Knopf, 2011.

Jayne, Allan. *Jefferson's Declaration of Independence: Origins, Philosophy, and Theology*. University Press of Kentucky, 2000.

Jordan, Winthrop D. *White over Black: American Attitudes Toward the Negro.* University of North Carolina Press, 1968.
Kammen, Michael. "The Meaning of Colonization in American Revolutionary Thought." *Journal of the History of Ideas* 31, no. 3 (July–September 1970): 337–58.
Kaplan, Sidney. "The 'Domestic Insurrections' of the Declaration of Independence." *Journal of Negro History* 61, no. 3 (July 1976): 243–55.
Kerber, Linda K. "From the Declaration of Independence to the Declaration of Sentiments: The Legal Status of Women in the Early Republic, 1776–1848." *Human Rights* 6, no. 2 (Winter 1977): 115–24.
Kettner, James H. *The Development of American Citizenship, 1608–1870.* University of North Carolina Press, 2005.
Keyssar, Alexander. *The Right to Vote: The Contested History of Democracy in the United States.* Basic Books, 2009.
Koch, Adrienne. *Philosophy of Thomas Jefferson.* Times Books, 1972.
Kloppenberg, James T. *Toward Democracy: The Struggle for Self-Rule in European and American Thought.* Oxford University Press, 2016.
Kloppenberg, James T. *The Virtues of Liberalism.* Oxford University Press, 1998.
Kramnick, Isaac. *Republicanism and Bourgeois Radicalism: Political Ideology in Late Eighteenth-Century England and America.* Cornell University Press, 1990.
Krohn, Wolfgang. *Francis Bacon.* C. H. Beck, 1987.
Larson, Carlton F. W. "The Declaration of Independence: A 225th Anniversary Re-interpretation." *Washington Law Review* 76, no. 3 (2001): 701–91.
Lepore, Jill. *These Truths: A History of the United States.* Norton, 2018.
Lewis, Jan. *The Pursuit of Happiness: Family and Values in Jefferson's Virginia.* Cambridge University Press, 1983.
Lienesch, Michael. *New Order of the Ages: Time, the Constitution, and the Making of Modern American Political Thought.* Princeton University Press, 1988.
Lovejoy, Arthur O. *The Great Chain of Being: A Study of the History of an Idea.* Harvard University Press, 1961.
Lovejoy, David S. *The Glorious Revolution in America.* Harper and Row, 1972.
Lucas, Stephen E. "Justifying America: The Declaration of Independence as a Rhetorical Document." In *American Rhetoric: Context and Criticism,* ed. Thomas W. Benson, 67–131. Southern Illinois University Press, 1989.
Lucas, Stephen E. "The Stylistic Artistry of the Declaration of Independence." *Prologue: Quarterly of the National Archives* 22 (Spring 1990): 25–43.
Lutz, Donald. *The Origins of American Constitutionalism.* Louisiana State University Press, 1988.

Macmillan, Ken. *Sovereignty and Possession in the English New World: The Legal Foundations of Empire, 1576–1640.* Cambridge University Press, 2006.

Maier, Pauline. *American Scripture: How America Declared Its Independence from Britain.* Knopf, 1997; Pimlico, 1999.

Maier, Pauline. "The Strange History of 'All Men Are Created Equal.'" *Washington and Lee Law Review* 56, no. 3 (Summer 1999): 873–88.

Malone, Dumas. *Jefferson and His Time.* 6 vols. Little, Brown, 1948–1981.

Marshall, John. *John Locke, Resistance, Religion, and Responsibility.* Cambridge University Press, 1994.

May, Henry. *The Enlightenment in America.* Oxford University Press, 1976.

McConville, Brendan. *The King's Three Faces: The Rise and Fall of Royal America, 1688–1776.* University of North Carolina Press, 2006.

McPherson, C. B. *The Political Theory of Possessive Individualism.* Oxford University Press, 1961.

Messer, Peter C. *Stories of Independence: Identity, Ideology, and History in Eighteenth-Century America.* Northern Illinois University Press, 2005.

Miller, Charles A. *Jefferson and Nature: An Interpretation.* Johns Hopkins University Press, 1988.

Miller, John Chester. *The Wolf by the Ears: Thomas Jefferson and Slavery.* Free Press, 1977; University of Virginia Press, 1991.

Miller, Robert J. *Native America, Discovered and Conquered: Thomas Jefferson, Lewis and Clark, and Manifest Destiny.* University of Nebraska Press, 2008.

Morgan, Edmund S. *Inventing the People: The Rise of Popular Sovereignty in England and America.* Norton, 1988.

Morgan, Edmund S. "The Puritan Ethic and the American Revolution." *William and Mary Quarterly* 64, no. 1 (January 1969): 3–43.

Morgan, Edmund S., and Helen M. Morgan. *The Stamp Act Crisis: Prologue to Revolution.* University of North Carolina Press, 1953.

Mumford Jones, Howard. "The Declaration of Independence: A Critique." *Proceedings of the American Antiquarian Society* 85, no. 1 (January 1975): 55–72.

Mumford Jones, Howard. *The Pursuit of Happiness.* Harvard University Press, 1953.

Nash, Gary B. *The Forgotten Fifth: African Americans in the Age of Revolution.* Harvard University Press, 2006.

Nelson, Eric. *The Royalist Revolution: Monarchy and the American Founding.* Harvard University Press, 2014.

Newman, Richard S. *The Transformation of American Abolitionism: Fighting Slavery in the Early Republic.* University of North Carolina Press, 2002.

Norton, Mary Beth. *1774: The Long Year of Revolution*. Knopf, 2020.
Norton, Mary Beth. *The British Americans: The Loyalist Exiles in England, 1774–1789*. Little, Brown, 1972.
O'Brien, Jean M. *Firsting and Lasting: Writing Indians Out of Existence in New England*. University of Minnesota Press, 2010.
O'Gorman, Frank. "The Parliamentary Opposition to the Government's American Policy, 1760–1782." In *Britain and the American Colonies*, ed. H. T. Dickinson, 97–123. Routledge, 1998.
Onuf, Peter S. "A Declaration of Independence for Diplomatic Historians." *Diplomatic History* 22, no. 1 (January 1998): 71–83.
Onuf, Peter S. *Jefferson and the Virginians: Democracy, Constitutions, and Empire*. University of Virginia Press, 2018.
Onuf, Peter S. *Jefferson's Empire: The Language of American Nationhood*. University of Virginia Press, 2000.
Onuf, Peter S. *Statehood and Union: A History of the Northwest Ordinance*. Indiana University Press, 1987.
Onuf, Peter S., and Nicholas P. Cole, eds. *Thomas Jefferson, the Classical World, and Early America*. University of Virginia Press, 2011.
Onuf, Peter S., and Robert M. S. McDonald, eds. *Revolutionary Prophecies: The Founders and America's Future*. University of Virginia Press, 2021.
O'Shaughnessy, Andrew J. *The Illimitable Freedom of the Human Mind: Thomas Jefferson's Idea of a University*. University of Virginia Press, 2021.
Ostler, Jeffrey. "'Just and Lawful War' as Genocidal War in the (United States) Northwest Ordinance and Northwest Territory, 1787–1832." *Journal of Genocide Research* 18, no. 1 (February 2016): 1–20.
Ostler, Jeffrey. *Surviving Genocide: Native Nations and the United States from the American Revolution to Bleeding Kansas*. Yale University Press, 2019.
Ostler, Jeffrey, and Nancy Shoemaker. "Forum: Settler Colonialism and Early American History." *William and Mary Quarterly* 76, no. 3 (July 2019): 361–450.
Pagden, Anthony. *The Burdens of Empire, 1539 to the Present*. Cambridge University Press, 2015.
Parkinson, Robert G. *The Common Cause: Creating Nation and Race in the American Revolution*. University of North Carolina Press, 2016.
Parkinson, Robert G. *Thirteen Clocks: How Race United the Colonies and Made the Declaration of Independence*. University of North Carolina Press, 2021.
Pincus, Steve. *1688: The First Modern Revolution*. Yale University Press, 2009.
Pincus, Steve. *The Heart of the Declaration: The Founders' Case for an Activist Government*. Yale University Press, 2016.

Pocock, J. G. A. *The Ancient Constitution and the Feudal Law: A Study of English Historical Thought in the Seventeenth Century.* Cambridge University Press, 1957, rev. ed., 1987.

Pocock, J. G. A. *The Machiavellian Moment: Florentine Political Thought and the Atlantic Republican Tradition.* Princeton University Press, 1975.

Pole, J. R. *Political Representation in England and the Origins of the American Republic.* St. Martin's Press, 1966.

Polgar, Paul J. *Standard Bearers of Equality: America's First Abolition Movement.* University of North Carolina Press, 2019.

Prior, Charles W. A. "Settlers among Empires: Conquest and the American Revolution." In *Remembering Early Modern Revolutions: England, North America, France, and Haiti,* ed. Edward Vallance, 79–94. Routledge, 2019.

Rahe, Paul A. "Cicero and the Classical Republican Legacy in America." In *Thomas Jefferson, the Classical World, and Early America,* ed. Peter S. Onuf and Nicholas P. Cole, 248–64. University of Virginia Press, 2011.

Rakove, Jack N. *The Beginnings of National Politics: An Interpretative History of the Continental Congress.* Johns Hopkins University Press, 1979.

Reck, Andrew J. "The Enlightenment in American Law I: The Declaration of Independence." *Review of Metaphysics* 44, no. 3 (March 1991): 549–73.

Reid, John Phillip. *The Ancient Constitution and the Origins of Anglo-American Liberty.* Northern Illinois University Press, 2005.

Reid, John Phillip. *Constitutional History of the American Revolution: Abridged Edition.* University of Wisconsin Press, 1993.

Reid, John Phillip. *Constitutional History of the American Revolution: The Authority of Law.* University of Wisconsin Press, 1993.

Reid, John Phillip. *Constitutional History of the American Revolution: The Authority of Rights.* University of Wisconsin Press, 1986.

Reid, John Phillip. *Constitutional History of the American Revolution: The Authority to Legislate.* University of Wisconsin Press, 1991.

Reid, John Phillip. *Constitutional History of the American Revolution: The Authority to Tax.* University of Wisconsin Press, 1987.

Reid, John Phillip. "The Irrelevance of the Declaration." In *Law in the American Revolution and the Revolution in Law,* ed. Hendrik Hartog, 46–89. New York University Press, 1981.

Ritz, Wilfred J. "From the Here of Jefferson's Handwritten Rough Draft of the Declaration of Independence to the There of the Printed Dunlap Broadside." *Pennsylvania Magazine of History and Biography* 116, no. 4 (October 1992): 499–512.

Rogin, Michael. "The Two Declarations of American Independence." *Representations* 55 (Summer 1996): 13–30.

Roosevelt, Kermit, III. *The Nation That Never Was: Reconstructing America's Story*. University of Chicago Press, 2022.

Roney, Jessica Choppin. "An Expansion of the Same Society: Republican Government and Empire in the Early Republic." *Journal of American History* 111, no. 1 (June 2024): 15–38.

Rossiter, Clinton. *The Political Thought of the American Revolution: Part Three of Seedtime of the Republic*. Harcourt, Brace, 1963.

Rosen, Jeffery. *The Pursuit of Happiness: How Classical Writers on Virtue Inspired the Lives of the Founders and Defined America*. Simon and Schuster, 2024.

Rothman, Adam. *Slave Country: American Expansion and the Origins of the Deep South*. Harvard University Press, 2005.

Sadosky, Leonard. *Revolutionary Negotiations: Indians, Empires, and Diplomats in the Founding of America*. University of Virginia Press, 2009.

Saler, Bethel. *The Settlers' Empire: Colonialism and State Formation in America's Old Northwest*. University of Pennsylvania Press, 2015.

Sarson, Steven. *Barack Obama: American Historian*. Bloomsbury, 2018.

Sarson, Steven. "Harmonizing the 'Sentiments of the Day': The Declaration of Independence and the Forging of a Revolutionary Consensus." *Journal of the Société des Etudes Romantiques et Dix-neuviémistes*. Open Edition, Special edition, *Discours des révolutions, discours sur les révolutions*, ed. Habran Augustin and Hélène Parent, 2024.

Sarson, Steven. *The Tobacco-Plantation South in the Early American Atlantic World*. Palgrave Macmillan, 2013.

Sarson, Steven. "'A total contradiction to every principle laid down at the time of the revolution': American revolutionaries and the Glorious Revolution." In *Remembering Early Modern Revolutions: England, North America, France, and Haiti*, ed. Edward Vallance, 61–78. Routledge, 2019.

Schlesinger, Arthur M. "The Lost Meaning of 'The Pursuit of Happiness.'" *William and Mary Quarterly* 21, no. 3 (July 1964): 325–27.

Schwoerer, Lois. *The Declaration of Rights, 1689*. Johns Hopkins University Press, 1981.

Sesay, Chernoh M. Jr. "The Revolutionary Black Roots of Slavery's Abolition in Massachusetts." *New England Quarterly* 87, no. 1 (March 2014): 99–131.

Shaffer, Arthur H. *To Be an American: David Ramsay and the Making of the American Consciousness*. University of South Carolina Press, 1991.

Shaffer, Arthur H. *The Politics of History: Writing the History of the American Revolution, 1783–1815*. Routledge, 1975, rev. ed., 2017.

Shalev, Eran. *Rome Reborn on Western Shores: Historical Imagination and the Creation of the American Republic*. University of Virginia, 2009.

Shalev, Eran. "Thomas Jefferson's Classical Silence, 1774–1776: Historical Consciousness and Roman History in the Revolutionary South." In *Thomas Jefferson, the Classical World, and Early America*, ed. Peter S. Onuf and Nicholas P. Cole, 219–47. University of Virginia Press, 2011.

Sinha, Manisha *The Slave's Cause: A History of Abolition*. Yale University Press, 2016.

Sneff, Emily. "When the Declaration of Independence Was News." PhD diss., College of William and Mary, 2024.

Sosin, J. M. *English America and the Revolution of 1688: Royal Administration and the Structure of Provincial Government*. University of Nebraska Press, 1982.

Spahn, Hannah. *Black Reason, White Feeling: The Jefferson Enlightenment in the African American Tradition*. University of Virginia Press, 2024.

Spahn, Hannah. *Thomas Jefferson, Time, and History*. University of Virginia Press, 2011.

Stanton, Grant. "The Freedom Petitions: Black Patriotism, Black Politics, and the Abolition of Slavery in Massachusetts, 1773–1783." *Early American Studies* 22, no.2 (Spring 2024): 262–304.

Stanwood, Owen. *The Empire Reformed: English America in the Age of the Glorious Revolution*. University of Pennsylvania Press, 2011.

Steele, Brian. *Thomas Jefferson and American Nationhood*. Cambridge University Press, 2012.

Strauss, Leo. *Natural Right and History*. University of Chicago Press, 1953.

Thompson, C. Bradley. "John Locke and the American Mind." *American Political Thought* 8, no. 4 (Fall 2019): 575–93.

Thompson, Peter. *Rum Punch and Revolution: Taverngoing and Public Life in Eighteenth-Century Philadelphia*. University of Pennsylvania Press, 1999.

Trouillot, Michel-Rolph. *Silencing the Past: Power and the Production of History*. Beacon Press, 1954, rev. ed., 2015.

Tsesis, Alexander. *For Liberty and Equality: The Life and Times of the Declaration of Independence*. Oxford University Press, 2012.

Vallance, Edward. *The Glorious Revolution of 1688: Britain's Fight for Liberty*. Little, Brown, 2006.

Vallance, Edward. *A Radical History of Britain: Visionaries, Rebels and Revolutionaries—The Men and Women Who Fought for Our Freedom*. Little, Brown, 2010.

Valsania, Maurizio. *The Limits of Optimism: Thomas Jefferson's Dualistic Enlightenment*. University of Virginia Press, 2011.

Veracini, Lorenzo. *Settler Colonialism: A Theoretical Overview*. Cambridge University Press, 2010.

Waldstreicher, David. *In the Midst of Perpetual Fetes: The Making of American Nationalism, 1776–1820*. University of North Carolina Press, 1997.

Waldstreicher, David. *Slavery's Constitution: From Revolution to Ratification*. Hill and Wang, 2010.

Wallace, Anthony F. C. *Jefferson and the Indians: The Tragic Fate of the First Americans*. Harvard University Press, 1999.

Walton, Craig. "Hume and Jefferson on the Uses of History." In *Hume: A Reevaluation*, ed. Donald W. Livingston and James T. King, 389–403. Fordham University Press, 1976.

Ward, Lee. *The Politics of Liberty in England and Revolutionary America*. Cambridge University Press, 2004.

Webb, Stephen Saunders. *Lord Churchill's Coup: The Anglo-American Empire and the Glorious Revolution Reconsidered*. Knopf, 1995.

White, Morton. *The Philosophy of the American Revolution*. Oxford University Press, 1978.

Wilcox, Daniel J. *Measures of Times Past: Pre-Newtonian Chronologues and the Rhetoric of Relative Time*. University of Chicago Press, 1987.

Wills, Garry. *Inventing America: Jefferson's Declaration of Independence*. Doubleday, 1978; Houghton Mifflin, 2002.

Wilson, Douglas L. "Jefferson vs. Hume," *William and Mary Quarterly* 46, no. 1 (January 1989): 49–70.

Witgen, Michael. "A Nation of Settlers: The Early American Republic and the Colonization of the Northwest Territory." *William and Mary Quarterly* 76, no. 3 (July 2019): 391–98.

Witgen, Michael. "'Settler Colonialism': Career of a Concept." *Journal of Imperial and Commonwealth History* 41, no. 2 (June 2013): 313–33.

Wolfe, Patrick. "Settler Colonialism and the Elimination of the Native." *Journal of Genocide Research* 8, no. 4 (December 2006): 387–409.

Wolfe, Patrick. *Settler Colonialism and the Transformation of Anthropology: The Politics and Poetics of an Ethnographic Event*. Continuum, 1999.

Wolfe, Patrick. *Traces of History: Elementary Structures of Race*. Verson, 2016.

Wood, Gordon S. *The Creation of the American Republic, 1776–1787*. University of North Carolina Press, 1969.

Wood, Gordon S. *The Radicalism of the American Revolution*. Vintage, 1993.

Wright, Benjamin Fletcher Jr. *American Interpretations of Natural Law: A Study in the History of Political Thought*. New edition with a foreword by Sidney Pearson Jr. Russell and Russell, 1962; Taylor and Francis, 2016.

Yirush, Craig *Settlers, Liberty, and Empire: The Roots of Early American Political Theory, 1675–1775*. Cambridge University Press 2011.

Zuckert, Michael P. *Launching Liberalism: On Lockean Political Philosophy*. University Press of Kansas, 2002.

Zuckert, Michael P. *The Natural Rights Republic: Studies in the Foundation of the American Political Tradition*. University of Notre Dame Press, 1996.

Zuckert, Michael P. "Thomas Jefferson and Natural Morality: Classical Moral Theory, Moral Sense, and Rights." In *Thomas Jefferson, the Classical World, and Early America*, ed. Peter S. Onuf and Nicholas P. Cole, 56–77. University of Virginia Press, 2011.

INDEX

abdication, 126, 127, 128
abolitionism, 112, 188–92, 208–11
Abraham, 25
Acosta, José de, 29
Act in Restraint of Appeals, 81
Act of Supremacy, 62
Act of Union, 82, 98, 178
Adam, 3, 24, 25, 144, 160, 187–88
Adams, Abigail, 169–70, 188
Adams, John: and British and Irish history, 61–62, 96, 97, 98; as co-author of the Declaration of Independence, 8, 45, 47, 61; and the Continental Congress, 103, 127; and democracy, 164–70; and forms of government, 164–66; and the Great Seal of the United States, 204–5; and the imperial constitution, 61–64, 96–100, 123; and monarchy, 161–62; and the origins and development of the colonies, 62–64, 96, 199; as President of the United States, 156; and public education, 149–50; and rebellion and revolution, 133–34; and the rule of law, 161, 165; and slavery, 182, 188; and trade regulation, 96–97, 99, 123; and women, 169–70, 211
Adams-Onis Treaty, 203
Africa, 46, 112, 182, 189, 205

African Americans: and abolitionism, 188–93, 208–11; as enemy others, 6, 11, 18, 113, 129, 130, 168–69, 174, 178, 179–80, 181–88, 205; and equality, 144, 180, 186–88; and the US Constitution, 192–94; and voting rights, 146, 173. *See also* Declaration of Independence; Jefferson, Thomas; slavery; slave trade
Albany Congress, 150
Alexander, 101
Alien and Sedition Acts, 156
Allen, Danielle, 8, 20–21
Ammonites, 28
ancient constitution, 56, 82, 116, 123, 205
Anderson, Benedict, 2
Andros, Edmund, 53
Anglican Church, 114
Anglo-Saxons, 47–48, 49, 50, 52, 56, 82, 201, 205
Anne, 87, 89, 158
Appalachian Mountains, 11, 196, 203
Appomattox Courthouse, Virginia, 157
Aristotle, 6, 86, 223n5
Arlington, Lord (Henry Bennet), 52
Articles of Association, 40, 145, 151, 154–55, 162
Articles of Confederation, 154, 155, 156, 162
Ashley, John, 191
Asia, 205

Bacon, Francis, 19–20, 21, 61, 150
Baltimore, Lords, 32
Barbeyrac, Jean, 134
Barons' Wars, 123
Barton, William, 206
Becker, Carl, 2
Berkeley, William, 58
Bernard, Francis, 32, 115
Bill of Rights (English), 110, 114, 115, 123
Bill of Rights (United States), 154, 156
Black founders, 188–92, 208–10
Blackstone, William, 22, 35, 45–46, 167, 218n9
Bland, Richard, 55–58, 59, 90–92, 123, 155, 156–57, 199
Board of Trade, 82, 88, 113
Bolingbroke, Henry, 21, 149
Bollon, William, 36
Boston, Massachusetts, 35, 53, 64–65
Boston Massacre, 84, 111, 122, 126
Boston Port Act, 84
Boston Tea Party, 84, 115, 116, 120, 122
Brazil, 29, 83
Britain: border treaties, 203; colonies separating from, 15, 17, 40, 175–77, 202; constitution of, 80–85; liberties of, 32, 33, 37, 38, 148–49; power of, 43; relationship to American colonies, 42–74, 77–106, 204. *See also* Declaration of Independence; George III; Parliament
Brom and Bett v. Ashley, 191
Brunswick, House of, 103
Bulkley, John, 197–98
Burke, Edmund, 83
Burlamaqui, Jean-Jacques, 22, 34, 215n6
Burnet, Gilbert, 165

Caesar, Julius, 101, 149
Caldwell, James, 191–92
Caldwell, John, 191–92
Caldwell, Seth, 191–92

Calhoun, John C., 156
Calvin's Case (Robert Colville), 31, 37–38
Camden, Lord (Charles Pratt), 64
Campbell, William, 39
Canada, 152, 203
Cape Breton, 32
Care, Henry, 31
Caribbean, 152
Carr, Peter, 219n13
Catholicism, 62, 81, 114, 125, 148
Cato's Letters, 149, 215n6
Cato the Younger, 149
Charles I, 57, 63, 65, 117, 120, 158
Charles II, 52–53, 58, 63, 88, 90–91, 158
Chesapeake, 167–68, 182
children, 169
Chiriguanos, 29
Cicero, 6, 21–22, 41, 86, 223n5
Civil War (English and Three Kingdoms), 57–58, 122, 123
Civil War (US), 157
Coercive Acts, 34, 65, 66, 79, 84, 100, 116, 150, 151
Coke, Edward, 22, 31, 37–38, 45–46
Colonies, British American: historical development of, 4, 5, 80–106, 153–55, 179–80, 181–85; historical origins of, 4, 5, 9, 11, 42–74, 79–80, 145, 151–53, 180, 194–202. *See also under* Declaration of Independence; Dickinson, John; Jefferson, Thomas
Columbian Magazine, 206
Columbus, Christopher, 2
committee of five, 8, 17–19, 44–45, 78–79, 115, 122, 126, 134, 136–37, 159, 176–77, 181–82
committee of thirteen, 155
Concord, 85, 105, 127
Confederation Congress, 156, 203
Connecticut, 63, 67, 159, 172, 173, 197
Constitutional Convention, 73, 154, 156, 157, 162–63, 164, 171–72, 192

Constitution of the United States, 145, 153, 154, 156, 162–64, 166, 171–72, 192–94
Continental Congress (First), 40, 46, 102–3, 110, 150, 151, 157
Continental Congress (Second), 40–41, 47; and the Declaration of Independence, 8, 17–19, 44–46, 69–73, 78–79, 115, 122, 126, 137–38, 159, 176–77, 181–84; and the Declaration of the Causes and Necessity of Taking Up Arms, 68–69, 200; as a government, 128–29; and the Great Seal of the United States, 204–6; and petitions, 69, 85, 102–5; Resolution of May 1775, 127; and union, 150, 155, 157
creation, 2, 5, 9, 15, 17–18, 26, 32, 41, 74, 107–8, 110, 134, 135, 160, 188, 202
Culpeper, Lord (Thomas Culpeper), 52
Cushing, William, 192, 208, 209
Customs Commissioners, Board of, 84, 119–20
Customs House oath, 120
Cyrus, 101

David, 25, 29
debt funding, 156
Declaration and Resolves of the First Continental Congress, 40, 102–3, 110
Declaration of Independence: accessibility and appeal of, 8–9, 31, 79, 106, 109–12, 133–40, 145; and African Americans and slavery, 6, 11, 18, 46, 74, 112–13, 129, 130, 144, 174, 178, 179–81, 181–94, 208; ambiguities and silences in, 8–9, 42–46, 69–74, 77–78, 78–79, 109–11, 137, 177, 201–2; and the British people, 4, 18, 42, 79, 84, 130–31, 176, 177, 178; as a civics lesson, 145, 147–50, 173; and Creation, 2–3, 5, 9, 41, 107, 110, 139; creedal interpretation of, 1–2, 6, 10, 12, 108–9, 144, 160, 173–74, 175, 180, 190–92, 194–95, 206, 207–11; and democracy, 6, 146–47, 164–73; and emigration and settlement of the colonies, 4, 5, 8, 9, 11, 41, 42–46, 69–74, 79–80, 85, 106, 125, 130–31, 139, 145, 151–54, 176, 177, 180, 183, 195, 196, 202, 206; and equality, 1, 2, 9, 10–12, 16, 17–18, 27, 107–8, 144, 146–47, 157, 159, 174, 175, 180–81, 194–95, 207–8; and George III, 3–4, 5, 41, 46, 77–81, 85, 89, 104–6, 107–34, 145, 154, 159, 162, 164, 176, 178, 181–85; and grievances, 3–4, 5, 9–10, 17, 42, 71–72, 77, 105–6, 107, 108–32, 153, 159, 176; grievances, number of, 78, 121–22, 226n1; grievances nos. 1 through 12, 111, 112–21, 128, 176, 203; grievance no. 13, 78, 105–6, 111, 121–26; grievances nos. 14 through 18, 71–72, 111, 126–30, 136, 178, 180–81; and intention, 4–5, 16–17, 41, 77, 104–5, 111–12, 130–32, 135, 139; and the laws of nations, 1, 2, 15, 16, 109–10, 132, 176; and loyalists, 18, 129–30, 135, 137–38, 174, 178–79; and monarchy, 6, 146, 157–64, 174; and Native Americans, 6, 11, 18, 43, 46, 74, 129–30, 174, 178, 180–81, 194–95, 201–2, 202–3, 208; and natural law, 2–5, 6, 9, 10–12, 15–19, 20–21, 41, 42, 106, 107, 108, 109, 110–39, 145, 147, 154, 174, 181–82; and natural rights, 1, 2–6, 9, 10–12, 16–18, 27, 42, 45, 46, 73, 106, 107–8, 110–39, 145, 153, 157, 173–74, 175, 181–82, 194–95; and necessity, 2, 4–5, 15, 41, 78, 105, 106, 107, 108, 111–12, 113, 126–27, 131–35, 138–39, 143, 175, 176; and one people, 2, 5, 6, 15, 17, 46, 74, 138, 145, 150–57, 175, 176, 177, 178–81, 186, 204–5, 206; and the origins of government, 3, 5, 9, 10–11, 16, 27, 41, 43–44, 107–8, 110, 139, 140, 157, 158, 173–74, 175; orthography of, 18–19, 45,

Declaration of Independence (*continued*)
125, 135–36, 210; and Parliament, 9, 43, 72, 77–78, 78–79, 105–6, 121–26, 127, 177, 202; and petitions, 4–5, 77, 85, 104–5, 106, 108, 111–12, 115–16, 126–27, 130–32, 134, 159, 176; rhetoric of, 135–38; and the right to revolution, 3–4, 9, 16–17, 30–31, 41, 104–6, 108, 111–12, 126–35, 139, 143, 144, 153–54, 157–58, 175–76, 207; signing of, 138; and the slave trade, 8, 46, 112–13, 130, 179, 180, 181–86, 194; and the state of nature, 2–3, 5, 10–11, 16, 41, 43–44, 107, 110, 128–29, 143, 146–47, 157, 174, 175, 180, 195, 207; structure of, 2–5, 15–17, 41, 42–43, 107–8, 110–11, 121–22, 175–76, 215n5; title of, 137–38, 155; and union, 150–57; versions of, 213n1, 216n10; and the War of Independence, 4–5, 11, 71–72, 104–5, 111, 120, 126–30, 138, 139, 159, 173, 178–81, 194–95; writing and revising of, 6–9, 17–19, 31, 39, 41–46, 47, 69–74, 78–79, 115–16, 119, 122, 124–25, 126–27, 128–30, 134–35, 136–38, 159, 176–77, 179, 181–84

Declaration of Rights and Grievances, 37–38, 101–2, 151. *See also* Stamp Act Congress

Declaration of Sentiments, 173, 211

Declaration of the Causes and Necessity of Taking Up Arms, 40–41, 59, 68–69, 104, 110, 126, 200

Declaratory Act, 79, 80, 81–82, 83, 98, 99, 102, 125–26, 126

Delaware, 73, 172, 173

Delaware Indians, 204

Dickinson, John: and the constitution of empire, 58–59, 88, 92–93, 101–2, 114, 123, 152, 157–58, 159; and the Continental Congress, 46; and the Declaration of the Causes and Necessity of Taking Up Arms, 40–41, 68–69, 200; disparaged for moderate opinions, 64, 73, 224n28; and the origins of the colonies, 41, 44–46, 58–59, 68–69, 92, 151–52, 156–57, 157–58; political career after independence, 73; and the Stamp Act Congress, 101–2; and trade regulation, 58–59, 88, 92, 123

dispensing power, 114

Dissolution of assemblies, 87, 115–17, 125, 162

Dominion of New England, 53, 96, 100

Douglass, Frederick, 210–11

Dulany, Daniel the Elder, 31–32, 54–55

Dulany, Daniel the Younger, 34, 55

Dummer, Jeremiah, 53–54, 197

Dunlap, John, 47, 139

Dunlap Broadside, 139, 177

Dunmore, Lord (John Murray), 116, 130

eagle (symbol), 206

East India Company, 123

East Jersey, 152

Egypt, 25

Electoral College, 156

eleven years' tyranny, 117

Elizabeth I, 31, 54, 57, 61, 82, 197

E Pluribus Unum, 154, 204–6

equality: and civil society, 9, 10–11, 12, 18, 27–31, 74, 107–8, 144, 146–74, 175, 180–206, 207–11; creedal interpretation of, 1–2, 10–11, 12, 109, 144, 174, 175, 180, 194–95, 206, 207–11; equal status with Britain, 2, 15, 17, 86, 87, 106, 107, 109–10, 175, 177, 178; as self-evident, 24; and the state of nature, 3, 9, 10–11, 16, 17–18, 22, 24–27, 29, 31, 32, 34, 51, 107–8, 123–24, 134, 135, 144, 157, 160, 161, 170–71, 174, 175, 180, 181–82, 184, 185–86, 188, 191, 192–93, 207. *See also under* Declaration of Independence; Locke, John

Eve, 187–88

Exclusion Crisis, 148
Exodus (book of), 120
expatriation (right of), 43, 47–48, 51, 52, 55, 56, 60, 69–71, 180, 182

Fairfax Resolves, 65–66, 200
federalism, 6, 145, 150–57
Federalist Papers, 156
feudalism, 49–52, 124
Fifteenth Amendment, 173
Filmer, Robert, 3, 6, 7, 24–25, 40, 124, 128, 144, 158, 160
Florida, 29, 152, 203
France, 62, 170–71, 183, 205
Franklin, Benjamin: as co-author of the Declaration of Independence, 8, 45; and the Great Seal of the United States, 204–5; in London, 104; Plan of Union, 150; and rebellion and revolution, 134–35; and slavery, 188; and voting rights, 171
Freeman, Elizabeth, 191, 209
free trade, 88–90, 91–92, 122–23
Fugitive Slave Acts, 193–94
fugitive slave clause, 193–94

Gage, Thomas, 84, 115, 121
Garrison, William Lloyd, 210
Genesis (book of), 11, 24, 25–26, 195, 197, 198
Geneva, 205
George I, 158
George II, 158
George III, 9, 39, 46, 50, 79, 80, 84, 87, 89, 90, 114, 128, 132, 139, 143, 149, 158, 159, 162, 164, 183, 184, 185. *See also under* Declaration of Independence
Georgia, 74, 83, 172, 182
Germany, 205
Gideon, 160
Gilbert, Humphrey, 50
Gileadites, 28

Glorious Revolution, 53, 79, 80, 81, 83, 84, 87–88, 93, 95–96, 99–101, 101, 110, 114, 116, 123, 128, 148, 163
Goddess of Justice, 206
Goddess of Liberty, 205
Gordon, Thomas, 149, 215n6
Great Seal of the United States, 147, 154, 204–6
Greece, 164, 205
Greene, Jack P., 43, 221n2, 234n14, 237n15
Grenada, 46
Grenville, George, 83
Grotius, Hugo, 22, 31, 33, 134, 183, 208
Gulf of Mexico, 203

Hakluyt, Richard (the Younger), 50–51
Hamilton, Alexander, 210
Hamilton, William, 210
Hancock, John, 139, 140, 143
Harrington, James, 165, 168
Hastings, Battle of, 49, 52
Hat Act, 89, 97
Haynes, Lemuel, 208–9, 211
Hengist, 205
Henry, Patrick, 103, 224n28
Henry VIII, 62, 124
Hercules, 205
Hessians, 129, 130
Hicks, William, 34, 59–60, 93–94, 114
Higginson, John, 196–97
Hillsborough, Lord (Wills Hill), 83
Hoadley, Benjamin, 165
Holland, 205
Holmes, John, 185
Hooker, Richard, 22, 23–24
Horsa, 205
Howard, Lord (Francis), 52–53
Howell, Samuel, 184
Hume, David, 21, 149
Hutcheson, Frances, 215n6
Hutchinson, Thomas, 80, 109, 115–16

Impartial Administration of Justice Act, 84, 122, 124
indentured servitude, 167, 184
Intolerable Acts. *See* Coercive Acts; Quebec Act
Ireland, 45–46, 62, 98, 205
Iron Act, 97
Isaac, 25
Israel, 28, 205

Jacob, 25
Jacobites, 87
James I and VI, 31, 57, 61, 63
James II, 88, 93, 110, 114, 117, 128, 148, 158
Jamestown, 57
Jefferson, Thomas: as author of the Declaration of Independence, 6–8, 17–18, 19, 31, 39, 41–46, 47, 57, 69–72, 78, 90, 114, 115, 116–17, 118, 120–21, 123, 127, 129–30, 134–37, 149, 176–77, 179; and the constitution of Britain and its empire, 43, 57, 62, 71, 86–90, 91, 94, 95, 97, 114, 115, 116–17, 118, 155, 158–59, 177, 179; and Declaration on the Causes and Necessity of Taking Up Arms, 40–41, 47, 68–69, 200–202; and democracy, 167–68, 170–71; and English and British history, 47–50, 56, 62, 87–90, 116–17; and the Great Seal of the United States, 204–5; library of, 19; and monarchy, 86–90, 95; and the moral sense, 24, 218–19n11, 219n13; and Native Americans, 68–69, 171, 196, 200–203; and natural law and rights, 19–22, 47–50, 134–35, 149, 181–88, 210, 211; and the origins of the colonies, 41–51, 59, 68–69, 71, 118, 151, 152–53, 158–59, 190, 224n28; and public education, 150; and the pursuit of happiness, 70–71, 210; and race, 185–88; and rebellion and revolution, 134–35; and religion, 19–20; and slavery, 112, 113, 129–30, 170–71, 181–88, 189, 190, 210, 211; and the slave trade, 112, 113, 122–23, 129–30, 170, 181–86; and state sovereignty, 152, 155; and trade regulation, 88–89, 91, 97, 123; and union of the colonies and states, 152–54; and the University of Virginia, 19–20; and women, 170–71
Jennison, Nathaniel, 191–92
Jephthah, 28, 132, 133
Jeremiah (book of), 120
Jim Crow, 173
Johnson, Samuel, 181
Judges (book of), 28–29
Justin, 28

Kentucky, 173
Kentucky Resolutions, 152, 156
Keyssar, Alexander, 167
Knox, William, 83

land banks, 97, 112
land ordinances, 172, 203, 204
Leclerc, Jean, 134
Lee, Henry, 6, 7–8
Lee, Richard Henry, 21, 72, 79, 103
Leonard, Daniel, 97, 133–34
Lexington, 85, 105, 127
Liberator, 210
Liberty Affair/Riot, 120
Library of Congress, 19
Lincoln, Abraham, 156
Lind, John, 80–81
Livingston, Robert, 8
Locke, John: citations of, 31–32, 32, 33, 37, 56, 84, 133–34, 165, 197–98; and conquest, 51–52; and the consent of the governed, 3, 26–29, 37, 121–22, 126, 157–58, 179; and equality, 2–3, 24, 25, 29–30, 51–52, 144; influence on Declaration of Independence,

2–3, 6–7, 19, 21–31, 37–38, 43–44, 86, 121–22, 131–34, 144, 160; and liberty, 22–31; and monarchy, 23, 24–25, 28–29, 30, 40, 160, 161; and Native Americans, 23, 29, 195–96; and natural law and rights, 6–7, 21–31; and the origins of government, 23, 26–29, 29–30, 157, 158; and popular sovereignty, 157–58; and property, 25–26, 123–24; and the right to revolution, 29–31, 131, 134, 157–58; and slavery, 183, 184, 208; and the state of nature, 2–3, 22–26, 28, 29; and Whiggism, 149
locusts, 119–20
London, 36, 52, 84, 95, 101
Lords of Trade, 52–53, 82, 88
Louisiana Purchase, 203
Lovell, James, 64, 199
Loyalists, 18, 73, 80–81, 109, 129–30, 135, 138, 174, 178–79, 236n1

Machiavelli, Nicolo, 215n6
Madison, James, 21, 154, 171, 172, 194
Magna Carta, 119, 123
Maier, Pauline, 109, 216n10, 221n1, 225n46
Manduit, Jasper, 36
Manhattan, 139
Manners, John, 70–71
Mansfield, Lord Chief Justice (William Murray), 46
Mary II, 37, 88, 96, 100, 148, 158
Maryland, 32, 54–55, 88, 93, 155, 159
Massachusetts: and abolition of slavery, 188–92, 208–9; Circular Letter, 38; colonial charters of, 37, 53, 67, 84, 96, 100, 116, 121, 125, 165–66; colonial origins and development of, 96–98, 99–101, 148, 196–97; General Court, 36–37, 112, 116; and Glorious Revolution, 53, 88, 93, 99–100; and loyalism, 109; Resolves (1765), 38, 67; response to the Sugar Act, 150–51; state constitution, 172, 191–93; town meetings, 121
Massachusetts Government Act, 84, 116, 121, 125
Massasoit, 62
Matlack, Timothy, 18–19, 125, 135, 177, 210, 213n1
Mexican-American War, 203
Micah (book of), 100–101
Michigan, 203
Milton, John, 165
Mississippi River, 11, 196, 203
Missouri, 203
Missouri Crisis, 152, 185
Mizpah, 28–29
Mohegans, 198
monarchy, 6, 23–29, 30, 47–52, 79–106, 144, 145, 146, 147–49, 158–64, 174
Montesquieu, 82
Monticello, 170
moral sense, 24
Morris, Gouverneur, 171–72
Moses, 160, 205

National Bank, 156
Native Americans, 6, 11, 18, 29, 43, 46, 54, 55, 62–63, 64–65, 66, 74, 129, 130, 169, 171, 178, 179, 180–81, 194–206. *See also under* Declaration of Independence
Navigation Acts, 58, 82, 85, 88, 91, 96–97, 123
Nedham, Marchamont, 165
Netherlands, 183
Neville, Henry, 165
New England, 53–54, 55, 96, 98, 100, 123–24, 125, 164, 182, 196–97
New England Restraining Act, 122–23
New Hampshire, 39, 115, 172
New Haven, 63
Newton, Isaac, 19, 20–21, 149

New Jersey: election districts, 115; Convention, 139; Resolves (1765), 38; state constitution, 39, 172–73
New York, 66, 67–68, 88, 93, 98, 101; authorizes independence, 137; British army in, 120; election districts, 115; state constitution, 172, 173; and Vermont, 152
New York African Society for Mutual Relief, 210
New York Restraining (Suspending) Act, 93, 113–14, 116
Nineteenth Amendment, 173
Noah, 25
non-importation, 40, 151
Norman Conquest, 49–50, 51–52, 82
North, George (Lord), 104
North Carolina, 118, 164, 172
Northwest Ordinance, 172, 194, 203
Norumbega, 50
Novus ordo seclorum, 140, 147

Old Saybrook, 63
Olive Branch Petition, 85, 103, 105
Onuf, Peter, 186
origins of government, 3, 5, 32, 35–36, 144, 147–48, 157, 158. *See also under* Declaration of Independence; Locke, John
Otis, James, 32–34, 55, 100, 199

Pacific Ocean, 196, 203
Paine, Thomas, 35–36, 160–61, 162
Palentus, 28
Parkinson, Robert, 130
Parliament: absence and limits of authority in the colonies, 17, 33, 34, 38–39, 40, 43, 44, 45, 48, 58–64, 80, 84–106, 107–30, 148, 151, 177; "cult of," 82, 84, 94; history of, 56, 86–89, 96–97, 116–17, 123, 128, 148–49, 158, 163, 178; as incidental to causes of the American Revolution, 9, 72, 77–79, 121–22, 159; power to regulate trade, 44, 58–59, 88–92, 93–94, 96–97, 99, 120, 123; relationship to crown, 46, 50, 57, 79–89, 90–91, 101–6, 121–26, 128, 148–49, 159, 163; usurps powers of colonial assemblies, 4, 34, 42, 46, 51, 57, 61, 77–78, 79, 80, 82–85, 88–106, 110, 111, 114, 118, 120, 121–26, 127, 158, 163. *See also under* Declaration of Independence
partus sequitur ventrem, law of, 184
Pennsylvania, 38, 70, 73, 93, 98; and declaring independence, 127–28; as a proprietary colony, 159; state constitution of 1776, 164, 172
Pennsylvania Gazette, 93
Peru, 23
petitions, 4, 10, 42, 52–53, 66–67, 69, 77, 83, 84, 85, 86, 102–5, 106, 108, 110, 111, 112, 116, 123, 126–27, 130–32, 133, 134, 151, 159, 176, 188–91, 196, 200, 208, 209. *See also under* Declaration of Independence
Pharaoh, 205
Philadelphia, 46, 47, 139, 188
Philistines, 28–29
philosophical history, 21, 149
pilgrims, 2, 65
Pitt, William (Lord Chatham), 64, 83
Plantation Act, 118
Plymouth Colony, 63, 96, 152
Post Office Act, 89, 97
Poyning's Law, 60, 98
presidency of the United States, 163
Privy Council, 52–53, 57, 82, 87, 113, 118
Privy Seal, 91
Prohibitory Act, 79, 105, 123, 127
Prorogation, 87, 117, 125, 162
Provisions of Oxford, 123
Psalms (book of), 25
Pufendorf, Samuel von, 22, 31, 33, 134
Puritans, 65

Quakers, 96
Quartering Act (1765), 93, 114, 122
Quartering Act (1774), 122
Quebec Act, 124–25
Quiescence, period of, 126
Quock Walker Case, 191–92
quo warranto, 100

Raleigh, Walter, 50–51, 54, 56–57
ratification of Constitution, 156
Rawson, Edward, 53, 100, 196–97
Read Sea, 205
republicanism. *See* monarchy
Restoration era, 58, 82, 85, 96, 100
Revelation (book of), 25, 120
Rhode Island, 159, 172
Richard I, 61
Richard II, 60, 116
Roanoke, 2, 50, 56–57
Roman Empire, 35, 81, 99, 101, 147, 148, 149, 206
Rome, 28
Rothman, Adam, 194
Royal African Company, 183
Royal Proclamation (1763), 79, 118
Royal Proclamation (1775), 79, 105, 111, 127, 203
Rush, Benjamin, 161–62
Russia, 203

Samuel, 160
Samuel (books of), 28
Sancho, Ignatius, 187
Saratoga, 85
Saul, 28–29
Scotch-Irish settlers, 152
Scotland, 31, 45–46, 98, 147
Scottish Militia Bill, 87
secessionism, 204
Shalmaneser, 28
Sedgwick, Theodore, 191
Seneca Falls Conference, 173

settler colonialism, 200, 222n2, 238n24
settler imperialism, 43, 45, 46, 47, 54, 55–56, 59, 60, 64, 73, 159, 200, 222n2
Seven Years' War, 48, 82–83, 97, 99
Sewall, Jonathan, 97
Sherman, Roger, 8
Sidney, Algernon, 22, 134, 165
Simitière, Pierre-Eugène, 205
slavery, 6, 11, 18, 112, 113, 117, 130, 156, 168–69, 173, 178, 179–80, 181–94, 205, 208–11; as a political condition, 30, 32, 33, 35, 37, 90, 100, 115, 148, 166, 189. *See also under* African Americans; Declaration of Independence; Jefferson, Thomas; Locke, John
slave trade, 8, 46, 112, 113, 130, 137, 170, 180, 181–84, 185, 189, 194, 205. *See also under* Declaration of Independence
Society for the Relief of Free Negroes Unlawfully Held in Bondage, 188
South Carolina: Constitution, 39; Resolves (1765), 38; and the slave trade, 182
Southwest Ordinance, 203
sovereign immunity, 79, 94
Spahn, Hannah, 20–21, 209, 217n7
Spain, 183
Sparta, 28
Stamp Act, 32, 34, 38, 59, 67, 79, 83, 91, 97, 102, 112, 123, 126, 151
Stamp Act Congress, 37–38, 66–67, 101–2, 126, 151, 200
standing armies, 120, 122
Stanton, Elizabeth Cady
State Compact Theory, 156
state constitutions, 166, 172–73
state of nature, 2–3, 5, 10–11, 16, 18, 22, 23–30, 32, 33, 34, 37, 41, 43, 107, 110, 123, 124, 128, 144, 146, 157, 174, 175, 180, 188, 192–93, 195, 198, 199, 203, 207, 210. *See also under* Declaration of Independence; Locke, John
state sovereignty, 155, 156
states' rights, 156–57

Stuart, House of, 87–88, 100, 147
Suffolk Resolves, 65, 191, 200
Sugar Act, 32, 38, 78, 79, 119, 123, 124, 150–51
Sullivan, John, 168, 169
Suspending Act. *See* New York Restraining (Suspending) Act
suspending power, 87, 113–14, 116, 125

Tallagio non concedendo, statute of, 123
Tarentum, 28
Tea Act, 79, 123, 126
Tennessee, 173
Tenth Amendment, 156
Thirteenth Amendment, 192
Thomson, Charles, 147, 206
three-fifths clause, 193
Tories (English), 128, 148
Townshend Acts, 34, 38, 59, 79, 83–84, 119–20, 123, 126, 151
trade regulation, 44, 57, 58, 82, 85, 88–90, 91–92, 93–94, 96–97, 118, 123
Treaty of Paris, 85, 203, 204
Trenchard, John, 149, 215n6
Tresillian, Robert, 116
Trouillot, Michel-Rolph, 201–2
Twenty-fourth Amendment, 172

union of the crowns, 31

Vattel, Emer de, 22, 33, 56
Vega, Garcilaso de la, 23
Venice, 28
Vermont, 152, 172, 173
veto power, 80, 86–87, 95–96, 112–13, 116, 117
Vice-Admiralty Courts, 119, 120, 124
Virgil, 147
Virginia: Act to Establish Public Schools, 150; Bill of Rights, 6, 39–40; colonial charters of, 56–58, 63–64, 66; colonial development of, 57–58, 88, 90–92; election districts, 115; House of Assembly, 46–47, 52–53, 57–59, 66, 88, 90–91, 116, 196; Northern Neck, 52; Resolves (1765), 38; Revisal of the laws, 70–71; settlement of, 55–58, 63–64, 65–66; state constitution, 6, 39–40, 172; and western lands, 155; women in, 170–71
Virginia Company, 57
Virginia Resolutions, 156
Vortigern, 56
voting rights, 115, 166–73
Voting Rights Act, 173

Waldsteicher, David, 193
Wales, 45–46, 62, 98, 178
Walker, David, 210
Walker, Quock, 191–92
Wallaston, William, 56
War of 1812, 19, 209
War of Independence, 19, 65, 85, 104–5, 120, 126–30, 138, 139–40, 145, 150, 155. *See also under* Declaration of Independence
Warren, Joseph, 35, 64–65, 100–101, 148, 199–200
Washington, George, 139–40, 156, 170–71
Webster, Daniel, 156
West Jersey, 152
Westminster, 116
westward expansion (after 1776), 202–4
William I (the Conqueror), 49–50, 52
William III, 37, 88, 93, 96, 100, 148, 158
Williamsburg, 47
Wilson, James, 34–35, 60–61, 95–96, 199
Wirt, William, 224n28
Wisconsin, 172, 203
witchcraft, 96
women, 11, 144, 146, 160, 169–71, 172–73, 174, 211

Xerxes, 28

Yirush, Craig, 31, 196, 222n2

THE REVOLUTIONARY AGE

Napoleon in America: Bonaparte and the Rhetoric of US Empire
Mark F. Ehlers

Before Manifest Destiny: The Contested Expansion of the Early United States
Nicholas G. DiPucchio

Revolutionary Diplomacy: Spanish Statecraft and the Birth of the United States
Thomas E. Chávez

Declarations of Independence: Indigenous Resilience, Colonial Rivalries, and the Cost of Revolution
Christopher R. Pearl

Dishonored Americans: The Political Death of Loyalists in Revolutionary America
Timothy Compeau

The American Liberty Pole: Popular Politics and the Struggle for Democracy in the Early Republic
Shira Lurie

European Friends of the American Revolution
Andrew J. O'Shaughnessy, John A. Ragosta, and Marie-Jeanne Rossignol, editors

The Tory's Wife: A Woman and Her Family in Revolutionary America
Cynthia A. Kierner

Writing Early America: From Empire to Revolution
Trevor Burnard

Spain and the American Revolution: New Approaches and Perspectives
Gabriel Paquette and Gonzalo M. Quintero Saravia, editors

The American Revolution and the Habsburg Monarchy
Jonathan Singerton

Navigating Neutrality: Early American Governance in the Turbulent Atlantic
Sandra Moats

Ireland and America: Empire, Revolution, and Sovereignty
Patrick Griffin and Francis D. Cogliano, editors

www.ingramcontent.com/pod-product-compliance
Lightning Source LLC
Chambersburg PA
CBHW030612230426
43661CB00053B/1945